READING CULTURE AND WRITING PRACTICES
IN NINETEENTH-CENTURY FRANCE

Reading Culture and Writing Practices in Nineteenth-Century France

MARTYN LYONS

UNIVERSITY OF TORONTO PRESS
Toronto Buffalo London

© University of Toronto Press Incorporated 2008
Toronto Buffalo London
www.utppublishing.com
Printed in Canada

ISBN 978-0-8020-9357-8

Library and Archives Canada Cataloguing in Publication

Lyons, Martyn
   Reading culture and writing practices in nineteenth-century France /
   Martyn Lyons.

   (Studies in book and print culture)
   Includes bibliographical references and index.
   ISBN 978-0-8020-9357-8

   1. Books and reading – France – History – 19th century.   2. Written
   communication – France – History – 19th century.   3. Book industries and
   trade – France – History – 19th century.   I. Title.   II. Series.

   Z1003.5.F7L96 2008   028′.9094409034   C2008-900102-8

University of Toronto Press acknowledges the financial assistance to its
publishing program of the Canada Council for the Arts and the Ontario
Arts Council.

University of Toronto Press acknowledges the financial support for its
publishing activities of the Government of Canada through the Book
Publishing Industry Development Program (BPIDP).

TO
M.N.R.

Contents

Tables, Maps, Images ix

Acknowledgments xi

Abbreviations xiii

1 Introduction: The Importance of the Nineteenth Century 3

The Statistical Approach

2 In Search of the Bestsellers of Nineteenth-Century France, 1815–1850 15

3 Towards a National Literary Culture in France: Bookshops and the Decline of the Colporteur 43

Censorship and Commemoration

4 Fires of Expiation: Book-Burnings and Catholic Missions in Restoration France 65

5 Literary Commemoration and the Uses of History: The Gutenberg Festival in Strasbourg, 1840 92

Readers

6 The Reading Experience of Worker-Autobiographers in Nineteenth-Century Europe 111

7 Oral Culture and the Rural Community: The *Veillée d'Hiver* 139

8 Why We Need an Oral History of Reading   151

Writers

9 Reading Practices, Writing Practices: Intimate Writings in
   Nineteenth-Century France   167

10 French Soldiers and Their Correspondence: Towards a History of
    Writing Practices in the First World War   184

Appendix   Calculating Bestsellers in Early Nineteenth-Century
             France   201

Notes   207

Select Bibliography   231

Index   239

Tables, Maps, Images

Table 2.1   French bestsellers, 1811–15   20
Table 2.2   French bestsellers, 1816–22   21
Table 2.3   French bestsellers, 1821–5   21–2
Table 2.4   French bestsellers, 1826–30   22–3
Table 2.5   French bestsellers, 1831–5   23–4
Table 2.6   French bestsellers, 1836–40   24–5
Table 2.7   French bestsellers, 1841–5   25–6
Table 2.8   French bestsellers, 1846–50   26–7
Table 2.9   Place of publication of selected titles, 1846–50   41

Map 3.1   Density of bookshops in provincial France, 1841   53
Map 3.2   Density of bookshops in provincial France, 1881   54

Table 4.1   Book-burnings, 1817–29   68
Table 4.2   Publishing history of Voltaire's *Complete Works*, 1816–30   80
Table 4.3   Publishing history of Rousseau's *Complete Works*,
             1816–30   81

Fig. 5.1   The Gutenberg statue in Strasbourg   98
Fig. 5.2   The Gutenberg Monument – the frontal frieze   99
Fig. 5.3   The Gutenberg Monument – the American panel   100
Fig. 5.4   The Gutenberg Monument – a contemporary
            postcard   103

Acknowledgments

Chapter 2, 'In Search of the Bestsellers of Nineteenth-Century France, 1815–1850,' is a reshaped and updated version of chapter 5 of my *Le Triomphe du Livre: une histoire sociologique de la lecture dans la France du 19e siècle* (Paris: Promodis and Cercle de la Librairie, 1987).

Chapter 4, 'The Fires of Expiation: Book-Burning and Catholic Missions in Restoration France,' was first published in *French History*, 10.2 (June 1996): 240–66. I have translated the citations into English for this edition, and added the stories about Lamartine's mother, and the inflammable edition of Voltaire.

Chapter 6, 'The Reading Experience of Worker-Autobiographers in Nineteenth-century Europe' is adapted from 'La Culture Littéraire des Travailleurs: Autobiographies ouvrières dans l'Europe du 19e siècle,' *Annales – Histoires, Sciences Sociales*, 4–5 (2001): 927–40, and from 'La experiencia lectora y escritora de las mujeres trabajadoras en la Europa del siglo XIX,' *Cultura Escrita y Sociedad* 1.1 (2005): 158–76.

Chapter 7, 'Oral Culture and the Rural Community: The *Veillée d'Hiver*,' appeared in *Australian Journal of French Studies* 23.1 (1986): 102–14.

Chapter 8, 'Why We Need an Oral History of Reading,' includes some material which appeared in Martyn Lyons and Lucy Taksa, *Australian Readers Remember* (Melbourne: Oxford University Press, 1992).

Chapter 10, 'French Soldiers and Their Correspondence: Towards a History of Writing Practices in the First World War,' appeared in *French History* 17.1 (2003): 79–95. A Spanish version was published as a chapter in *La Conquista del Alfabeto: Escritura y clases populares* (Madrid: TREA, 2002), 225–46, and appears here with the kind permission of the editor, Antonio Castillo Gómez. I have translated the citations into English for this edition.

Abbreviations

AD	Archives départementales
AESC	*Annales – économies, sociétés, civilisations*
AN	Archives Nationales
BN	Bibliothèque Nationale de France
FH	*French History*
JMH	*Journal of Modern History*
Naf	Nouvelles acquisitions françaises
Rfhl	*Revue française d'histoire du livre*
Rhmc	*Revue d'histoire moderne et contemporaine*
SHAT	Service historique de l'Armée de la Terre

READING CULTURE AND WRITING PRACTICES
IN NINETEENTH-CENTURY FRANCE

1 Introduction: The Importance of the Nineteenth Century

This book brings together a series of studies on the history of reading and writing practices, written over a twenty-year period. Some have been published in places relatively inaccessible to book historians (for example, chapters 4, 7, and 10). Some have never been published before in English (for example, chapters 2 and 6), and three recent studies have never been published at all (chapters 5, 8, and 9). All the previously published work has been brought up to date, thoroughly revised, and sometimes expanded. The result is a book of essays revolving around common concerns and approaches to the history of reading and writing. Its unity and coherence lies in its principal focus on nineteenth-century Europe, and in two themes in particular that define this era in the history of the book. The first of these is the development of a mass market in fiction publishing, brought about by technological changes which industrialized book production, by economic changes which allowed publishing entrepreneurs to flourish as never before, and by social and cultural changes which expanded the reading public. From at least the 1830s, book production in western Europe was experiencing a revolution which led by the 1890s to the emergence of a mass literary culture. This revolution was driven by the press. It went hand in hand with the appearance of daily newspapers with wide circulation and of early illustrated magazines, which attracted advertising revenue and were no longer exclusively dependent on expensive subscriptions. Until this period, the essential conditions of publication had changed very little since Johannes Gutenberg invented the printing process in the fifteenth century. The industrialization of production in the early nineteenth century, however, marked a watershed: in political terms, the Old Regime had ended in 1789, but the typographical Old Regime expired in the 1830s.

The rate of book production increased rapidly. In Britain, between 2000 and 3000 titles were published annually in the 1840s, surging to over 5000 titles annually in the 1850s. Not only did more titles appear, but the size of print-runs increased as well. At the beginning of the nineteenth century, the average print-run for a novel was only 1000 or 1500 copies. The first edition of Stendhal's *Le Rouge et le Noir* appeared in Paris in 1831 in only 750 copies. A second edition quickly followed, but it too had a run of only 750 copies. By the 1840s, however, some bestselling authors like Victor Hugo appeared in editions of 5000. The French publisher Charpentier pioneered a revolution in the 1830s, by producing novels in small in-18o (octodecimo) format, rather than the customary larger and multi-volume in-octavo format, which had been designed for sale to circulating libraries.[1] Charpentier made the text more compact, and reduced novels to one instead of three volumes, thereby reducing the price and expanding the clientele of purchasers. This was an important early breakthrough in the expansion of a mass reading public for cheap fiction. It was followed by the progressively cheaper fiction series produced by Lévy in the 1850s and by Flammarion and Fayard in the 1890s.

The second great theme of the nineteenth century is the acquisition of mass literacy in the advanced Western world. By the last decade of the century, over 95 per cent functional literacy had been achieved in the West, before national systems of free, primary education had been established in Britain and France. The influence of formal education in this process was no more than intermittent in Western countries until the 1880s. Without formal schooling, the beginners used a multiplicity of extra-curricular avenues to reading, which enabled them to start their apprenticeship in literacy with family members, neighbours, workmates, priests, and employers, to name just a few resources available. New categories of readers joined the reading public, which expanded to include first the lower middle class of shopkeepers, clerical workers, artisans and craftsmen, but eventually unskilled workers as well. By the end of the century, even the European peasantry was learning to use the instruments of written culture.

Mass culture, however, had its critics and prophets of doom. The appearance of 'new readers,' such as workers and peasants, not to mention the increase in the number of female readers at all social levels, was regarded as a social problem. The masses were considered easily susceptible, and it was feared they could be manipulated by unscrupulous publishers and propagandists. Conservatives blamed the Revolutions of 1848 on the distribution of dangerous socialist literature. Today we are sometimes worried that people do not read enough; in the nineteenth century, the problem was the opposite – people were reading *too much*, and too unwisely. Political elites, social conservatives, and the churches saw mass readership as a dangerous social innovation. New readers, in their view, needed guidance, control, and censorship if social stability was to be maintained.[2]

While a mass reading public developed, so too, ordinary people enjoyed improved access to writing. With new readers came new writers, and this, too, was part of the nineteenth-century transition to a modern mass society. Research over the last twenty years has exposed the myth that writing was unknown to peasants and workers. In fact it was a very generalized practice, and the explosion of popular writing in the First World War, discussed in chapter 10, was clear evidence of this. There was never a clear separation between the literate and illiterate. In fact the border between the two was very fluid, as was the boundary between the oral and the written: many everyday writings were produced by people who were partially illiterate or at least imperfectly able to master writing skills. Nevertheless, the Western world was learning to write as well as read, and access to written culture in general forms the essential context for the essays which follow.

I treat the 'long nineteenth century' in European history, which began in 1815 with the fall of the Napoleonic Empire and extended up to and including the First World War. Occasionally, as in chapter 8, I have strayed further into the early twentieth century. My geographical focus is principally on France and occasionally it widens to include Western Europe more generally. As a cultural historian I believe that national frontiers sometimes impose artificial constraints, and international comparisons are often instructive. I make such comparisons not only to contrast different national trajectories, but also and more importantly to stress the cultural practices common to the Western world as a whole. National contexts remain important but changes in the shared cultural practices of the West rarely respect national borders.

Although the studies which follow are not presented in chronological order, they nevertheless tell a story. They mark the changing priorities and concerns of *l'histoire du livre*, illustrating some important historiographical developments since the 1970s. Book history, for example, has moved since then from a search for statistical sources towards more qualitative assessments of reader responses. The first chapters illustrate a statistical approach to book production, reflecting a historiographical moment when quantitative methods seemed capable of opening up new ground in many fields of historical inquiry, and not just in economic history where sophisticated uses of statistical data were already well advanced. The great French revolutionary historian Michel Vovelle quantified the contents of wills and bequests in eighteenth-century Provence to build a magisterial thesis about the decline of traditional religious practices.[3] In so doing he showed that quantification could make a contribution even to cultural history. Historians used the signature test in parish records to compile literacy figures and, in the examination of postmortem inventories, they counted the presence of books and of individual titles in private libraries.[4] The fashion for quantitative methods was vigorously promoted by the historians of the Annales school. My own calculations of the bestselling titles of early nineteenth-century France (in chapter 2) did not require any mathematical genius, but they answered a need to know in numerical terms what was produced by the nineteenth-century book trade. In chapter 3 I turn briefly from the statistics of book production in France to a summary of numerical data on bookshop density. Like Robert Darnton on eighteenth-century France, I am interested in the circuit of distribution, above all to libraries and bookshops.[5] Unlike Darnton, my concern is not with the clandestine trade, but with the mainstream and the everyday. Today the need for a statistical account is felt less urgently, if indeed it is felt at all. Statistical studies, however, were not an irrelevancy, but an essential preliminary phase in the study of book production and distribution. They made possible a well-grounded overview of the whole field of production. This was a necessary foundation for future work. But it would be imperative at some point to go beyond it.

The central chapters of this collection do go beyond it, taking us from the study of production and distribution to the less tangible and often unquantifiable study of reading history. The sequence thus reflects an important switch in the focus of book historians. While many came to the discipline from the important specializations of bibliography and palaeography, and while others focused on the publishing industry as a branch of economic history, my angle of approach – that of a cultural historian – is different. To some extent the change of emphasis from publishing history to the history of reading reflected a change within the Annales school itself in its post-Braudel era, away from quantification and towards the new history of *mentalités*. Reading and reception, it seemed, might offer clues about collective assumptions and profound cultural shifts. In the search for such clues, the skills of the historical anthropologist seemed potentially more fruitful than the tools of demographers and economic historians.

Admittedly, there was a difficulty here: how could the responses of readers become accessible to the historian, when little obvious trace of their responses survives in documentary form? I have emphasised two approaches in answer to this question which are represented here. The first is the study of what readers, or constituencies of readers in the past, were encouraged to read or were discouraged from reading. These are the 'normative sources' produced by elites, churches, trade unions, feminists, and others to recommend desirable reading and to warn against dangerous literary temptations. Chapter 5 shows how literary commemorations promote official and orthodox views, while chapter 4 examines book-burnings in France under the restored Bourbon regime of 1815–30. These are chapters on the literary canon and ways to promote and defend it.

For a closer glimpse of readers' responses, the historian of reading and of reading practices needs to turn to a second set of valuable sources: the autobiographies and personal accounts which are the basis of chapters 6–8. In diaries, autobiographies, and oral testimonies, individual readers describe their reading experiences and allow us to appreciate their enormous diversity. The exponents of German reception theory gave us the putative reader, whether 'hidden' or 'implied,' whose presence was deduced from (usually canonical) literary texts, but they failed to satisfy the social or cultural historian's thirst for contact with actual readers.[6] Personal sources lead us to real flesh-and-bone readers, who write or speak of their books, preferences, loves, and hates, and inform us consciously or unconsciously about the status and function of reading in different phases of their lives.

Reception theorists lacked a historical dimension. They tended to assume that literary texts are static and immutable, whereas they are constantly reedited over time, in different versions and formats and at different prices. Each reincarnation of a text targets a new public, whose participation and expectations are guided not just by authors but by publishing strategies, illustrations, and all the other physical aspects of the book. My concern is not with the implications of canonical texts fossilized in time but with real readers in specific historical circumstances, who can provide us with what Janice Radway calls 'an empirically-based ethnography of reading.'[7] Using the rich conceptual insights of Roger Chartier, the book historian can investigate reading as a cultural practice, to examine what readers bring to their texts, and how they 'appropriate' meaning through the act of reading.[8]

The autonomy of the individual reader is a fundamental principle here. We can make no prior assumptions about the reader's response. The reader never comes to the text passively or empty-handed, and never absorbs the text without resistance or criticism. Since the celebrated and oft-quoted case of Menocchio, the sixteenth-century Friulian miller who staggered the Inquisition with his version of the origins of the earth, we have been warned: we predict the reader's response at our peril. Nothing apparently in Menocchio's reading authorized his bizarre vision of the world as a curdled cheese, harbouring large worms which transformed themselves into angels.[9] How had Menocchio acquired these notions? His singular views cannot be directly connected to his reading of the Koran, the Decameron, Mandeville's Travels, or the medieval chronicles which came briefly into his possession. For Carlo Ginzburg, his unpredictable views were the result of a coming together of popular and learned sources. On one hand, there was the contribution of an archaic, oral tradition of peasant protest, rooted in a dim pagan past. On the other hand, Menocchio had selected and reworked information received from learned sources: the books which he told the Inquisition so much about. It was the mutual imbrication of the oral with the printed, the popular with the erudite, which produced his very personal heresy.

In Michel de Certeau's metaphor, the reader is a poacher.[10] The reader as consumer hides as it were in the text, but not in the sense understood by the reception theorists. The reader is a trespasser, creeping about the proprietor's estate for his or her own nefarious purposes. The estate is not his property; the landscape has been laid out by other hands; but, undetected, he takes what he needs from it, a hare here, a thrush there, even a deer if he's lucky, and escapes without leaving a trace on the page. In this way, the individual reader insinuates his own meanings and purposes into another's text. Each individual reader has silent and invisible ways of subverting the dominant order of consumerized culture. With these ideas in mind, we can bring together both the normative and the autobiographical sources and elucidate the connections and disparities between the experiences of an individual reader and the ideal reading models presented in a given sociocultural context.

The final chapters of this collection represent another shift towards the history of writing practices. Sometimes known as *écritures ordinaires* or 'ego-documents,' the everyday writing practices of ordinary people are increasingly under the microscope. Ordinary people have not been as silent through historical time as has often been asserted – their written traces can be uncovered and their voices are there if we make the effort to listen. Their writings, whether in the form of correspondence, diaries, autobiographies, written prayers, scrapbooks, or private notebooks, tend to be ephemeral and respond to peculiar situations like emigration, exile, war, and prison. 'Ordinary writing' is often infused with dialect, sitting somewhere in-between the oral and the written, often combined with drawings and portrait sketches. The untutored writer may commit grammatical errors and have difficulty in holding the line straight.

This recent interest in writing practices, and in the history of popular access to writing, is indebted to Philippe Lejeune, whose concept of the 'autobiographical pact' has informed much analysis of first-person writing.[11] Whereas *l'histoire du livre* has a distinctively French ancestry, dating back most notably to Lucien Febvre and Henri-Jean Martin's *L'Apparition du livre*, the history of writing practices is inspired by other sources.[12] Spain and the Hispanic world currently lead the way in this field, with no fewer than three Spanish journals publishing work on the history of written culture, namely *Litterae*, *Syntagma*, and *Cultura Escritura y Sociedad*. It is therefore fitting in a collection which traces the changing historiography of written culture that the final chapter should have appeared in Madrid.

The framework for my examinations of the history of reading and writing practices owes a considerable debt to Chartier and de Certeau, Bourdieu and Lejeune, among other gurus of this interdisciplinary field. In spite of the importance of their theoretical insights, however, my own primary concern has always been with the individual, actual reader and his or her perceptions and experiences. I have consistently exploited autobiographical sources. These have included a range of genres, such as nineteenth-century workers' autobiographies, whether published in journals or in books, or the *journaux intimes* produced by middle-class women or by young girls anxiously facing the ordeal of marriage, or the recorded oral testimonies solicited from elderly readers about their childhood and family memories.

At this point, however, I run into a serious practical problem. If, as I have argued, individual readers engage in a dynamic interaction with what is read, and share in the production of meaning, and if, in addition, they develop private interpretations which are not in any way predetermined, then how are we to write their personal histories? The danger is that we will be faced with a multiplicity of individual stories, all of them unique. If we dissolve the history of reading into a myriad of free agents, all arriving at unexpected conclusions, we have a state of subjective anarchy in which no generalizations are either possible or legitimate. The notion of 'interpretive communities' of readers may offer a constructive way out of this trap.

Stanley Fish, the American literary critic to whom we owe this idea, offers a useful corrective to the anarchic tendencies of reading history just mentioned.[13] To adapt a much-used phrase, readers make their own meanings, but they do not make them entirely as they wish. Readers do so as members of a community which makes certain assumptions about literature and what it constitutes. Members of a reading community may not know each other or even be aware of each other's existence, and this fact alone stretches our conventional ideas of community. Members of a reading community, however, have a common set of criteria for judging what is 'good' and 'bad' literature, for categorizing texts as belonging to certain genres, and for establishing their own genre hierarchies. Reading communities may be readers of the same newspaper, they may have an institutional basis like a literary society or a university faculty, or they might be defined more loosely in terms of gender or social class. Perhaps as women readers, or as militant workers, they employ similar interpretive strategies in attributing meaning to their books. Individual readers may of course belong to several reading communities at once.

In the nineteenth century, for example, self-educated and self-improving workers formed a distinctive interpretive community of readers. Janice Radway gave us another reading community in her study of female romance readers in the American Midwest.[14] They read as individuals, but with common aims, and in a common sociocultural context for, as Robert Darnton reminded us, ascribing meaning to texts is a social activity.[15] The process is not wholly individual and random, but relies on broader social and cultural conditioning factors. The expectations brought to the book by readers are formed through shared social experience. These expectations may also be encouraged by publishers who adopt marketing strategies aimed at particular communities of readers. This already goes beyond Fish's own formulations, but his ideas need a broad interpretation if we are to extract most profit from them.

In a sense, the style of reading history demonstrated in this book is a form of 'history from below.' Its main focus is the reading and writing histories of ordinary people, and the ways they experienced and grappled with the acquisition of literacy, reading and writing. The spread of mass literary culture in the nineteenth century was neither smooth nor uniform; it met resistance. The cultural homogeneity of any nation up to

1914 was mitigated by geographical and linguistic diversity and by the imperfect integration of literacy skills by the lower classes. In examining the advent of reading for all and of writing for all, a gendered dimension also needs to be taken into account. Differences between male and female cultural practices, as well as differences in the ways gendered practices were represented, are indicated in the central chapters of the book.

In conclusion, I hope to demonstrate that *l'histoire du livre* intersects with historical issues of broad social or cultural significance. In their studies of eighteenth-century Europe, Robert Darnton and Roger Chartier made book history a key element in renewing old debates about the impact of the Enlightenment and its possible connections to the outbreak of the French Revolution.[16] Similarly, a study of bestsellers in nineteenth-century Europe has a direct bearing on our evaluation of the so-called Romantic Movement, while the history of the 'battle of the books' in Restoration France takes us to the heart of political and intellectual conflicts in post-revolutionary French society. The continuing vigour of book history will depend on its ability to illuminate significant historical issues in this way.

The Statistical Approach

2 In Search of the Bestsellers of Nineteenth-Century France, 1815–1850

Today, lists of best-selling books and CDs, and audience ratings of television programs are published weekly, for the benefit of retailers, manufacturers, publishers, and advertisers. Students of mass culture, who treat the box office as their oracle, should find them invaluable. So, too, should the cultural historians of the future. The book historian can only dream of the enormous possibilities which would open up if he or she could lay hands on accurate lists of best-selling fiction and non-fiction in the eighteenth or nineteenth centuries. We can construct such lists, but only from indirect evidence. They can provide an invaluable guide to popular preferences, and to the fluctuating tastes of an emerging mass consumer market. Our evidence is based not on actual sales, but on production statistics, details of print-runs and re-editions of individual titles. Establishing from such sources which titles were bestsellers is an important step towards defining the basic values and assumptions which form the consensus of a whole society. With this idea in mind, I have attempted here to compile approximate lists of the best-selling books in early nineteenth-century France.

It is dangerous to generalize about popular literary taste or about French literary culture on the basis of novels chosen by literary critics on purely aesthetic or stylistic grounds. For the cultural historian, a history of French literary culture in the nineteenth century based on Stendhal, Balzac, Flaubert, and Zola would have little to recommend it. The evidence of popular taste would dictate a very different choice, made according to the more mercenary criteria of sales and output. A more representative choice of nineteenth-century French novelists would have to include Walter Scott, Pigault-Lebrun, Eugène Sue, Alexandre Dumas, Erckmann-Chatrian, Jules Verne, and Pierre Loti – a list of best-selling authors comprising those who are, in the eyes of today's reader, unfamiliar, unread, and in some cases unreadable. To a historian, however, who is trying to mine information about cultural patterns, these novelists have their own legitimate claims to attention, based on frequent and widely disseminated editions of their works. Placing early nineteenth-century bestsellers on a solid, quantitative basis is an indispensable preliminary for any social history of reading in the period.

1. The Methods

The Sources

Compiling lists of bestsellers in this period has required some methodological innovation, and a more detailed explanation of the approach will be found in the appendix (see pp. 201–5). It relies substantially on the official printers' declarations, required in advance of publication by Napoleonic legislation, which are the best available guide to consumer habits. They are in fact the only source of print-runs we have, and important inferences can be made from them. The evidence they provide, however, is not evidence of sales but of production output. Estimated quantities sold over the counter in early nineteenth-century Paris can be deduced from assessing editions and re-editions of the same titles. By counting the number of editions published of any given title, and estimating the print-runs of these editions, we can estimate how many copies had been put into circulation. Proceeding in this way, I have tried to distinguish the contours of the book market and of the reading public. The relative importance, for example, of fiction and non-fiction, of modern, eighteenth-century and foreign novels, the legacies of seventeenth-century classicism and the eighteenth-century Enlightenment, together with the relative impact of romanticism are all themes which acquire a clearer definition, when illuminated by the circulation figures for best-selling works.

The main sources in my search for the historical bestseller are twofold: the *Bibliographie de la France* gives the number of editions published of any title and author, while the printers' declarations give the print-runs (*tirages*).[1] The *Bibliographie de la France* was established by Napoleon in 1811 to codify production records, but also to facilitate government supervision of undesirable literature. The *Bibliographie* listed all books legally published in France, and deposited, according to regulations, in the *dépôt légal*. Unfortunately, the *Bibliographie* is incomplete. In its early years, before it became an established institution published at regular intervals, many titles were omitted. During times of political and administrative upheaval, like the defeat of Napoleon in 1815 or the revolutionary years of 1848–9, there was a similar tendency to under-report, as the bureaucratic organs of the state ceased to function with their accustomed consistency. Even in good years, some printers, out of negligence or deliberate evasion, failed to make the statutory deposit in the *dépôt légal*. In spite of these problems, however, the *Bibliographie de la France* provides a basic starting point for any survey of what was actually published in France. It is full of useful information, compiled with impressive erudition. Without its list of editions published, my study of the reading public could not have been undertaken.

The dusty, green-bound tomes of Series F18 in the Archives Nationales contain the declarations which the government required all printers to make in advance of the publication of any book. They detail the printer's name, the title of the proposed work, its format, the number of volumes and folios, as well as the *tirage*. Its unique value lies in the fact that it gives the intended print-runs. By matching these print-runs with the editions listed in the *Bibliographie de la France*, I embarked on a quantitative study of what was offered for literary consumption in early nineteenth-century France. Taken separately, the *Bibliographie de la France* and the printers' declarations would each be an invaluable historical source in its own right. Used in tandem, they offer an incomparable opportunity to set the architecture of French book consumption on firmer foundations than have yet been attempted.

As well as the declarations of Parisian printers, I have also consulted the declarations of some provincial printers, of which fragments are kept in the Archives Nationales.[2] Better provincial records exist on the spot, and my data include printers' declarations from the departments of the Vaucluse, the Nord, and the Maine-et-Loire.[3] These departments include some of the principal centres of publishing outside the capital: Avignon, Lille, and Angers. Paris dominated the book trade, but a provincial angle can enhance the value of the search for the bestseller.

My study concludes in 1850. The exact mid-point of the century may seem an arbitrary moment at which to halt the investigation. In the second half of the century, however, the sheer volume of material becomes a deterrent for a single-handed researcher using the methods of an artisan. We enter a domain where so much is produced that even data-entry specialists have not ventured there. This is not the main reason for closing in 1850. Even with the benefits of computerization, historians would find their investment yielding diminishing returns in the latter part of the century. The value of the printers' declarations was already decreasing. Novels were frequently first published in serialized form in the newspaper press. They appeared later as novels, in complete bound editions, but only after the work's first, fresh impact had been absorbed by the public. In the mid-1840s, the printers' declarations of runaway successes by Eugène Sue and Alexandre Dumas only give a limited idea of their total readership. For a more accurate picture, we would need to follow Pierre Orecchioni's advice, and consider published editions in conjunction with newspaper circulation figures.[4] The printers' declarations, therefore, are at their most useful precisely in the period between the First Empire and the eve of the 1848 Revolution. Beyond this point, the declarations, although more voluminous, are less valuable as a measure of commercial success.

Authors

I searched the sources just described to reconstruct the publishing histories, over half a century, of fifty-six different authors. Among them, these authors were responsible for about 3000 relevant publications between 1813 and 1850, for which I made a search for the print-runs. Authors and titles were selected on an essentially empirical and sometimes intuitive basis. One group of authors was chosen for survey because modern secondary sources have frequently and loosely described them as bestsellers of their age. This applies, for example, to the works of Walter Scott, Béranger, Lesage, Eugène Sue, and Pigault-Lebrun. The success of Lamennais's *Paroles d'un Croyant* in the early 1830s, and of Voltaire's complete works under the Restoration, are also well known, although this has never been substantiated on a quantitative basis.

A second group of authors and titles was included because they seemed possible indicators of the popularity of romantic literature. This consideration dictated the choice of, for example, Byron, De Vigny, and the *Méditations* of Lamartine. It soon emerged, however, that some authors like Alfred de Vigny were not printed in sufficiently frequent editions or in large enough print-runs to be ranked as bestsellers. The omissions from the bestselling lists are sometimes as interesting as the literary successes, especially when such omissions involve works highly valued by literary critics.

Literary critics are also responsible for a third category of authors surveyed, consisting simply of those hallowed by posterity as the greatest creative geniuses of the epoch. This survey could not afford to neglect the publishing histories of Balzac, Sand, Hugo, De Staël, Chateaubriand, or Stendhal.

In 1866, the Minister for Education, Duruy, conducted a questionnaire addressed to prefects, which investigated reading habits in the French countryside. This produced a further list of titles, compiled by the prefects, which seemed potential candidates for the bestseller lists.[5] A few years later, the Franklin Society began to publish the reports of local librarians on lending preferences all over France.[6] The *Bulletin de la Société Franklin* suggested some additional titles for the survey, even though it was published thirty years after the period which directly concerned me. These later sources were responsible for the inclusion in the survey of works such as *Mille et Une Nuits*, the *Contes* of Canon Schmid, and the histories of France by Anquetil and Madame de Saint-Ouen.

Finally, many authors were selected for inclusion on a purely empirical basis. A reading of the printers' declarations produced a further choice, suggested by frequent encounters with repeated editions of the same titles. Some works, therefore, were added during the course of the investigation itself, because constant reprints could not be ignored. This method accounted for the inclusion of Madame Cottin, Bérenger, Fleury, Massillon, and Tasso, to name only a few. This empirical method may not be foolproof or exhaustive, but it was certainly the one which produced the biggest surprises and the greatest sense of discovery. In this way, the reading preferences of the contemporary public could be distinguished from the preferences of later literary criticism. The popular tastes of French men and women could be rescued from under the feet of those plaster heroes erected by a subsequent academic tradition.

The Tables of Bestsellers

The data are summarized in the tables which follow. After the author and title of the work detailed, the third column T shows the total number of editions recorded in the *Bibliographie de la France*, with some additions from the general catalogue of the *Bibliothèque Nationale*. The fourth column P indicates how many of those editions were published in Paris. The following column P/B shows the number of editions published either in the provinces or in Belgium. This enables us to guess at the provincial readership of certain titles.

The final two columns give the 'minimum known *tirage*' and the 'total known or estimated *tirage*.' I located the exact print-run in the printers' declarations for between one-half and two-thirds of the editions recorded in the *Bibliographie de la France*. The success ratio was higher for editions published in Paris, lower for titles which regularly relied on provincial sources of publication. The *tirages* are practically complete for the works of Walter Scott, which have been analysed elsewhere.[7] They are nearly complete for the works of Stendhal, Reybaud's novel *Jérôme Paturot*, and for Victor Hugo, for whom I located over 80 per cent of *tirages*. The success ratio was below average, on the other hand, for Ducray-Duminil, Canon Schmid, and for *Don Quichotte*. For these publications, I located less than 40 per cent of *tirages*. The penultimate column of 'minimum known *tirage*' consists of the aggregate number of copies for those editions for which I located the *tirages*. The last column is based on the known minimum print-run plus a figure for the unknown editions, based on a conservative but educated guess.

As already explained, this aggregate does not represent a sales figure, but an estimate of the number of copies produced for sale. It is a safe assumption, however, that a title which was regularly re-edited did not sit for very long on a bookseller's shelf. In spite of their lack of precision, the figures allow the historian to assess the relative significance of each author and genre within the book market as a whole. In the tables of bestsellers which follow, print-runs have been added in five-year periods. Statistics are available from 1811 onwards, and the breakdown of quinquennia from this starting date conveniently coincides with important political turning points in 1815 and 1830. This chronological division allowed a judgment on the degree to which the Empire, Bourbon Restoration, and July Monarchy were culturally, as well as politically, distinct.

2. The Results

Table 2.1
French Bestsellers, 1811–15

Author	Title	No. of Editions T = P + P/B	Minimum Known *Tirage*	Total Known or Estimated *Tirage*
La Fontaine	*Fables*	24 = 11 + 13	35,600	40–45,000
Fénelon	*Télémaque*	21 = 8 + 13	15,500	26–32,000
Fleury	*Catéchisme historique*[a]	15 = 4 + 11	21,250	23–25,000
Perrault	*Contes des fées*	15 = 5 + 10	17,700	20–22,000
Florian	*Fables*	10 = 6 + 4	8,600	11–15,000
Bérenger	*La Morale en action*	6 = 1 + 5	10,000	12,000
Racine	*Théâtre/Oeuvres comp.*	8 = 6 + 2	8,930	10,000
Massillon	*Petit Carême*	8 = 4 + 4	6,000	9–11,000
Barthélemy	*Voyage du jeune Anacharsis*	6 = 4 + 2	5,600	8,600
Molière	*Oeuvres complètes*	6 = 5 + 1	4,000	6–7,000
Lesage	*Gil Blas*	5 = 5 + 0	4,900	6,000
Buffon	*Le Petit Buffon des enfants*	3 = 3 + 0	3,500	5,000

a Includes the abbreviated version, *Petit catéchisme historique*.

Table 2.2
French Bestsellers, 1816–20

Author	Title	No. of Editions T = P + P/B	Minimum Known Tirage	Total Known or Estimated Tirage
La Fontaine	Fables	29 = 16 + 13	22,100	38–48,000
Fleury	Catéchisme historique[a]	16 = 9 + 7	29,000	36–42,000
Fénelon	Télémaque	14 = 5 + 9	11,000	21–35,000
Mme Cottin	Claire d'Albe	11 = 11 + 0	19,000	25–30,000
B de St-Pierre	Paul et Virginie	3 = 3 + 0	18,000	20–30,000
Mme Cottin	Elisabeth	10 = 10 + 0	14,500	20–25,000
Massillon	Petit Carême	12 = 9 + 3	14,500	20–24,000
Perrault	Contes des fées	14 = 7 + 7	13,000	19–24,000
Tasso	La Jérusalem délivrée	9 = 7 + 2	17,650	20–22,000
Florian	Fables	12 = 8 + 4	10,000	16–18,500
Anon	La Cuisinière bourgeoise	7 = 5 + 2	15,000	18,000
Voltaire	Oeuvres complètes	9 = 8 + 1	11,800	15–19,000
Rousseau	Oeuvres complètes	8 = 8 + 0	13,200	14–15,000
Barthélemy	Voyage du jeune Anacharsis[b]	8 = 5 + 3	8,500	11–12,000
Florian	Estelle	9 = 5 + 4	5,800	10–12,000
Volney	Les Ruines	5 = 5 + 0	10,000	10,000
Racine	Théâtre/Oeuvres comp.	9 = 8 + 1	3,900	10,000
Lesage	Gil Blas	6 = 5 + 1	4,750	8–10,000
Anquetil	Histoire de France	5 = 5 + 0	7,600	8–9,600
De Staël	Corinne	6 = 6 + 0	7,025	8–8,500

a Includes the abbreviated version, Petit catéchisme historique.
b Includes the abbreviated version, Abrégé du voyage du jeune Anacharsis.

Table 2.3
French Bestsellers, 1821–5

Author	Title	No. of Editions T = P + P/B	Minimum Known Tirage	Total Known or Estimated Tirage
La Fontaine	Fables	44 = 24 + 20	80,250	95–105,000
Fleury	Catéchisme historique[a]	32 = 3 + 29	38,100	58–80,000
Fénelon	Télémaque	32 = 12 + 20	42,800	60–78,000
Florian	Fables	21 = 10 + 11	38,000	47–55,000
Anon	La Cuisinière bourgeoise	10 = 4 + 6	32,000	38–44,000
Massillon	Petit Carême	19 = 16 + 3	25,800	35–42,000
Racine	Théâtre/Oeuvres comp.	18 = 14 + 4	20,600	31–40,000
Molière	Théâtre/Oeuvres comp.	21 = 21 + 0	20,200	28–35,000

Table 2.3   (*Continued*)

Author	Title	No. of Editions T = P + P/B	Minimum Known *Tirage*	Total Known or Estimated *Tirage*
Rousseau	*Oeuvres complètes*	15 = 15 + 0	20,935	25–32,000
Voltaire	*Oeuvres complètes*	12 = 12 + 0	21,850	23–26,000
Béranger	*Chansons*	4 = 4 + 0	18,300	20–25,000
Barthélemy	*Voyage du jeune Anacharsis*[b]	13 = 9 + 4	18,400	22–24,000
Tasso	*La Jérusalem délivrée*	9 = 6 + 3	15,000	18–22,000
Defoe	*Aventures de R Crusoé*	9 = 7 + 2	4,000	18–25,000?
Bérenger	*La Morale en action*	12 = 1 + 11	9,000	17–22,000
Cervantes	*Don Quichotte*	6 = 6 + 0	17,300	19–21,000
Lesage	*Gil Blas*	10 = 8 + 2	15,900	17–18,000
Perrault	*Contes des fées*	6 = 2 + 4	12,200	13–16,000
Lamartine	*Méditations poétiques*	7 = 7 + 0	9,000	12–16,000
Voltaire	*Théâtre*[c]	6 = 6 + 0	6,000	10–18,000
Volney	*Les Ruines*	5 = 5 + 0	15,000	15,000
Buffon	*Petit Buffon des enfants*[d]	7 = 4 + 3	11,500	12–14,000
Lascases	*Mémorial de Ste Hélène*	4 = 4 + 0	9,000	12,000
Anon	*Lettres d'Héloïse et d'Abelard*	6 = 4 + 2	8,000	10–12,000

a Includes the abbreviated version, *Petit catéchisme historique*.
b Includes the abbreviated version, *Abrégé du voyage du jeune Anacharsis*.
c Includes Voltaire's *Chefs-d'oeuvre dramatiques*.
d Includes *Le Buffon des enfants*.

Table 2.4
French Bestsellers, 1826–30

Author	Title	No. of Editions T = P + P/B	Minimum Known *Tirage*	Total Known or Estimated *Tirage*
Béranger	*Chansons*	16 = 15 + 1	135,000	140–160,000
Fénelon	*Télémaque*	52 = 26 + 26	58,500	90–120,000
Fleury	*Catéchisme historique*[a]	39 = 6 + 33	55,000	80–130,000
La Fontaine	*Fables*	33 = 22 + 11	65,100	80–110,000
Florian	*Fables*	22 = 9 + 13	34,650	48–62,000
Defoe	*Aventures de R Crusoé*	18 = 15 + 3	23,000	43–53,000
Perrault	*Contes des fées*	11 = 0 + 11	13,000	27–40,000
Massillon	*Petit Carême*	15 = 9 + 6	17,000	28–34,000
Voltaire	*Oeuvres complètes*	16 = 16 + 0	20,850	25–33,000
Rouvière	*La Médecine sans médecin*	9 = 9 + 0	4,000	20–36,000?

Table 2.4   (*Continued*)

Author	Title	No. of Editions T = P + P/B	Minimum Known *Tirage*	Total Known or Estimated *Tirage*
Anon	*La Cuisinière bourgeoise*	8 = 8 + 0	22,000	25–29,000
Racine	*Théâtre/Oeuvres comp*	11 = 10 + 1	18,700	22–30,000
Bérenger	*La Morale en action*	13 = 0 + 13	0	13–40,000?
Molière	*Oeuvres complètes*	13 = 12 + 1	12,000	20–28,000
Scott	*Ivanhoé*	10 = 8 + 2	20,800	20,800
Scott	*L'Antiquaire*	10 = 8 + 2	20,800	20,800
Scott	*L'Abbé*	9 = 9 + 0	20,000	20,000
Scott	*Quentin Durward*	9 = 8 + 1	20,000	20,000
Buffon	*Histoire naturelle*[b]	7 = 7 + 0	12,000	16–24,000
Rousseau	*Oeuvres complètes*	8 = 8 + 0	9,000	17–21,000
B de St-Pierre	*Paul et Virginie*	4 = 4 + 0	18,000	18,000
Chateaubriand	*Génie du christianisme*	6 = 6 + 0	17,000	18–19,000
Lesage	*Gil Blas*	12 = 11 + 1	4,600	15–20,000
Buffon	*Le Buffon des enfants*[c]	8 = 1 + 7	0	8–24,000
Young	*Les Nuits*	5 = 3 + 2	14,500	14,500
Volney	*Les Ruines*	3 = 3 + 0	10,000	12–16,000
Tasso	*La Jérusalem délivrée*	2 = 1 + 1	10,000	11–15,000
Barthélemy	*Voyage du jeune Anacharsis*	7 = 7 + 0	9,500	12–14,000
Byron	*Œuvres*	4 = 4 + 0	10,500	10,500
Anquetil	*Histoire de France*	6 = 6 = 0	8,500	10–11,500

a Includes the abbreviated version, *Petit catéchisme historique*.
b Includes Buffon's *Œuvres complètes*.
c Includes *Le Petit Buffon des enfants*, *Le Buffon de l'enfance*, and *Buffon de premier âge*.

Table 2.5
French Bestsellers, 1831–5

Author	Title	No. of Editions T = P + P/B	Minimum Known *Tirage*	Total Known or Estimated *Tirage*
Fleury	*Catéchisme historique*[a]	45 = 16 + 29	64,000	110–130,000
La Fontaine	*Fables*	23 = 8 + 15	75,500	95–120,000
Fénelon	*Télémaque*	28 = 13 + 15	33,700	60–80,000
Béranger	*Chansons*[b]	9 = 8 + 1	42,000	52–75,000
Saint-Ouen	*Histoire de France*	5 = 5 + 0	46,000	52–66,000
Florian	*Fables*	14 = 4 + 10	27,000	30–40,000

Table 2.5   (*Continued*)

Author	Title	No. of Editions T = P + P/B	Minimum Known *Tirage*	Total Known or Estimated *Tirage*
Lamennais	*Paroles d'un croyant*	10 = 10 + 0	28,300	29–30,000
Bérenger	*La Morale en action*	15 = 3 + 12	8,000	34–50,000
Pellico	*Mes Prisons*	15 = 11 + 4	17,450	22–30,000
Defoe	*Robinson dans son île*	5 = 5 + 0	13,000	20–30,000
Jussieu	*Simon de Nantua*	5 = 5 + 0	17,000	21–23,000
B de St-Pierre	*Paul et Virginie*	8 = 7 + 1	16,000	21–26,000
Chateaubriand	*Oeuvres*	9 = 9 + 1	12,000	18–23,000
Lesage	*Gil Blas*	5 = 5 + 0	12,500	15–18,000
Rousseau	*Julie, ou la Nouvelle Héloïse*	6 = 5 + 1	12,000	15,000
Hugo	*Notre-Dame de Paris*	8 = 8 + 0	8,400	11–14,000
De Kock	*Le Cocu*	5 = 4 + 1	9,600	11–14,000
Defoe	*Aventures de R Crusoé*	7 = 7 + 0	0	14–22,000
Molière	*Œuvres*	8 = 7 + 1	7,300	9–14,000
Scott	*Woodstock*	4 = 4 + 0	13,000	13,000
Thiers	*Histoire de la Révolution française*	3 = 3 + 0	8,000	10–15,000
Tasso	*La Jérusalem délivrée*	7 = 5 + 2	500	4–20,000?
Perrault	*Contes des fées*	6 = 3 + 3	1,000	6–20,000?
Lamartine	*Œuvres*	3 = 3 + 0	7,000	9–12,000
Anquetil	*Histoire de France*	4 = 3 + 1	6,000	9–12,000
Scott	*Château périlleux*	3 = 3 + 0	9,300	9,300
Barthélemy	*Voyage du jeune Anacharsis*[c]	5 = 4 + 1	5,250	8–11,000

a Includes the abbreviated version, *Petit catéchisme historique*.
b Includes Béranger's *Œuvres complètes* and *Chansons nouvelles et dernières*.
c Includes the abbreviated version, *Abrégé du voyage du jeune Anacharsis*.

Table 2.6
French Bestsellers, 1836–40

Author	Title	No. of Editions T = P + P/B	Minimum Known *Tirage*	Total Known or Estimated *Tirage*
Fénelon	*Télémaque*	41 = 20 + 21	29,850	78–120,000
Fleury	*Catéchisme historique*[a]	38 = 14 + 24	27,300	70–110,000
La Fontaine	*Fables*	32 = 14 + 18	23,500	58–85,000
Saint-Ouen	*Histoire de France*	3 = 3 + 0	22,000	35–45,000
B de St-Pierre	*Paul et Virginie*	22 = 12 + 10	13,000	30–55,000
Lamennais	*Paroles d'un croyant*	4 = 4 + 0	30,000	30–33,000

Table 2.6   (*Continued*)

Author	Title	No. of Editions T = P + P/B	Minimum Known *Tirage*	Total Known or Estimated *Tirage*
Pellico	*Mes Prisons*	11 = 7 + 4	21,500	28–40,000
Chateaubriand	*Génie du christianisme*	12 = 11 + 1	18,500	28–38,000
Bérenger	*La Morale en action*	14 = 3 + 11	4,000	30–58,000
De Staël	*Corinne*	11 = 5 + 6	13,000	22–35,000
Defoe	*Aventures de R Crusoé*	15 = 11 + 4	4,500	19–40,000
Defoe	*Robinson dans son île*	5 = 3 + 2	11,000	14–25,000
Schmid	*Contes*[b]	13 = 4 + 9	7,500	20–38,000?
Chateaubriand	*Oeuvres complètes*	7 = 7 + 0	13,500	16–24,000
Florian	*Fables*	12 = 6 + 6	1,400	18–35,000?
Anquetil	*Histoire de France*	10 = 9 + 1	7,000	12–30,000
Béranger	*Oeuvres complètes*	3 = 3 + 0	10,000	15–25,000
Tasso	*La Jérusalem délivrée*	15 = 8 + 7	2,000	15–30,000?
Perrault	*Contes des fées*	8 = 4 + 4	500	8–24,000?
Mme Cottin	*Elisabeth*	5 = 4 + 1	11,000	15–18,000
Anon	*Lettres d'Héloïse et d'Abelard*	7 = 6 + 1	3,500	9–20,000?
Lesage	*Gil Blas*	6 = 3 + 3	6,000	13–16,000
Thiers	*Histoire de la Révolution française*	4 = 4 + 0	3,300	9–18,000
Rousseau	*Julie, ou la Nouvelle Héloïse*	4 = 2 + 2	8,000	11–15,000
Racine	*Œuvres*	8 = 5 + 3	2,500	10–20,000?
Anon	*Mille et Une Nuits*	4 = 3 + 1	7,000	9–14,000

a Includes the abbreviated version, *Petit catéchisme historique*.
b Includes Schmid's *Nouveaux petits contes*, *Sept nouveaux contes*, *Cent nouveaux petits contes*, *Nouveaux contes*, etc.

Table 2.7
French Bestsellers, 1841–5

Author	Title	No. of Editions T = P + P/B	Minimum Known *Tirage*	Total Known or Estimated *Tirage*
La Fontaine	*Fables*	31 = 17 + 14	53,400	88–125,000
Fleury	*Catéchisme historique*[a]	26 = 8 + 18	50,500	80–100,000
Fénelon	*Télémaque*	27 = 16 + 11	62,200	82–98,000
Schmid	*Contes*[b]	23 = 15 + 8	29,000	55–70,000
Saint-Ouen	*Histoire de France*	5 = 5 + 0	26,400	48–96,000
Anquetil	*Histoire de France*	6 = 6 + 0	39,000	40–43,000
Sue	*Le Juif Errant*	8 = 4 + 4	23,000	32–46,000

Table 2.7   (*Continued*)

Author	Title	No. of Editions T = P + P/B	Minimum Known *Tirage*	Total Known or Estimated *Tirage*
Bérenger	*La Morale en action*	15 = 4 + 11	21,900	35–40,000
Lesage	*Gil Blas*	9 = 9 + 0	22,000	30–42,000
Florian	*Fables*	12 = 6 + 6	21,000	30–50,000
Sue	*Mystères de Paris*	7 = 4 + 3	18,200	25–35,000
Pellico	*Mes Prisons*	11 = 9 + 2	18,500	25–35,000
Defoe	*Aventures de R Crusoé*	12 = 8 + 4	13,500	22–35,000
B de St-Pierre	*Paul et Virginie*	11 = 7 + 4	15,500	25–30,000
Defoe	*Robinson dans son île*	3 = 3 + 0	25,300	25,300
Ducray-Duminil	*Victor*	9 = 7 + 2	14,000	24–30,000
Perrault	*Contes des fées*	8 = 7 + 1	16,500	22–30,000
Molière	*Œuvres*	8 = 8 + 0	22,300	24–26,000
Béranger	*Oeuvres complètes*	4 = 3 + 1	20,000	22–30,000
Massillon	*Petit Carême*	12 = 11 + 1	18,100	20–25,000
Racine	*Théâtre*	12 = 11 + 1	3,500	13–30,000?
Lascases	*Mémorial de Ste Hélène*	3 = 3 + 0	14,000	16–20,000
Defoe	*Robinson de 12 ans*[c]	3 = 2 + 1	16,000	16,000
Cervantes	*Don Quichotte*	6 = 6 + 0	6,000	11–20,000
Reybaud	*Jérôme Paturot*	5 = 5 + 0	13,000	13,000
Tasso	*La Jérusalem délivrée*	6 = 5 + 1	11,500	13–18,000
Anon	*Mille et Une Nuits*	5 = 5 + 0	8,500	11–15,000
Scott	*Rob Roy*	2 = 2 + 0	12,000	12,000
Jussieu	*Simon de Nantua*	2 = 2 + 0	6,000	12,000
Scott	*Quentin Durward*	2 = 2 + 0	11,500	11,500
Barthélemy	*Voyage du jeune Anacharsis*	5 = 4 + 1	6,000	10–13,000

a Includes the abbreviated version, *Petit catéchisme historique.*
b Includes Schmid's *Nouveaux petits contes, Sept nouveaux contes, Cent nouveaux petits contes, Nouveaux contes,* etc.
c Includes *Le Robinson du jeune âge.*

Table 2.8
French Bestsellers, 1846–50

Author	Title	No. of Editions T = P + P/B	Minimum Known *Tirage*	Total Known or Estimated *Tirage*
Saint-Ouen	*Histoire de France*	8 = 8 + 0	144,000	230–320,000
La Fontaine	*Fables*	26 = 19 + 7	63,600	80–105,000

Table 2.8   (*Continued*)

Author	Title	No. of Editions T = P + P/B	Minimum Known Tirage	Total Known or Estimated Tirage
Florian	*Fables*	18 = 15 + 3	40,600	60–80,000
Fleury	*Catéchisme historique*[a]	17 = 9 + 8	41,000	65–80,000
Béranger	*Chansons*[b]	8 = 7 + 1	62,000	65–80,000
Anon	*Mille et Une Nuits*	8 = 8 + 0	35,500	45–60,000
Dumas	*Le Comte de Monte Cristo*	11 = 11 + 0	11,000	24–44,000?
Dumas	*Les 3 Mousquetaires*	7 = 6 + 1	15,500	24–35,000?
Fénelon	*Télémaque*	16 = 7 + 9	5,500	20–35,000
Defoe	*Aventures de R Crusoé*	14 = 11 + 3	2,000	15–40,000?
Lamartine	*Histoire des Girondins/ Oeuvres complètes*	6 = 6 + 0	21,000	30,000
B de St-Pierre	*Paul et Virginie*	4 = 4 + 0	23,000	25–28,000
Sue	*Mystères de Paris*	2 = 2 + 0	20,000	22–28,000
Sue	*Le Juif Errant*	2 = 1 + 1	20,000	25,000
Sue	*Mystères du peuple*	4 = 2 + 2	11,600	20,000
Ducray-Duminil	*Victor*	7 = 7 + 0	4,400	15–25,000?
Reybaud	*Jérôme Paturot*	3 = 3 + 0	15,000	18–20,000
Dumas	*Le Chevalier de Maison-Rouge*	5 = 5 + 0	14,000	16–19,000
Brillat-Savarin	*Physiologie du goût*	5 = 5 + 0	14,000	15–17,000
Schmid	*Contes*[c]	9 = 5 + 4	4,650	12–22,000?
Anquetil	*Histoire de France*	5 = 5 + 0	11,000	13–16,000
Cabet	*Voyage en Icarie*	4 = 4 + 0	14,000	14,000
Perrault	*Contes des fées*	8 = 7 + 1	13,000	18–26,000
Racine	*Théâtre/Oeuvres*	6 = 6 + 0	1,500	9–16,000
Hugo	*Notre-Dame de Paris*	3 = 3 + 0	12,500	12,500
Michelet	*Le Peuple*	3 = 3 + 0	9,000	11–12,000
Dumas	*La Reine Margot*	4 = 4 + 0	7,400	9–12,000
Defoe	*Robinson dans son île*	1 = 1 + 0	10,000	10,000

a Includes the abbreviated version, *Petit catéchisme historique*.
b Includes Béranger's *Œuvres complètes, Chansons choisies, Album Béranger*, and *Stances aux mânes de Manuel*.
c Includes Schmid's *Nouveaux petits contes, Sept nouveaux contes, Cent nouveaux petits contes, Nouveaux contes*, etc.

The Bestsellers of the Moment

By presenting the data in five-year periods, I have tended to obscure trivial or topical successes, which have been swamped by the titles which were regularly reprinted. An *histoire événementielle* of the transient bestsellers would include all kinds of short pamphlets and brochures on topical subjects. Since the historian cannot afford to neglect the *fait divers* completely, and even the passing concerns of the reading public may be of interest, some of them must be mentioned here.[8]

In 1815, for example, many ephemeral brochures appeared on the life and death of the recently executed Marshal Ney. Although Ney was soon forgotten by a fickle public, many other bestsellers of the moment illustrated popular interest in the Napoleonic saga. In the first years of the Restoration, many brochures against Napoleon appeared, often in the form of real or fictitious personal memoirs, or anecdotes about the emperor, his marshals or members of his family. On the death of Napoleon, this ephemeral Bonapartiana acquired a more serious and less scurrilous tone. In 1821, many pamphlets and odes to Napoleon or his tomb were published, usually printed in editions of 500 copies per broadsheet. Bonaparte was entering the ranks of myth in titles from 1821 such as *Bonaparte devant Minos* and *Bonaparte, Alexandre et Pertinax*. The transfer of his ashes to France in 1840 inspired another brief torrent of material. This was perhaps a kind of 'literature of the boulevard,' prefiguring the mass consumption of street literature in the 1880s and 1890s, discussed by Jean-Yves Mollier.[9]

Many ephemeral successes can be classed as official or semi-official literature. In every election year, the Paris publishing trade busied itself with the production of election addresses and candidates' manifestos. New pieces of legislation like the Forest Code of 1827 had to be publicized and commented on in ways that made them intelligible to the general public. There were polemical pamphlets too, such as Chateaubriand's *Opinion sur le projet de loi*, a tract on press freedom published in 1827. At least 30,000 copies appeared within two months. This genre hit a peak in 1848, when demand for political tracts and election manifestos was so intense that there was practically no time left in the Paris print-shops to produce anything else.

Publishing fashions changed from year to year. Lamennais's *Paroles d'un Croyant* had such a rapid success in 1833 that it immediately sparked a rush of imitators and parodists, producing titles such as the inevitable *Paroles d'un Voyant* and other satirical variations on the same theme. For a while there was a vogue for titles with medical metaphors. The number of medical handbooks was probably on the increase, especially in the cholera years of 1831–2. For publishers, 1841 was the year of physiology. After Brillat-Savarin's *Physiologie du goût* and Balzac's *Physiologie du mariage* came a range of similar titles.

Almanacs were of course annual productions, and a form of ephemera which is impossible to ignore. Perhaps the largest circulation was achieved by Stahl's *Double Liégeois*, printed in annual runs of 150,000 between 1820 and 1833. Stahl's competitor Eberhart had *Le Vrai Mathieu Laensberg* which attained runs of 25,000 or 30,000 in the late 1820s. Almost every provincial centre produced its own almanac. In Angers, three different printers together contributed about 50,000 copies of the *Almanac de Maine-et-Loire* in the 1840s.[10] In the Doubs, Deckherr produced the *Messager boiteux de Berne* in print-runs of 100,000 copies in the 1820s.[11] During the nineteenth century, such traditional forms of popular reading were ceasing to be the only type of literary consumption available in the countryside, but they still enjoyed massive sales.

The songs of Béranger have their place, too, in this brief survey of short-term successes. The popularity of his songs is a reminder that print had not yet eliminated all forms of popular oral culture; in fact print and oral culture could strengthen each other. The *Chansons* of 1830 were composed and published in order to be sung aloud, in public, on musical evenings, at clubs, *goguettes* and private gatherings. They included drinking songs, patriotic songs, and satires on the clergy. The dominant presence of Béranger at the head of table 4 is a clear example of literary output reinforcing traditional forms of cultural expression.

His father had called himself 'de Béranger' in aristocratic style, but in fact the poet's family were modest tailors from the Faubourg Saint-Antoine in the heart of revolutionary Paris. Béranger worked as a printer before getting a secretarial job in Napoleon's University. He began writing social satire under the Directory, and Napoleon's brother Lucien Bonaparte briefly gave him financial support. Béranger remained staunchly pro-Bonapartist and his poetry did much to nurture the Napoleonic legend in the years after 1815. Béranger was a nationalist troubadour whose songs expressed hatred of the English and supported liberal causes like Greek independence. He idealized poverty and the grape, treated the clergy with irreverence, and answered the Holy Alliance of the monarchs with *La Sainte Alliance des peuples*. He was twice imprisoned under the Bourbon Restoration, which made him a popular hero. 'My Muse,' he would say, 'is the people.' His populism and Bacchic tendencies, which belong to a continuing tradition of French popular song-making, were a little embarrassing to liberal intellectuals as well as to royalists. Alfred de Vigny detested Béranger's success as that of vulgar, bourgeois mediocrity. Béranger, however, reached a national audience, which included artisans and shopkeepers as well as eminent admirers like Michelet, Lamartine, and Chateaubriand.[12]

It is difficult to count Béranger editions: works entitled *Chansons* were sometimes reeditions but sometimes new collections. Some margin for error must be allowed, but print-runs seemed so large on the eve of 1830 that the Revolution of that year must have been a rich musical experience. Sales were boosted by the publicity of legal prosecution and Béranger's prison sentences, especially the nine months and huge fine he received in 1828. The July Revolution set him free from jail, but after 1830, Béranger was no longer the troubadour of the opposition. The wheel turned full circle in 1848 when Béranger was elected against his will as one of the deputies he had earlier lampooned in songs like *Le Ventru*. He soon resigned.

The Bonapartist flavour of many of his songs (for example, *Le Vieux Drapeau*) adds weight to David Pinckney's thesis that a Bonapartist revival, rather than the promise of republicanism, lay at the heart of the 1830 Revolution.[13] His print-runs subsided under the July Monarchy, but experienced a moderate resurgence at the time of the 1848 Revolution. Béranger was a best-selling author who literally had his moments, and those moments were revolutionary ones. He was a songster of the revolutionary *conjonctures* of 1830 and 1848.

There can be little doubt about the most gripping titles of the 1840s which ensured short-term publishing success. In the wake of Eugène Sue's *Le Juif errant*, the best-selling topics of 1845 were firstly the Jews and secondly the Jesuits. In 1847, the death of O'Connell, the grievances of the Poles, and the unpopular missionary, Pritchard, in the Pacific all captured the attention of readers. In 1849 and 1850, the sudden but short-lived fascination with California gold contrasted with the intense politicization of the revolutionary years of 1848–9.

Contemporary Novelists

The impact of bestselling novels is apparent in the tables. Table 2 suggests that Sophie Cottin was extremely popular after 1816, but that her popularity was limited to the early years of the Restoration. Her frequently reedited *Claire d'Albe* was a partly autobiographical love story, told in the eighteenth-century epistolary style. The heroine, like the author, entered a marriage of convenience at the age of twenty-two with a considerably older man. She fell in love with a passionate nineteen-year-old, their affair was consummated and Claire died of remorse for her infidelity. Cottin's most popular title, however, was *Elisabeth ou les exilés de Sibérie*, in which the pure and devoted daughter of a Polish nobleman finds rehabilitation at the hands of a merciful tsar. This legitimist novel, first published in 1806, celebrated monarchical justice and filial piety – values officially endorsed by the Bourbon Restoration.

The enormous impact of Walter Scott is illustrated in table 4. Four of his most popular titles appear on the bestseller list for 1826–30, when his vogue was at its peak in France. Scott again appears in table 5, but the titles listed here for 1830–5 were the last to be published before his death. In the absence of new novels, Scott production assumed a regular and less spectacular rhythm.

After Scott, the novelist's baton was taken up by Victor Hugo, whose *Notre-Dame de Paris* was one of the best-selling novels of the period. Printings were at their height in the first years of publication shown in Table 5. At the end of the period, Eugène Sue and Alexandre Dumas broke new records for novel production, as tables 7 and 8 suggest.

Eugène Sue is an example of a writer who enjoyed enormous popularity in his own time but is now considered unbearably tedious. Sue came from a middle-class family who worried about his unruly escapades and sent him off travelling as a naval surgeon. In 1830 he inherited his father's money and became a cynical Parisian dandy, frequenting high society and writing adventure novels on the side. In 1841, at the age of thirty-six, he discovered the medium of the serialized novel (*roman-feuilleton*) of which he was the master. First in *Les Mystères de Paris* and then in *Le Juif errant*, he fed the popular taste for melodrama, and nurtured interest in criminality and the dark underside of the fashionable Paris he knew so well. He indulged his vague sentimental attachment to socialism.[14] His hero Prince Rodolphe of Gerolstein (in *Les Mystères de Paris*) was a deus ex machina who rescued oppressed prostitutes and seamstresses and punished the villains. He produced novels of immense length which well suited the demands of producing biweekly instalments for the newspapers. Sue kept his suspenseful stories going interminably; readers who wanted satisfying closure were constantly disappointed. Sue's readers, who produced a significant body of correspondence with the author, appreciated his title *Les Mystères de Paris*.[15] For them, Sue was unveiling the mysteries of poverty, crime, and social injustice hidden beneath the elegant social life of the capital. They debated Sue's morality (should a prostitute be a heroine?) but embraced his sympathy for social reform.

On the strength of his fiction, Sue was elected a deputy in 1850, but was forced into exile by Louis-Napoleon's seizure of power in 1851. Sue's *Le Juif errant* and *Les Mystères de Paris* had enjoyed a great initial burst of success but, as Pierre Orecchioni pointed out, reeditions became rarer after 1854, when Sue was in exile, and the popular novel went through a phase of 'depoliticization' under the Second Empire.[16] Depoliticization may, however, be an inappropriate label for Dumas, whose novels had noticeable Bonapartist tendencies.

Orecchioni estimated a total print-run before 1850 of 60,000 for *Les Mystères de Paris*, and 50,000 for *Le Juif errant*. It is unclear whether these figures include editions of Sue's complete works. In any case, they rely on a hazardous average of 5000 copies assumed printed for each edition. They do not account for readers of the serialized version of Sue's novels. According to Véron, the serialization of *Le Juif errant* increased the circulation of *Le Constitutionnel* from 3,600 in June 1844 to 25,000 in July 1845. The initial cost of reading Sue indicates an essentially bourgeois readership: an octavo volume of his novels cost between 7fr50 and 10fr in the mid-1840s, which was four or five times the average daily wage of a Parisian labourer. A subscription to *Le Constitutionnel* was not cheap either (40 francs per year). In 1844, however, *Le Juif errant* appeared not only in an expensive octavo edition of ten volumes, but also in illustrated instalments costing only 50 centimes per episode, which were later bound in four volumes. Sue's readership was perhaps widening to include the Parisian *petit-bourgeois*.

Judging by the complaints of Second Empire prefects, Sue's influence spread into rural areas as well by the 1860s, long after he had disappeared from the bestseller lists. The sales figures of writers like Sue, Cottin, Scott, and Hugo are evidence of the expansion of novel reading, and the growing audience for fiction amongst the bourgeoisie and lower middle class, which was an essential feature of the transformation of the nineteenth-century reading public.

A few celebrity novelists are conspicuous by their absence from the bestseller lists. Pigault-Lebrun, Ducray-Duminil, and Paul de Kock appear only rarely in the five-year tables. Their claim on our attention is based on the prolific number of titles they produced rather than by the outstanding success of any one of them. The complete works of Paul de Kock ran into well over 100 volumes in duodecimo format. In 1842 alone, seventeen titles were recorded under his name in the *Bibliographie de la France*, but their print-runs were modest compared with those of his main rivals.

The omission of Stendhal is perhaps no surprise to those who count themselves among the 'Happy Few' to whom Stendhal dedicated his few novels. Happy or not, his readers were certainly few in his lifetime, for *Le Rouge et le Noir* appeared in only 750 copies in its first edition, and only another 750 in the second, while *La Chartreuse de Parme* was issued in a

modest run of 1200 copies. The most popular Stendhal works were probably the *Vie de Rossini* (two editions in 1823), *Rome, Naples et Florence* and
De l'amour (two editions each, 1817–33).

Balzac is a slightly less surprising absentee, but since he was often serialized in the press, some of his success may have escaped the survey.
Printers' declarations identify his best-selling titles of this period as *La
Peau de Chagrin* (eight French editions before 1850), and *La Physiologie du
mariage* (seven French editions before 1850). The aggregate print-run
for both of these titles, however, did not exceed 20,000 copies.

The print-runs of George Sand's novels were equally limited in comparison to those of Sue and Dumas. Even the relatively successful series
of *romans champêtres*, often reedited, was produced in runs of 1500 or
2000 in 1850, while her earlier successes, *Indiana* and *Valentine*, had
begun their careers in the 1830s with runs of less than 1000 copies each.

Romantic Literature

The success of Lamartine's *Méditations* in the early 1820s was a notable
indication of the audience for romantic literature, and quite exceptional
for a work of poetry. The bestseller lists, however, suggest that popular
romanticism was better represented by Walter Scott and Victor Hugo, by
the medieval love story of Abelard and Héloïse, and by Tasso's crusading
epic *Jérusalem délivrée*. Sylvio Pellico's *Mes Prisons* and Lamennais's *Paroles
d'un Croyant* were immediately popular on their release in 1833 and 1834
respectively, illustrating the strength of the romantic religious sensibility.

Alfred de Vigny fitted the romantic stereotype of the writer ignored in
his own lifetime by a philistine public. The genius, however, did not go
completely unrecognized. By 1846, *Cinq-Mars* had reached its ninth edition, which implied a circulation of between 16 and 20,000 by then. In
addition, De Vigny's *Servitude et grandeur militaires* had been published in
four editions by 1846.

Bestsellers in the *longue durée*

A selection of long-term bestsellers reveals in outline the deepest mental
structures of modern French society. They illustrate literary tastes and
cultural values which were traditional and enduring. Bibles, like De
Sacy's New Testament, have not been counted here; nor have dictionaries like that of Lhomond. Not surprisingly, these were very slow sellers
with long careers. Lhomond's French grammar appeared in occasional
editions of 20,000 or 30,000 copies under the Restoration, and De Sacy's

Bible in editions of 10,000 copies almost annually. The bestseller tables do, however, represent for us the handful of creative and non-fictional works which French society had chosen over the centuries as most representative of itself. The bestseller lists suggest that this culture was, in the nineteenth century, profoundly marked by the achievements of seventeenth-century classicism and, to a slightly lesser extent, of the eighteenth-century Enlightenment.

Almost every one of the five-year tables is dominated by the same three titles: La Fontaine's *Fables*, Fénelon's *Télémaque*, and the Abbé Fleury's *Catéchisme historique*. A second group of titles which appear very regularly in the tables without scaling the heights includes Florian's *Fables*, *Paul et Virginie*, *Robinson Crusoe* in different versions, and the works of Buffon from the eighteenth century, together with Racine, Molière, and Perrault's fairy tales from the seventeenth.

The classical theatre of the seventeenth century is represented by Racine and Molière, always in that order, rather than by Corneille, whose plays were outsold in this period by those of Voltaire. The outstanding example of the abiding influence of French classical culture in the so-called age of romanticism is that of La Fontaine, whose *Fables* stood head and shoulders above all other titles. Between 1816 and 1820, the *Bibliographie de la France* recorded over 240 editions of the *Fables*. I have located the print-runs for 58 per cent of these editions, and they add up to a minimum aggregate of 419,000 copies. Most of the missing *tirages* are for provincial editions, which cannot be expected to have had very large print-runs. In the first half of the nineteenth century, copies of La Fontaine produced in France certainly exceeded half a million, and probably approached 750,000.

Total print-runs for both Fénelon and Fleury also hovered close to the half-a-million mark, but on this evidence, La Fontaine was the most widely read French author of the nineteenth century, or at least of the hundred years which preceded the era of Jules Verne and Pierre Loti. The conclusion is inescapable that, in spite of the fame of Rousseau, Lamartine, Byron, and Scott, French culture remained classical to its core, and the aesthetics of *Le Grand Siècle* left an indelible mark on the history of French taste.

The Legacy of the Eighteenth Century

In the 1820s, the market became saturated with the complete works of Voltaire. Alongside Racine, Molière, and Rousseau, he had achieved canonical status, and could be considered henceforth as a best-selling author in the *longue durée*. The publication history of Voltaire during the Bourbon Restoration was, however, exceptional. No fewer than six complete editions were launched in 1825 alone. All were published in Paris, for only the largest enterprises of the capital had the huge initial resources required to launch the customary seventy-five volumes in-octavo of a complete Voltaire. Ventures of this grandeur were not on the whole destined for a popular audience. Doyen's edition of 100 volumes, which started in 1827, was priced at 300 francs; Didot's earlier production of 1824–33, annotated by Arago, cost 450 francs. Only in the 1830s did Pourrat manage to produce a cheaper edition for about 160 francs all told.

Owning a complete Voltaire was perhaps a sign of bourgeois cultural aspirations, but it was also, in the context of the Bourbon Restoration, to make a political statement. Voltaire was heavily implicated in the 'battle of the books,' in which Catholic missionaries denounced his influence and organized public burnings of his works, while liberals used Voltaire as a badge of their anticlerical resistance against the excesses of post-revolutionary bigotry (see chapter 4).[17]

The overall legacy of the eighteenth century to the nineteenth-century reading public was a mixture of the classical, the picaresque, and the literature of sensibility. Voltaire's stories and plays were probably still the most published part of his oeuvre. Diderot and Montesquieu did not play such a central role in nineteenth-century perceptions of the Enlightenment. Buffon, on the other hand, was very popular. Daniel Mornet demonstrated years ago the strong eighteenth-century demand for Buffon as a reference work.[18] Now his *Histoire naturelle* was becoming more accessible to a new and a younger public. Iknayan stressed the importance of *Gil Blas de Santillane* as an archetypal *roman de moeurs* for nineteenth-century critics.[19] Lesage's novel, valued for its moral instructiveness and for the elegance of its prose, was a steady seller in the best-seller tables.

The literature of sensibility had its readers in the romantic era. Rousseau's *Julie ou la Nouvelle Héloïse*, shown by Mornet to have been the best-selling novel of the eighteenth century, was steadily republished in the early nineteenth century.[20] The *Bibliographie de la France* recorded fifty-five editions, either on its own or as part of Rousseau's complete works, between 1816 and 1850. These produced a total print-run for *La Nouvelle Héloïse* of at least 75,000, and probably between 100,000 and 120,000 copies. This was more than Lesage's *Gil Blas*, but fewer than Bernardin de Saint-Pierre's *Paul et Virginie*. This latter title was often produced in small format, and usually in larger print-runs than Rousseau enjoyed.

Florian's *Fables* were what nineteenth-century readers remembered best from the late eighteenth century. They were published regularly all over France, in short selections, or illustrated by Adam, together with some of Florian's novellas, or even together with some of La Fontaine's fables. The *Bibliographie de la France* recorded 121 editions of the many different versions of Florian's *Fables*. Sixty per cent of these editions yielded a minimum known print-run of over 180,000 copies between 1816 and 1850. The total *tirage* for this period can be reasonably estimated at about 300,000 copies. Florian was also known as the author of novellas like the pastoral *Estelle*, as well as the translator of *Don Quixote*. His influence on the early nineteenth-century reading public clearly surpassed the recognition he received from literary critics in the twentieth.

The Educational Market

The list of long-term bestsellers illustrates the secular preferences of the French reading public, but it also reflects a comparatively new development, namely, the growth of the educational market. Many titles mentioned above were produced specifically for educational purposes. The *Aventures de Robinson Crusoé*, for example, appeared in various editions for children of different ages. The same was true of Buffon's *Histoire naturelle*, which became *Le Petit Buffon*, and *Le Buffon des enfants*. The expansion of educational institutions in nineteenth-century France was clearly having an influence on book production, opening a new market in the schools and adding new readers who, the publishers hoped, would not lose the reading habit after their school years.

The Abbé Barthélemy's *Voyage du jeune Anacharsis*, first published in 1788, was a young student's guide to the civilization of ancient Greece.[21] The author was a student of oriental languages, a numismatist, and an ancient historian who knew Winckelmann, the art critic of neoclassicism. Anacharsis's fictional journey provided an excuse to discuss the arts, religion, and science of Greece in the age of Philip of Macedon. Anacharsis conversed with great philosophers, saw a vast panorama of Greek institutions, and visited the islands. This was potentially a multivolume work, but it was abbreviated, and was most popular in the 1820s.

Télémaque, of course, was an explicitly educational work. La Fontaine's *Fables* had a school readership, and in 1847 they appeared in Boulé's *Bibliothèque du baccalauréat* series as well as in children's editions. The high print-runs of Saint-Ouen's *Histoire de France* are also explained by its status as a textbook. Demand for Madame de Saint-Ouen's *Histoire de France* soared in the later years of the July Monarchy. Her straightforward account of French monarchs emphasized financial economies and the love of peace – values very appropriate to the regime of Louis-Philippe, the so-called bourgeois king. Mollier has traced how Hachette laid the basis for his publishing fortune in exploiting the educational market with titles like this during the 1840s.[22] In spite of its intentions, Guizot's Education Law of 1833 did not create a primary school in every commune at a single stroke. Nevertheless, the evidence from the publishing trade shows the growing importance of educational institutions as consumers of books from the 1830s onwards.

Religious Works

Book historians have charted a decline in the proportion of theology titles published in the eighteenth century.[23] On this basis, they have argued for a gradual and widespread secularization of mentalities in the age of Enlightenment. Religious works, however, were still an important part of the book market. They were not necessarily polemical works, like the attacks on religious holidays and on religious intolerance which had been prerevolutionary obsessions. Nor are the bestseller lists concerned with theological disputes which engaged an erudite but limited clientele. The religious bestsellers were the catechisms and prayer books which served the daily needs of practising Catholics. Religious literature of this kind was a structural feature of nineteenth-century publishing.

Good examples from the Tables are Massillon's *Petit carême* and Abbé Fleury's catechism. Although Massillon's popularity waned after the Bourbon Restoration, Fleury's held strong. His was the most widely used catechism in France, regularly produced in provincial centres, usually in small format for portability and easy reference. It cost only 40 to 60 centimes. From the 1830s onwards, Delalain was producing a *petit catéchisme historique* for use in primary schools, and Moronval issued editions of 10,000 copies every few years, presumably for sale outside Paris by colporteurs. Devotional works and catechisms were typical colportage literature. They were being taken over by large Parisian publishers, and they found their way into new schools, while remaining a permanent reflection of the practices of *la France profonde*.

Moralizing Works

As the primary school population multiplied, and the reading pubic expanded, so the need for improving literature became more urgent in the eyes of both the Catholic and secular authorities. A series of moralizing works met the need to promote moral standards amongst the young. They were usually short pieces for easy digestion, as a pithy message was best embodied in a brief fable, *conte*, or didactic tale. This rule of brevity was demonstrated successfully by La Fontaine and Florian, as well as the *contes* of Canon Schmid, and Bérenger's *La Morale en action*.

Bérenger's *La Morale en action* qualified as a bestseller by virtue of the eighty editions listed by the *Bibliographie de la France* between 1816 and 1860. According to the general catalogue of the *Bibliothèque nationale*, Moronval's edition alone was reprinted twenty times between 1824 and 1863, while Caron's Amiens edition had 137 reprints between 1810 and 1899. An exact estimate of the print-run of Bérenger's anthology will not be attempted, because it is very difficult to identify this title from many others like it in the printers' declarations.

The work, adopted by secondary schools, had as its full subtitle '*faits mémorables et anecdotes instructives.*' It was a compilation of short moral tales usually about children. Little is known of Bérenger himself, except that the first edition of the work appeared in Lyon in 1785, and that the author died in 1822. Even this information came to light by accident, for publishers had assumed that the work was anonymous, and reprinted it thus for years, not realizing that Bérenger was still alive and had some legal rights over the manuscript. The stories had exotic settings to capture the young imagination, and all had a happy and a moral ending. A few had an explicitly religious content, but the majority advanced a secular morality, emphasizing kindness to animals (which figured prominently), courage, honesty, and fidelity. They warned against avarice and gambling and emphasized family solidarity. Many stories featured wealthy merchants: *Jeannot et Colin* praised the usefulness of commerce, but warned against ostentation and reckless social climbing. Here a traditional message was transposed into a middle-class setting, in which Catholicism played a very unobtrusive role.

Later in the century, morally edifying tales for children were produced by the German cleric Christophe (von) Schmid. Schmid's works were adopted by the Catholic educational establishment, and given the blessing of the archbishop of Paris. They had a regular audience in the east of France, and were often reprinted in Nancy, Toul, and Metz. Schmid produced ponderous and sickly parables in which animals and flowers took on symbolic value.[24] His young heroines, uniformly modest and innocent, all had one remediable fault. In *Myosotis*, she was forgetful; in *Les Ecrevisses*, she was cured of gluttony. His girls were *marguérites*, delicate flowers in need of careful cultivation to keep the weeds at bay. Schmid's fictional children were kind to animals, strangers, and the poor. They kept their word, always repaid a good turn and were never tempted by money. They lived in a rural, timeless world populated by hunters, shepherds, and soldiers. Schmid's rather nauseating and insipid fare makes even Bérenger look interesting. Unlike Bérenger, Schmid included explicitly religious references, which perhaps helps to explain his popularity with the proclerical prefects of the Second Empire.

Cooking and Other Manuals

One further category of book must be briefly mentioned: the practical manual, in the form of cookery books and medical handbooks. *La Cuisinière bourgeoise*, or the *Nouvelle cuisinière bourgeoise*, was produced in thirty-two editions between 1815 and 1840, the period of its greatest popularity. The minimum known print-run for these editions amounted to 74,500 copies, and the total number produced was probably about 100,000. The book had been a triumphant innovation of the late eighteenth century. For Alain Girard, it typified the cooking of the Enlightenment, embodying a more scientific approach to dietetics, and a rejection of both aristocratic luxury and coarser plebeian tastes.[25] It represented a wider social diffusion of culinary refinement, and articulated a bourgeois sense of distinction at table. It gave advice on table settings, the proper subjects of conversation, and the etiquette of serving and drinking wine. In these ways, the nineteenth-century bourgeoisie, and those aspiring to join it, were shown a distinctive style of social behaviour and a distinctive gestural code which allowed it to recognize its own and to identify interlopers. Unlike its predecessors *Le Cuisinier royal* and *Le Cuisinier impérial, La Cuisinière bourgeoise* was female, and the book was usually edited by women. But bourgeois women were not necessarily expected to read it. They needed rather to pass it on to their domestic staff.[26] The book's real readership, then, may have been even more democratic than its title implied; it was destined not just for the personal use of the lady of the house, but also for those who sought to serve her better.

Rouvière's *La Médecine sans médecin* had a wide appeal in the 1820s, going into thirteen editions between 1823 and 1830. It was an early medical handbook which discussed a wide range of complaints from apoplexy and asthma to menstrual disorders, migraine, and worms.[27] The author recommended his own purgative remedies, proclaimed as a great advance on bleeding the patient and applying leeches. This advice was couched in language which suggested a Rousseauist stress on natural medicine, fresh country air, and a frugal diet. Rouvière approvingly cited Cato the Elder, who wrote that he was the doctor of his own family, household, and slaves. Rouvière quoted letters he had received from grateful patients, mostly from members of the well-to-do bourgeoisie, *rentiers*, landowners, lawyers, and manufacturers, with a lesser number from clerks and urban craftsmen. These two handbooks therefore both contained internal clues about their readers, real or intended. They came from established or aspiring middle-class families, although they could reach out as well to a readership of the urban *petite bourgeoisie*.

3. Conclusion – Paris and the Provinces

Under the surface of short-term trends and instant literary fashions, we can detect four permanent characteristics which form the irreversible constants of French literary culture. These consisted, first, of the dominant classicism of *Le Grand Siècle*, best represented here by La Fontaine, the outright bestseller of this half-century. Second, the tables suggest the process of canonization of a certain eighteenth-century legacy, represented by Voltaire and the novel of sensibility, best illustrated by *Paul et Virginie* and *La Nouvelle Héloïse*. Third, a group of books especially produced for schools was significant, among them notably *Télémaque*. Fourth, religious and moralizing titles endured as steady sellers, such as Fleury's catechism.

In the nineteenth century, the reading pubic expanded and it became more homogeneous on a national scale. An enormous gulf still existed, according to the five-year tables, between publishing in Paris and in the provinces. The classics, like Voltaire and Molière, were published almost exclusively in Paris, and so too were contemporary novelists like Hugo and Balzac (although for a time Walter Scott was printed in Avignon). If the place of publication is any indication, romantic authors like Lamartine also had their main readership in the capital. Titles which originated in the provinces, which by implication enjoyed a wide provincial readership, were the 'stayers,' the bestsellers in the *longue durée*.

Table 9 illustrates the provincial origins of selected titles. The three titles already identified as the long-term bestsellers of their epoch, namely La Fontaine's *Fables*, Fénelon's *Télémaque*, and Fleury's *Catéchisme historique*, all achieved that status because of their huge provincial audiences. The provincial popularity of secondary authors, like Defoe and Perrault, show that provincial publishers were taking what advantage

Table 2.9
Place of Publication of selected titles, 1846–50

Author	Title	No. of Editions	Publication Paris/ Provinces	% in Provinces
La Fontaine	*Fables*	242	131 / 111	45.9
Fénelon	*Télémaque*	231	107 / 124	53.7
Fleury	*Catéchisme historique*	228	69 / 159	69.7
Florian	*Fables*	121	64 / 57	47.1
Defoe	*Aventures de R Crusoé*	81	50 / 31	38.3
Massillon	*Petit carême*	81	61 / 20	24.7
Bérenger	*La Morale en action*	80	13 / 67	83.75
Racine	*Théâtre*	77	65 / 12	15.6
Perrault	*Contes des fées*	76	35 / 41	53.9
B de St-Pierre	*Paul et Virginie*	57	41 / 16	28.1
Tasso	*Jérusalem délivrée*	51	34 / 17	33.3

they could of the new market of young readers and schoolchildren. It is no doubt significant that the two works with the largest proportion of provincial editions were a catechism and a work of moral edification (*La Morale en action*).

The search for underlying continuities thus leads us to provincial France, for it was there, in the small towns and hamlets of *la France profonde*, that traditional preferences endured longest, and religious practices maintained their strong grip. The evidence of book production presented here gives the impression that the structural features of French literary consumption were essentially provincial features. The provinces absorbed, and for a time also produced, educational books, religious books, and works of moral edification. Paris, by contrast, produced innovation and new fiction. Paris offered publishers high risks and the chance of quick profits. It was here that the forces of modern publishing capitalism would develop.

From Paris, too, came the literature of romanticism, represented in the five-year tables by the poems of Lamartine and Byron. Popular romantic taste, however, preferred Tasso's chivalric poem *Jérusalem délivrée* and Young's melancholic and macabre *Les Nuits* (*Night Thoughts*). If the output of these titles is compared to the constant, regular publication of La Fontaine, Fleury, and Fénelon, literary romanticism appears as quite a marginal factor in French literary consumption. When primary schools were being fed La Fontaine, and when catechisms and almanacs still held an impressive readership, romanticism does not seem an adequate concept to define the era. It appeared, rather, as an evanescent crest of surf on a deep ocean of classicism and Catholicism.

3 Towards a National Literary Culture in France: Bookshops and the Decline of the Colporteur

In the mid-eighteenth century, the only books which reached genuinely national audiences were Bibles, prayer books, and catechisms. By the end of the nineteenth century, readers all over France were buying or borrowing novels like Hugo's *Notre-Dame de Paris*, or Dumas's *Les Trois Mousquetaires*. A homogeneous reading public had been created, and the distinctive audiences of learned literature on one hand, and the popular texts of the Bibliothèque bleue on the other had become merged in the formation of a new mass audience. To adapt Eugen Weber's phrase, readers had become Frenchmen.[1]

The expansion of the French reading public in the nineteenth century remained geographically uneven. Reading French, for instance, was still a much rarer accomplishment in the far western departments than in the north and east of France. Novels became part of everyday life sooner in the southern crescent, formed by the valleys of the Rhône and Garonne, than they did in the rural areas of the Midi. Social status, too, inevitably had an influence on reading habits, for a member of the professional bourgeoisie was far more likely to be a regular reader and book owner than a peasant or factory worker. These geographical and social differences, however, were becoming increasingly blurred in the expansion of the national reading public. The growing population, the advent of mass literacy, and the development of the retail bookshop network tended to erode cultural particularism and the cultural gap between the social classes.

Changes in the World of Publishing

Many factors brought about these changes: the rise of literacy, the decline of *patois*, and the growth of primary education were among them. In addition, developments in printing technology and the appearance of a new entrepreneurial attitude in publishing opened the way to the greater commercialized and capitalistic exploitation of an expanding readership. As a result, fiction writers like Jules Verne could reach a vast national and global audience from the end of the century.

Between 1789 and 1791, the French Revolution had succeeded in destroying the structure and organization of the Ancien Regime book trade. New legislation removed the ancient regulations designed to control, police, and restrict publishing in the interests of the monarchy and privileged corporations. On 2 March 1791, the Constituent Assembly resolved to abolish the guilds. The French Revolution thereby swept away the corporative system which had governed the book trade and the printing industry for centuries, just as it also brought to an end the royal privileges which had limited opportunities for publishers.

The royal administration of the book trade in the Ancien Regime was centralized and repressive, but not always efficient. The apparatus of royal censorship expanded rapidly during the century. In the early 1730s, there were only forty-one royal censors, but by the eve of the Revolution, their number had increased to 178.[2] The censors were unpaid officials, lawyers, intellectuals, and librarians and they were in close touch with the authors they were censoring. Some writers like Condillac also acted as censors, and it was common for writers to discuss their work with their censor, to ensure that it defended religion, monarchy, and *les bonnes moeurs* to official satisfaction.[3]

In the Ancien Regime, printing and publishing were governed by the grant of a royal *privilège*. A *privilège* conferred fiscal rights, for books were tax-free, and in principle guaranteed a home market. A *privilège* was thus an authority to publish which conferred a virtual monopoly on the successful publisher. Armed with a royal *privilège*, a publisher could begin to print in the knowledge that he would be immune from any official prosecution or domestic competition for the duration of the *privilège*. A *privilège* might be limited to twenty, ten, or just a few years – enough to allow the publisher to produce not just one edition, but the repeated editions which alone could make a book profitable. Until 1777 *privilèges* were renewable. Printers before the French Revolution thus worked within a protected system of temporary monopolies, and the book trade was at the mercy of the royal pleasure.

By 1791, however, the Ancien Regime had been practically defunct for some time as far as the book trade was concerned. The monarchy's attitude alternated between authoritarianism and paternalism and the rules were periodically relaxed. The first relaxation is usually associated with the tenure of office of Malesherbes as Directeur de la Librairie (1750–63), although it was continued by others, including his immediate successor, Sartine.[4] The desire to loosen royal control stemmed from a recognition that the government was powerless to prevent an outpouring of pirated and illegally imported works. The government itself began to issue informal authorizations to print (*permissions tacites*), circumventing its own system of *privilèges*.

Meanwhile the late eighteenth-century reading public consumed an increasing amount of recreational literature, and showed a healthy appetite for modern novels as well as the classics. Readers favoured contemporary writers like Madame Riccoboni, and fashionable English novelists like Defoe, Fielding, and Richardson. In a later period, their attention turned to Gothic novels, again of English origin, by 'Monk' Lewis and Anne Radcliffe. The novel was finding new readers further and further down the social scale.

The Revolution accelerated these trends. The crisis of 1787–9 had inspired an outbreak of pamphlets, journals, and political broadsides, defying the legal restrictions which technically still operated. This interlude of press freedom was unparalleled and short-lived, for censorship was to be reimposed by the Republic and subsequent regimes. Nevertheless, the changes wrought by the Revolution were momentous and decisive. They opened up publishing and every other industry to the forces of free enterprise and open competition, making possible the future expansion and capitalist organization of the industry in the nineteenth century.

The publisher who best exploited the situation in the late eighteenth century was Panckoucke, who stands out as a large-scale entrepreneur and press magnate of the preindustrial book trade. Panckoucke was a major press impresario, who came to own seventeen journals, of which seven had been created by himself. He developed the Rupert Murdoch-like technique of buying up minor journals, either to absorb them or just to make them disappear altogether.[5] His printing works were the largest in France before the period of industrialization. He owned twenty-seven presses, and estimates of his labour force range between 100 and 200 employees, which was then an enormous figure.[6] He published Prévost, Voltaire, and Buffon, and before his involvement with the famous quarto *Encyclopédie* (of D'Alembert) was over, he was already planning his own bigger, better, and more systematic encyclopedia. He was the 'Atlas' of the French book trade.[7]

Panckoucke exploited the old system up to the hilt. He used his connections in high places to further his enterprises, presenting complimentary copies of philosophical works to ministers and royal Intendants. He still defended the notion of an industry controlled by guilds, however, to maintain standards, keep the workers docile, and eliminate obscene publications. His career therefore illustrates the limits of economic development within the Ancien Regime. He was a dynamic force but he had not escaped the traditional mould. According to Robert Darnton, 'To follow Panckoucke and his *Encyclopédie* into the Revolution is to watch a cultural system being overthrown.'[8]

In postrevolutionary France, the pace of change was uneven but inescapable. In the 1830s, the introduction of Charpentier's series of small-format novels was crucial for the output of cheap popular fiction; and the Guizot Law of 1833 on primary education laid the basis for the future development of schooling. The serialization of fiction in the press, in the form of *romans-feuilleton*, enabled Eugène Sue and Alexandre Dumas to reach readers who may never have bought a book. The steady fall in production costs brought about a continuing reduction in the price of popular fiction to the consumer. In 1855, Michel Lévy launched his collection of contemporary novels at only one franc; in the mid 1890s, Flammarion and Fayard priced their new series of fiction even lower. Meanwhile the reduction of working hours in the last quarter of the century created a little more leisure time for reading, although progress in this direction was slower in France than it was elsewhere. After 1899, the Waldeck-Rousseau government reduced the working day to eleven hours. The labour movement continued to campaign for an eight-hour day, which was achieved in 1919.

These were important landmarks indicating the need to produce cheaper books for a widening reading public. More and more sophisticated financial management was required for publishers to keep afloat in a world of cut-throat competition. A pioneer like Flammarion could succeed with an initial capital of only 2000 francs and a bookstall by the Odéon theatre, but others like Charpentier, who had shown the way ahead in the 1830s, did not ultimately prosper because their financial grasp left something to be desired.[9]

By 1830, Louis Hachette had seen the potential of exploiting the expanding national demand for school textbooks, at first at the primary but subsequently also at the secondary level. He produced a journal for the teaching profession (*Le Lycée*) which was his own best publicity medium. Hachette benefited from the support of Minister of Education Guizot and by the early 1840s, he produced an average of 110 titles every

year.[10] In the Second Empire, he pursued the franchise on railway station bookstalls, inspired by the English example of W.H. Smith. This was
a step out of educational books into general literature as well as a step
towards greater control of distribution. In the decade of the 1860s,
Hachette's company produced the huge total of 4406 titles.[11] Hachette
was a ruthless boss with a very demanding work ethic, but when he died
in 1864 he was an enormously rich example of the self-made man.

Family firms still dominated French publishing; indeed powerful
dynasties emerged, like the Panckoucke-Dalloz and the Didot families.
Family firms, however, did not always have the resources to remain self-
financing, and they were increasingly transforming themselves into
limited companies, as Paul Dupont did in 1871 and Hachette in 1919.
Of course there was no income tax in the nineteenth century and this
helped to prolong the possibility of self-financing. Other publishers
developed the 'vertical concentration' of the industry, combining not
only printing and publishing, but also buying paper manufacturers at
one end of the production process and bookshops at the other. Publishers developed greater links with business and finance capital. They
invested in land and industrial shares. The Garnier brothers, for example, made a fortune from the sale of erotic and obscene books under the
July Monarchy, but they were also moneylenders and book exporters to
South America.[12] They invested massively in real estate in the Montpar-
nasse district, and by the Third Republic they owned more than forty
Parisian apartment buildings. In fact, their income from real estate was
four times greater than their profits from publishing. Similarly, after
1890, Calmann-Lévy moved his money into railways, public utilities, the
Banque de France, and Rio Tinto mining.[13] Publishing was now an integral part of the capitalist world.

The Transformation of French Cultural Geography

Today's publishers sell books through many different channels. They sell
directly to schools and other educational institutions. They sell directly to
the reader by mail, or through a book club. They sell to supermarkets,
department stores, and to specialized retail bookshops. In the nineteenth
century, many of these various and sophisticated sales outlets did not
exist. The growth of the retail bookshop, however, was a nineteenth-century phenomenon, which made an enormous contribution in assimilating readers into a homogeneous literary culture. At the same time, it
assimilated them as consumers into a national market. By the end of the
nineteenth century, readers all over France were buying or borrowing the

same popular fiction titles. Readers of erudite works and readers of cheap, popular colportage literature came together to form a mass reading public.

Bookshops and lending libraries in small towns and suburbs were powerful mechanisms of cultural integration. In his book on the nationalization of the French peasantry, Eugen Weber emphasized that the period after 1870 was the most important era in the formation of a homogeneous national culture.[14] As far as the growth of the bookshop network is concerned, he was mistaken. I would prefer instead to focus on the decade of the 1850s as the key period.

The establishment of a bookshop in a small provincial town linked the provincial reader with Parisian literary culture and opened up possibilities for literary and cultural standardization all over France. In small towns with a retail bookshop, the cheap popular novels rolling off the presses in Paris were rapidly accessible to all social classes. The spread of the bookshop network, together with its changing pace, rhythm, and geography enable us to outline the changing cultural geography of nineteenth-century France. In the mid-nineteenth century, sale by subscription seemed an antiquated and limited system. Hiring books from a *cabinet de lecture* survived in the provinces, but the colporteur belonged to a dying race. The public library existed only in embryonic form. For a brief historical moment, the retail bookshop became a vital agent of cultural uniformity, as well as a generator of publishers' and newspaper editors' profits. The creation of the national bookshop network, therefore, can be approached as a vital step in the building of a national, if not yet quite a global, village.

What determined the installation of a new retail bookshop? The map of French bookshops reflects growing urbanization. The bookshop was an essential service, which formed part of the familiar infrastructure of city life. Everywhere, therefore, the expansion of the bookshop network was linked to the existence of towns. Not all towns, however, were identical in either their size or function. The size of the town is a vital factor in this investigation. In the nineteenth century, the growth in the number of bookshops occurred in part in the largest towns which were already well served by the bookshop network. In addition, bookshops spread to smaller provincial towns and villages, which lends weight to the argument about the acculturation of remote provinces. The quality of bookshop provision also varied in traditional, administrative centres, in comparison with those in more industrial urban centres with new, proletarian suburbs.

The installation of a bookshop is connected at the same time to the presence of a large, dense, and literate population. Thus, the spread of the bookshop network and its cultural implications must be understood in relation to population density and to the local rate of literacy, wherever this can be determined. Urbanization, the size and function of towns, and the density and literacy of the population must all be taken into account. Regional cultural differences emerge very clearly. Many features, like the comparative backwardness of Brittany or the Massif Central, are very familiar aspects of French regional history. The general argument, however, is that during the nineteenth century, regional differences were slowly diminishing. The expansion of reading in both social and geographic terms was slowly eliminating wide gaps in literacy and in consumption patterns between distant provinces. France's many regional reading publics were being integrated into a more homogeneous national readership.

It is hard to generalize about the scope and sophistication of bookshops and their owners. They include the grocers' shops, which might have sold or lent a few volumes of almanacs, as well as establishments which were probably little more than newspaper kiosks, like the bookstall which appeared in 1880 in a café in Roger Thabault's village of Mazières-en-Gâtine.[15] But even this was a major event for a small community. A few booksellers were not even literate, judging by the case of Pigne-Chateau, who pleaded illiteracy as his defence when accused of selling a legitimist almanac in Angers in 1837. I just look after a grocer's shop, he told the authorities, and leave my wife and children to sell a few books.[16] It is hard to see such individuals as active agents of acculturation. As far as the government was concerned, giving a *brevet* (licence) to an illiterate 'is like putting gunpowder in the hands of a child' – a warning which suggests that it had actually been done.[17] In the little town of Saintes, according to Constans, booksellers could not make a living selling literature alone, and they doubled as dealers in religious objects and school textbooks, as haberdashers, or hardware merchants.[18] The system of *brevets*, furthermore, only reveals to us the legally approved booksellers. Many others operated without a *brevet*, and they remain an unknown quantity, although occasionally, as in Chartres, the local administration noted their presence as clandestine dealers.[19] At the other end of the scale, the official lists of authorized booksellers included shops which, in time, supported thriving publishing houses, like Edouard Privat of Toulouse, who received his *brevet de libraire* in 1836.

Many booksellers clung to a narrowly specialized clientele. In an old ecclesiastical and administrative centre like Toulouse, many bookshops of the Restoration period sold only *livres de piété*, law books, or almanacs. We can hardly regard such places as being in the vanguard of cultural change. They rarely promoted political change, either, it seems, for Dalles of Toulouse, who sold only *livres de piété*, was known to the police in 1822 as an excellent royalist, while his colleagues Manavit and Corne were equally *bien pensant*, being praised respectively as 'a pronounced royalist' and a man 'of good reputation.'[20] A bookshop often functioned as a political rallying point, for example for legitimist or liberals under the Restoration. In 1879, Jean-Baptiste Dumay, a former employee at Le Creusot, opened a bookshop there, displayed anticlerical posters, and tried to attract a workers' following. But workers who bought their newspapers in his shop were likely to be sacked by the Schneider factory, and Dumay had to close in 1881.[21] As far as changes in reading tastes are concerned, booksellers who handled a wider selection of stock are more interesting, like Vergnes of Toulouse, who sold pious works but also literature and science, or Douladoure and Bénichet the younger, who stocked only 'littérature,' which implied that they held fiction and poetry. Not surprisingly, the Restoration police found Vergnes and Bénichet 'in bad odour,' and Douladoure was dangerously 'inclined towards liberalism.'

It is necessary to state the obvious – that bookshops tend to differ – before embarking on an analysis of the official lists of authorized nineteenth-century bookshops. The official archives do not recognize subtle variations in speciality, clientele, or political bias. Instead, they illustrate one facet which all nineteenth-century bookshops had in common: they were all subject to identical policing and governmental supervision, exercised through the local prefect.

Prefectoral statistics on licensed bookshops in every department outside the Seine highlight the importance of this period as an era of capitalist expansion.[22] Between 1851 and 1877–8, the total number of active booksellers in France increased by 110 per cent, to a figure in excess of 5,000, despite the effects of war, revolution, and loss of territory. The bulk of this expansion was achieved in the eight years after 1851. The economic growth of the first ten or twelve years of Napoleon III made possible the assimilation of many small provincial towns into the French reading public.[23] This remarkable expansion did not proceed at an even pace. Statistics suggest two periods of relatively fast growth, with a shorter phase of relative stagnation sandwiched between them. A rapid rate of bookshop expansion in the 1850s was followed by a period of sluggish development in the early 1860s. Then, in the 1870s, expansion resumed, but at a steadier rate than that achieved in the 1850s.

Central Paris itself enjoyed an exceptional bookshop density of under 2000 inhabitants per bookshop in the 1830s and 1840s.[24] The prefectoral archives, however, do not permit a systematic survey of the capital. Instead, they enable us to focus on the Paris region as a whole. The surrounding departments of the Seine-et-Oise, Oise, and Seine-et-Marne formed a privileged area in terms of the location of cultural institutions, and they formed part of the national bookshop network from an early stage. By the middle of the nineteenth century, this was the region most densely provided with bookshops, and its facilities went on improving at an impressive pace, mainly in the 1850s, as far as the Seine-et-Oise was concerned, later on in the case of the Seine-et-Marne. By 1881, bookshop density had reached impressive levels here (3,583 inhabitants per bookshop in the Seine-et-Oise).[25] Only a handful of departments could improve on this.

The most striking feature of the expansion in the Paris region was the spread of bookshops into smaller towns and suburbs. Apart from Versailles and, to a lesser extent, Beauvais, there were no large, fast-expanding urban centres; instead smaller communes were gradually penetrated by the bookshop network. In 1851, forty-four communes in the three departments of the Paris region had active booksellers; but by 1877–8, 138 different communes had at least one. It was in the 1850s, above all, that the bookshop network spread into the future dormitory towns of the outer Parisian suburbs. Chantilly first acquired a bookshop in 1852, Palaiseau in 1854, Orsay in 1858, and Créteil got one in 1859. This geographical spread gave the Paris region its exceptional bookshop density during the Second Empire and made the readers of greater Paris a privileged elite among French readers.

The situation in the provinces is summarized in the accompanying maps. The 1841 map illustrates the areas most deprived of bookshops. In Corsica, the ratio was one bookshop per 27,000 inhabitants or more, but even this was far surpassed by the Ariège, with a bookshop: population ratio of almost 1:38,000. It seems that most of the southwest, except for Toulouse and Montpellier, had not yet been absorbed into the national network of bookshops. The same could be said of most of the west and the centre.

The 1881 map starkly confirms some structural features of the French cultural landscape, especially the solid bookshop network in the east, the north, around Paris, and in Normandy, contrasting with the more deprived areas of Corsica, Brittany, and the centre. All was not static, however: a few transformations were redefining France's cultural space. The emerging importance of the book trade in Bordeaux is one example. In general terms, the well-provided regions were no longer confined to a limited number of isolated but prominent urban centres. Enormous advances had occurred in the middle decades of the century to ensure better book provision throughout the southwest, especially in the Gers, Gironde, and the Pyrenees.

Although the east retained an exceptionally dense bookshop network, by virtue of its superior prosperity, literacy, and urbanization, regional variations were diminishing. By 1881, there were thirty-eight departments with a bookshop-to-population ratio of more than 1:7500. In 1841, there had been only ten.[26] A new geological pattern had emerged in France's cultural geography. A clearly defined southern crescent had arisen, curving south from the Bordelais in the southwest along the Garonne valley, then running eastward along the Mediterranean coast, to thicken at its Alpine extremity, and curve north up the Rhône valley to Lyon. Parts of the centre of France were still poorly provided with book outlets, but only inland Brittany and Corsica were still in 1881 unviolated by the pervasive commerce of the printed word.

To some extent, the departmental map of bookshops is also a map of nineteenth-century literacy. In 1881, the areas best-provided with bookshops in the north, east, Normandy, and the Paris region formed a solid block which roughly coincided with the most literate third of France. The frontiers of this block correspond to the famous Maggiolo line, which appeared to divide literate France from the rest.[27] Maggiolo had recruited 16,000 local schoolteachers to count signatures on marriage contracts in selected periods going back to the late seventeenth century. His ulterior motive had been to prove that the Catholic Church had done little to improve French literacy before the Revolution of 1789. The result was inconclusive, but he left to posterity a conception of France as two contrasting regions: the prosperous, educated and literate north and east, separated from the far less literate south and west by an imaginary line bisecting the country from St Malo to Geneva. This simple dichotomy was misleading, even on its own terms. It tended to ignore the urban, literate Midi, the southern crescent, already mentioned, which ran from Bordeaux to the Mediterranean and up the Rhône valley. This geological pattern emerged in the bookshop density map of 1881. It remained true that the lowest, but fastest rising, literacy rates were to found south and west of Maggiolo's line.[28] For many parts of the Midi, the nineteenth century was a period of catching-up with better-endowed areas. The west, in comparison, found it more difficult to catch up with the north, and it could be argued that even by 1914 it had failed

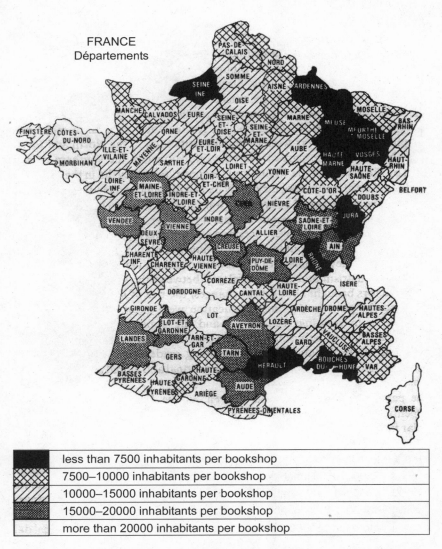

Map 3.1 Density of bookshops in provincial France, 1841. From Martyn Lyons, *Le Triomphe du Livre* (Paris: Promodis/Cercle de la Librarie, 1987). Reproduced by permission.

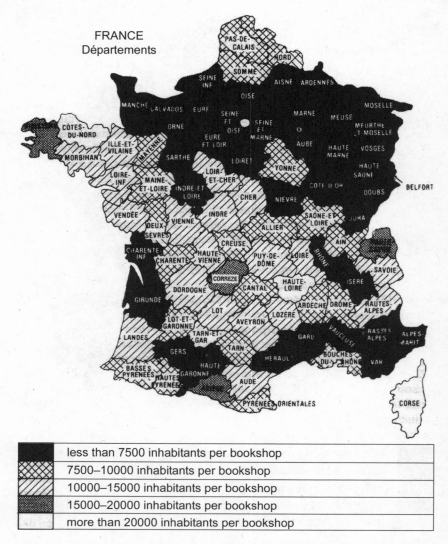

Map 3.2 Density of bookshops in provincial France, 1881. From Martyn Lyons, *Le Triomphe du Livre* (Paris: Promodis/Cercle de la Librarie, 1987). Reproduced by permission.

to do so. Some Bretons, however, would prefer to interpret this failure in terms of successful resistance against the colonizing impulses of the francophone state. Book outlets were rare in some parts of the Massif Central, the Limousin and the centre, together with inland Brittany and Corsica. At the same time, however, the expansion of basic literacy everywhere was obliterating historic differences between France's many and diverse regional cultures. The so-called Maggiolo line was vanishing from sight, just as soon as it had been revealed.

The Decline and Repression of Colportage

The development of a national literary culture contributed to the decline of popular cultural practices. Novels entered the sack of itinerant peddler (colporteur) alongside the almanacs, and the railway and local bookshop made the colporteur himself redundant. Popular literary culture could not long survive the industrialization of book production, the nationalization of the book market, and growing conformity in literary consumption.

Until the second half of the nineteenth century, the itinerant colporteur was a familiar and regular visitor to most parts of rural France. The chapbooks of the Bibliothèque bleue which he sold had catered for a world outside the domain of the book itself. As the book's influence spread socially and geographically, through serialized novels and illustrated magazines, the world of colportage literature correspondingly shrank. In the second half of the nineteenth century, it disappeared altogether.

It did not, however, disappear of its own accord. It was the victim of a campaign of active suppression in the early years of the Second Empire. It had always been officially regarded as a dangerous medium, which might encourage the politicization of the masses. Under the Bourbon Restoration, officialdom had blamed colportage for disseminating subversive Voltairean doctrines. Liberal intellectuals deplored the spread of Bonapartism through the same medium. In the 1850s, there was a strong reaction against any kind of politicization in the literature of the Bibliothèque bleue. Conservative critics reacted with moral revulsion against brochures on the occult sciences, or against the obscene humour of much popular entertainment. The excesses of the 1848 Revolution were blamed on the dissemination of obscene and anarchistic tracts amongst the susceptible masses. Thus, colportage literature had to be purged for political reasons. The almanac had indeed become politicized in 1848, while the songs of Béranger and miniature versions of Eugène Sue had found their way into the colporteur's basket, which reinforced official suspicion of the itinerants.

After 1849, the machinery of censorship and control was set in motion. Prefects were empowered to issue permits to colporteurs in 1849, and since the permits were only valid in the department where they were issued, itinerants were compelled to seek a whole series of prefectoral authorizations to complete their journeys.[29] This exposed the colporteurs to police and bureaucratic harassment. In 1852, a censorship commission was established, and its stamp of approval was necessary to legalize the sale of colportage literature. These measures effectively ruined the publishing industry of Troyes, which had been the main provincial production centre for the Bibliothèque bleue. Production declined, and the number of colporteurs declined, too, as hundreds every year were condemned for infringing the regulations in the 1850s.

Changes in Distribution Practices

The arrival of the railway, which brought newspapers like *Le Petit Journal* into the heart of the countryside, pushed the remaining colporteurs to the remotest rural areas of France. *Le Petit Journal*, founded in 1863 as a cheap, small-format daily selling for five centimes, was the first daily newspaper to conquer a provincial readership. By 1887, it had a print-run of 950,000, which made it the largest daily in the world.[30] In contrast to its predecessors, *Le Petit Journal* had very few subscribers: it sold directly to readers through a national network of outlets. It was sold at Hachette's new railway kiosks, and distributed from depots set up in small towns. Itinerant vendors on bicycles, who were paid employees of the paper, collected it from station depots, and then took it into the countryside.

The rise of *Le Petit Journal* was contemporary with the emergence of the press magnates, like Solar, the Péreire brothers, and Mirès, the model for Saccard in Zola's novel *L'Argent*. The modernization of the press and its readership cannot be understood outside the context of their investment priorities. The daily press extracted huge revenue from selling space to banks and financial consortia, who aimed to tap the savings of gullible small investors. Links between banks and the press were such that by 1880, Soubeyran, vice-governor of the Crédit Foncier bank, controlled the financial copy of sixty-four provincial newspapers.[31]

By this time, sophisticated distribution methods had made the itinerant peddler obsolete. In reporting *faits divers* like the execution of the notorious murderer Troppman, the daily press absorbed one of the staple genres of colportage literature. The retail bookshop allowed even the peasants to buy literature on market days in small towns.

Under the monopoly secured by Louis Hachette, railway bookstalls were another important departure. He created seven special series for the railway bookshops. Each one was cheap, relatively short, in the portable in-16o format, contained inoffensive material for a wide public, and was colour-coded, including his *bibliothèque rose* for schoolchildren.[32] Hachette's bookstalls also sold books produced by other publishers, but at Hachette's prices. Although Flammarion wrested the franchise from Hachette in 1896, Hachette won it back after 1903. Counterbidding from competing publishers had forced up rents, and Hachette was shrewdly buying up newspaper suppliers. By the end of the century the main business of the railway bookstalls was selling newspapers rather than books. Newspaper sales accounted for three quarters of their turnover.[33]

Jules Verne's *Voyages extraordinaires* and the Rise of 'Literary Cretinism'

By the early 1870s, one of the chief beneficiaries of this trend was Jules Verne. In 1871 his publisher Hetzel doubled Verne's fee to 6,000 francs per volume. In 1875, after the huge success of *Le Tour du monde en 80 jours*, Verne could enjoy royalties of 50 centimes per in-18o volume sold.[34] In the 1870s Verne was at the peak of his popularity. Up to 1879, his works were produced in *tirages* exceeding 30,000 copies each, although these figures apply only to the cheapest editions in the in-18o format. In 1904 the aggregated print-run for all Verne editions in-18o had reached the staggering level of 1.6 million copies. The most successful titles by 1905 were *Le Tour du monde en 80 jours* (133,100 copies in-18o), *Cinq semaines en ballon* (83,600), *Michel Strogoff* (59,400), and *20,000 Lieues sous les mers* (55,000).[35]

The work of Jules Verne towers like a colossus over the history of mass fiction, which is perhaps why Salvador Dali dubbed him 'one of the most fundamental cretins of our age.'[36] On the face of it, Verne may seem a transparent and predictable formula novelist. His interests in science and education were hardly exceptional in the second half of the nineteenth century. He was a man of obsessively regular habits, rising at six, working four or five hours a day, walking to his club to read his correspondence, and always calling at the same pastry shop on the way home in Amiens, where he was a member of the town council between 1888 and 1904, hardly missing a meeting.[37] Verne was a model of punctuality and reliability, always fulfilling his publisher's deadlines. He was a typical provincial bourgeois, which is what no doubt irritated Salvador Dali.

There was, however, a mysterious and even surrealist side to the life of the author of the *Voyages extraordinaires*. He maintained a secret relationship with his presumed Parisian mistress Madame Duchesne. His nephew Gaston shot him in the leg in 1887 after Verne refused to subsidize a trip to England – an incident which ended Verne's own travels. His son ran off with a singer. What, one wonders, was the significance of the four thousand cryptograms (word puzzles) left among his papers when he died? And why did he plead with his publisher Hetzel to beat him? 'Beat me,' he wrote in 1865, 'but know that I follow you with all my heart, my venerable master.'[38] These are merely a few of the shadows which obscure parts of Verne's life and work.

Critics have expended much energy on his works. There is a Freudian Verne, a Bachelardian Verne, a crypto-anarchist Verne, a racist and a mysogynist Verne. The notion of Verne as the ancestor of science fiction is the most familiar and hackneyed of his many persona. In fact, space exploration was a theme of a very small minority of his novels, and he was much more concerned with registering recent discoveries than in making fantastic prophecies. In *Cinq semaines en ballon*, for example, he used the explorations of Burton and Speke in a story of African travel whose pretext was the contemporary search for the sources of the Nile. *Voyage au centre de la terre* becomes a documentary about prehistory, reflecting contemporary debates on the origins of the planet and of humanity. The journey underground is a journey backwards in time to the quaternary era. Above all, Verne was interested in the realities of contemporary travel, as illustrated by many novels besides *Le Tour du monde en 80 jours*, constructed around the recent rail crossing of the American continent.

Verne's project also had a pedagogical dimension. The educational aspects of the *Voyages extraordinaires* were particularly stressed by his publisher Hetzel, who in 1862 enlisted Verne on a twenty-year contract as a contributor to his journal *Le Magasin d'Education et de Recréation*. Hetzel's aim was to present the wonders of nineteenth-century science in an entertaining and useful way, and he persuaded Verne to collaborate in developing this conception of children's literature.[39] There remains, however, a continuing tension between the educational aims of the *Voyages extraordinaires* and their role as adventure novels. Today's reader may well find the geography lessons pedantic and intrusive.

Working with Hetzel ensured the novels were marketable but some sacrifices were involved. Hetzel frequently intervened and altered Verne's
text. He was a pro-active editor and thus made a major contribution to
the finished work. He would persuade Verne to excise whole chapters,
alter their order, and change his plots and he would himself add sections
to the manuscripts. When Verne suggested that Captain Nemo was a Polish prince whose wife had died under Russian tyranny, Hetzel successfully
objected. He had his eye on Verne's growing Russian market, and before
releasing *Michel Strogoff*, he consulted both the novelist Ivan Turgenev
and the Russian embassy in Paris to make sure it would not cause offence
to tsarist readers.[40] Hetzel, keeping in mind the conservatism of his bourgeois public, also intervened on religious questions, which left Verne
quite indifferent. He demanded a token divine presence in Verne's
novels. He insisted on including a missionary in *Cinq semaines en ballon*.
Nemo's dying breath was originally 'Independence!' but Hetzel substi-
tuted the safer slogan 'God and the Motherland!' (*Dieu et la Patrie!*).[41] He
wrote to his own son about his role in the composition of *Les Indes noires*:

> The *Indes noires* has in fact become an interesting novel. But it had to be
> rewritten four times over. Besides, Verne wrote to me that he didn't recog-
> nize his original book any more. To which I would have liked to have
> replied: so much the better.[42]

Was Jules Verne indeed the 'author' of his novels? Clearly Hetzel, sometimes seen as Verne's substitute father from whom the author demanded
guidance and discipline, played an important creative role in them.

Jules Verne embodied the racist, imperialist, and sexist prejudices of
his era and perhaps this too contributed to his huge literary success.
Unlike Dumas, who was attracted to Mediterranean settings, Verne preferred the white-skinned inhabitants of northern and Baltic latitudes.
His novels helped to reinforce popular notions of their racial and
national characteristics. His Britons are proud, phlegmatic, and domi-
nating, and his Americans jovial and enterprising. The Germans, de-
picted in Verne's 1879 novel of *revanche*, *Les 500 millions de la Bégum*, love
beer and sauerkraut; they are well-disciplined but prone to bad temper.
The *Voyages extraordinaires* show traces of anti-Semitism, too, and Verne
was an anti-Dreyfusard. Verne's portrait of Isaac Hakabhut in *Hector Ser-
vadac* (1877) earned him an elegant letter of protest from the Grand
Rabbi of Paris, who reminded Verne of his responsibilities to the
younger generation.[43]

Imperialistic platitudes abound in the *Voyages extraordinaires*. Verne's interest in imperial expansion accounts for the Anglophilia of the series. Marie-Hélène Huet counted eighty-nine English characters and twenty-seven Scottish characters in the Vernian corpus. In addition, there are eighty-five Americans and only eighty-two French characters.[44] For Verne, the native energy and *sangfroid* of the Anglo-Saxons made them ideal explorers. The only exception is the eccentric Phileas Fogg, who, far from being an explorer, belongs to 'that English race which has their domestic servants visit the countries through which they travel.' Little sympathy is wasted on the victims of European colonialism. In *Cinq semaines en ballon*, to give one example, black Africans are savage, associated with cannibalism, and frequently described as 'apes' (*singes*). Only two subject nationalities attract Verne's sympathy: the Irish (in *P'tit bonhomme*) and the Canadians (in *Famille sans nom*).

Verne's novels have very few female characters, in fact the formula of his adventure narrative relied on a trio of male characters. The leader was often a scientist, like the humourless Professor Lidenbrook in *Voyage au centre de la terre*. These characters are phlegmatic and inscrutable. In fact the emotionless Phileas Fogg was such an enigma that he was mistaken for a celebrated bank robber. The learned leader has a younger assistant. Verne invited adolescent readers to identify with this character, for most of the adventures happen to him, to test his courage, nerve and intelligence. In *Voyage au centre de la terre*, it is the young Axel who deciphers the cryptogram revealing the passage through the Icelandic volcanoes into the bowels of the earth. The third member of the trio is resourceful but subservient. Affectionate relationships develop between the mad professor, the trusty servant, and the daring adolescent in a male bonding which has given rise to speculation about Verne's sexual inclinations. The rare females in his work typically include the patient fiancée who waits for her young man to return from his exciting initiation into adulthood to marry her, as Grauben waits for her Axel. Verne's heroes travel far in his imaginary universe, but however surreal their adventures, they always fall back to earth. They are sustained by what Isabelle Jan called 'la nostalgie de retour,' a yearning for the distant *foyer* kept warm by tender and devoted female hands.[45] In Amiens, Verne expressed antifeminist views when he was invited to present prizes at the local girls' school. There he discouraged girls from pursuing the study of science and from joining political campaigns.[46] The message was apparently appreciated because the invitation was repeated in following years.

By 1978, Jules Verne was by far the best-selling French author in the world, and probably the most-translated ever, with an estimated global *tirage* three times greater than that of his nearest rival, Shakespeare.[47] His fictional output is a culminating landmark in the story of the triumph of the book and the nationalization of the reading public in nineteenth-century France. His enormous popularity, attested by sales figures, and by lending reports for popular libraries, made him a leading factor in the diffusion of cheap mass fiction, continuing the path already marked out by Walter Scott, Eugène Sue, and Alexandre Dumas.

The Advent of Mass Culture

Many regretted the advance of cultural conformity. According to Flaubert, the democratization of culture was simply 'the raising of the working class to the level of stupidity attained by the bourgeoisie.'[48] Intellectuals, however, were as powerless as the readers of the Bibliothèque bleue to resist the pervasiveness of bourgeois cultural domination. By now, a clear distinction between 'popular' and 'mass' culture had emerged: mass culture drove out popular culture, borrowing from it, and occasionally absorbing it, but essentially relegating it to a quaint survival in a mass age.

The works of Jules Verne are in absolute contrast to the literature of colportage. Both have common features: they were cheap, and they produced a literature of fantasy; but whereas the novels of Verne reached bookshops throughout the world, the catechisms and almanacs of the Bibliothèque bleue were sold in French villages by travelling peddlers. Verne looked forward to a future built on science and technology; colportage literature, on the other hand, looked towards the past, with its traditions of medieval farce, religious devotion, and folk tales. These two very different literary universes could not coexist.

By the last quarter of the century, therefore, a mass literary culture had arrived. Jean-Yves Mollier has emphasised this development, while pointing to its unsavoury side, in his study of the ephemeral literature of the boulevard.[49] The street-sellers of newspapers and pamphlets, the *camelots de la rue*, were also used in the campaign against Dreyfus, disseminating anti-Semitic and stridently nationalist literature. The *camelots* were the descendants of the colporteurs, but unlike traditional peddlers, *camelots* were urban and less itinerant, more associated with the rapid rise of the daily press. The street-sellers were key figures in the dissemination of print culture in the modern city. They had an important role in the formation of a mass culture of print.

This chapter began with Eugen Weber's formula about transforming peasants into Frenchmen, and it has sketched a story of increasing cultural homogeneity which accords to some extent with Weber's vision. Theories of modernization, however, set several traps for the unwary historian. The process of increasing access to reading and writing is an essential aspect of the passage to modernity, but the process followed different rhythms in different contexts. It could take different routes, and a deterministic approach would be misleading. In addition, the acculturation of the masses has usually been seen in terms of the priorities and values set and promoted by the nation-state. National identity formation has been usually interpreted as a priority of the dominant bourgeoisie, concerned to incorporate the masses through a range of nationalizing institutions, including primary schools, the army, the newspaper press, and the communications infrastructure emphasised by Weber. None of this tells us how the masses themselves responded, whether they internalized national priorities, questioned them, or resisted them. Neither Eugen Weber nor this chapter have envisaged such a 'history from below': in order to judge how the lower classes may have assimilated the literature increasingly thrust upon them, we need a perspective very different from that of publishing and distribution history. We need a history of readers.

Censorship and Commemoration

4 Fires of Expiation: Book-Burnings and Catholic Missions in Restoration France

Book-Burning: A Strange Pleasure?

To members of a literate society, the act of burning books remains a particularly shocking and disturbing violation of cherished values. Somehow pulverizing a 'blue' movie, or smashing a television set (a cultural practice once favoured by certain English rock bands) do not produce the same *frisson* as applying a torch to the crisp pages of a well-stocked library. Images of the book-burnings perpetrated in 1933 by young Berlin Nazis are perhaps the most widely known twentieth-century example of this form of destruction. In spite of the familiarity it has acquired, this footage still fascinates, perhaps because it represents the vehement rejection of a whole culture, on the one hand, and because of the ultimate futility of the Nazis' response on the other.

Such thoughts are implicit in an interesting article on the phenomenon by Francisco Gimeno Blay provocatively entitled *Quemar libros ...!Qué extraño placer!* (Burning Books – What a Strange Pleasure!).[1] Gimeno Blay's brief but stimulating discussion starts from two fictional cases of book-burning, the destruction of Don Quixote's library of poetry and chivalric romances and Ray Bradbury's science-fiction classic *Fahrenheit 451*. He might also have included the fiery finale of Umberto Eco's novel *Il Nome della Rosa*, in which forbidden books do, quite literally, poison their readers before being burned like heretics and witches. The author also takes into account a variety of historical instances, ranging from the Inquisition to the obliteration of the National Library of Sarajevo in 1992, and including the attack on Rushdie's *Satanic Verses* in England in 1989.

Building on the ideas of Leo Lowenthal,[2] Gimeno Blay defined three essential characteristics of book-burning. Book-burning as a public act is distinguished, first, by the attempt to extinguish a historical memory, in order to rewrite the past. Second, it is conceived as an operation of social hygiene, designed to exterminate intellectual infections. Thus, in Cervantes' metaphor, not only did the housekeeper participate in the destruction of the books which generated dangerous fantasies in the mind of Don Quixote, but she also brought holy water and hyssop to purify and protect his room.[3] Third, book-burning signifies an attack on the individual author, and may be a premonition of his or her own destruction. Gimeno Blay argues in conclusion that as long as writing remains a weapon in the struggle to reshape social realities, the periodical destruction of literature is inevitable.

This chapter considers some neglected episodes of book-burning in Restoration France in the light of the analysis offered by Gimeno Blay. The book-burnings of this period were distinctive in that they were essentially voluntary acts of destruction. Although, as this chapter will show, Catholic missionaries exerted considerable psychological pressure on their congregations, the burnings remained personal acts of repentance. Although book-burnings were publicly orchestrated for maximum effect, they should be classed as private rather than official censorship.

The practice of book-burning, promoted by the Catholic missions of the Restoration, has been obscured from view by the reticence of the available sources. Three cartons in the Archives Nationales contain police reports about missionary activity between 1816 and 1830.[4] The priority for the government officials who wrote and received this documentation was simply the maintenance of public order, but the files contain valuable details of the missions' activities and the hostility they encountered. It is very surprising, therefore, that there is no mention here of *auto-da-fé*s, which included book-burnings. The standard texts on the period are equally silent about the phenomenon of book-burning. Bertier de Sauvigny's account ignores them.[5] Cholvy and Hilaire discuss the Catholic crusade against family limitation, and against dancing (to which we must return), but do not mention the public destruction of impious literature.[6] The abbé Sevrin, who published a history of the missions in 1948, made some attempt to come to terms with the repressive tendencies of early nineteenth-century Catholicism. He listed eleven book-burnings in this period, but the task clearly embarrassed him, and he sought rather unconvincingly to lay the blame solely on the Jesuits.[7] Perhaps with this aim in mind, Sevrin cited the biblical justification for the book-burnings, namely the verse from the Acts of the Apostles about the effects of Paul's preachings to the Ephesians. In the authorized King James version,

> Many of them also which used curious arts brought their books together, and burned them before all men: and they counted the price of them, and found it fifty thousand pieces of silver.[8]

This text was used in Jesuit book-burnings organized by the Inquisition in the sixteenth century.[9] There is no evidence, however, that it was cited by preachers in the 1820s.

Contemporary press reports, however, whether sympathetic or antagonistic towards catholic ultraroyalism, reveal at least some of the book-burning activities of the period. The principal journal consulted here is *L'Ami de la Religion et du Roi*, very ultraroyalist and ultramontane in its sympathies, and supportive of the Jesuits, although edited by a layman, Michel Picot. *L'Ami de la Religion* carried regular reports of missionary activity in the provinces, and of the war against *mauvais livres*. The liberal press, too, entered the polemic on subversive literature, and I have also consulted *La Minerve française, Le Constitutionnel, La Chronique religieuse*, which was a Gallican paper, and the *Gazette des Cultes*. Anonymous pamphlets and satirical brochures supplement these newspaper sources.

A study of these sources has enabled me to confirm some cases mentioned by Sevrin, and to add others of which he was unaware. Altogether, at least thirteen book-burnings can be documented, as shown in the table below. The table identifies the timing and location of the book-burnings, the missionary society responsible wherever this is known, and the main documentary source for the incident. The last column indicates whether or not Sevrin's account listed the book-burning in question. Sevrin lists a book-burning at Nogent-le-Rotrou in 1828: this is retrospectively confirmed by Arsène Meunier, the anticlerical schoolteacher of the Perche, although he (perhaps mistakenly) places it in 1829. I have not been able to verify one of the book-burnings listed by Sevrin, at Belle-Ile. If the abbé was right, this would bring the total number of known book-burnings to fourteen. This is probably no more than a sample of the Catholic Church's widespread attack on various genres of literature over a fifteen-year period.

This chapter argues that, in general terms, the book-burnings of the Restoration can be understood within the analytical framework offered by Gimeno Blay. Individual authors were targeted, especially Voltaire and Rousseau, although they were not the only writers fit for burning. The

Table 4.1
Book-burnings, 1817–29

Date	Time	Place Diocese/Dept	Mission	Source	Sevrin?
23.3.1817	Lent	**Bourges** dio Bourges	Laval diocese	ARR[a]	Yes
?05.1817	after Easter	**Nevers** dio Nevers	Laval diocese	ARR[b]	Yes
09/10.1817	pre-Xmas	**Vannes** dio Vannes	Laval diocese	ARR[c]	Yes
04.1818	Lent	**Clermont** dio Clermont	??	Minerve/ARR[d]	No
15.1.1819	pre-Mardi Gras	**Avignon** dio Avignon	??Miss'res de France	Minerve[e]	Yes
11.1819	pre-Xmas	**Orange** dio Orange	Missionnaires de France	Anon pamphlet[f]	No
02.1823	pre-Mardi Gras	**Chinon** dio Tours	Laval dio/St-Martin	ARR[g]	No
03/04.1823	Lent	**Amboise** dio Tours	St-Martin de Tours	ARR[h]	Yes
02.1825	Lent	**Richelieu** dio Tours	St-Martin de Tours	ARR[i]	Yes
02.1825	?Lent	**Romorantin** dio Blois	St-Martin de Tours	ARR[j]	Yes
1827	??	**Tréguier** Côtes-du-Nord	??	E. Renan[l]	Yes
05/06.1828	after Easter	**Chambon** dio Limoges	Limoges diocese	ARR[m]	Yes
	??	Belle-Ile dio Vannes	??	??	Yes
1828 or 1829	??	**Nogent-le-Rotrou** dio Chartres	??	Meunier22	Yes

a *L'Ami de la Religion et du Roi* (henceforth *ARR*) 11.285, (3 May 1817), 377–81.
b *ARR* 12.302 (2 July 1817), 235–7.
c *ARR* 14.343 (22 November 1817), 57–8.
d *ARR* 16.395 (23 May 1818), 58–61; *La Minerve française* 2.18 (1818), 242.
e *La Minerve française* 5.65 (April 1819), 632.
f *Mission donnée à Orange en novembre et décembre 1819, par MM. les Missionnaires de France* (Orange, 1819), 13–17.
g *ARR* 35.888 (12 February 1823), 10.
h *ARR* 35.907 (19 April 1823), 311.
i *ARR* 43.1102 (2 March 1825), 87.
j *ARR* 43.1107 (19 March 1825), 170.
k Ernest Renan, *Souvenirs d'enfance et de jeunesse*, 8th ed. (Paris: Calmann-Lévy, 1883), 97.
l *ARR* 56.1457 (26 July 1828), 345.
m Arsène Meunier, 'Mémoires d'un ancêtre ou les tribulations d'un instituteur percheron, 1801–1887,' *Cahiers percherons* 65–6 (1981), 57. I am grateful to Jean Hébrard for bringing this reference to my attention.

missionaries aimed to cleanse society of the moral corruption these authors had allegedly brought about. Finally, and most importantly, the book-burnings were inspired by an attempt to neutralize a powerful historical memory: the memory and the power of the French Revolution. In addition to this, book-burning was part of an intense effort of spiritual reconquest, aimed at reclaiming postrevolutionary France from atheism and unbelief. This effort had many characteristics of a cultural revolution in that it instilled collective guilt, urged collective repentance, and identified individual scapegoats. It made inflexible demands and insisted on uniform compliance, which was to be expressed through rigorously orchestrated public rituals.

'The Cossacks of fanaticism'

The targets and the perpetrators of book-burning, as well as the peculiar ambience of Restoration religiosity, cannot be understood without an account of the activities of the missions, which formed their essential context. One of the main purposes of a mission was to compensate for the shortage of priests. The Catholic Church had never fully overcome the crisis of clerical recruitment which had enfeebled it since the late eighteenth century. According to Bertier de Sauvigny, there were only 36,000 priests active in 1814, which was half the number of 1789. They were old and poorly trained, so that the clergy was lacking in quality as well as in quantity.[10] According to Cholvy, 42 per cent of the clergy active in 1814 were over the age of sixty. The church was inadequately prepared, in numerical terms, to mend what it saw as the ravages of the revolutionary period, or to combat the indifference of many local notables.[11] It is not surprising that book-burnings tended to occur in the central dioceses of Bourges and Nevers, as well as in the Loire valley, for these were areas where the churches were particularly poorly provided with local clergy.[12]

It was quite possible for local curés to get together and organize a mission among themselves, but the missions of 1817–29 usually involved inviting specialist preachers, with the local bishop's approval. They included the abbé Rauzan, a priest from Bordeaux and superior of the Société des Missionnaires de France, who had a spectacularly long beard, which was part of his charisma. Abbé Guyon and Abbé Forbin-Janson, the future bishop of Nancy, were also very active missionaries. In addition there were Jesuits, Lazarists, Montfortains, Coudrin's Prêtres des Sacrés-Coeurs, and De Mazenod's Oblats de Marie-Immaculée active in the Midi, as well as various diocesan missions.

Once the missionaries arrived, the *Ami de la Religion* explained, their aim was to expound some basic truths in accessible, non-academic language: they covered the main elements of Christian dogma, the duties of a Christian, and the meaning of Christian symbolism.[13] The zeal of many missionaries, however, far surpassed this innocuous program.

Their preaching encouraged religious observance, attendance at mass, confession, and penitence. Missionaries also hoped to effect some occasional conversions; a few Lutherans, for instance, were converted at Nancy in 1824,[14] and in Toulon a special effort was made to 'convert' convicts, and books were distributed to them.[15] The *Ami de la Religion* assiduously reported conversions of Lutherans, Jews, and Muslims, which were a valued performance indicator of a successful mission.

Missions organized processions, sometimes involving the whole community, the public authorities, and the National Guard. They conducted religious instructions and pious exercises, which started very early in the morning so that workers could attend before going to work, and sometimes went on until very late at night. At Rennes, where there were seven instructions daily in 1817, people turned up at 4 am so as not to miss the first instruction at five.[16] Participating priests had to be fit enough to deliver three sermons daily, and spend hours, and perhaps entire nights, in the confessional for the duration of the mission. (Missions in large towns usually lasted about six weeks.) The pious exercises over which they presided might include an *amende honorable* (a public apology) to Jesus Christ, in the mood of public repentance typical of the Restoration missions, the renewal of baptismal vows, the consecration of the Virgin, and establishing the Stations of the Cross.

The sermon in the cemetery was a striking and macabre component of many missions. In Barjols (Var), for example, four young missionaries from Aix exhumed a recently buried corpse, separated the head from the body, and exhibited it to the crowd to illustrate their dissertation on mortality.[17] Preachers emphasized the terrors of death and damnation as vividly as possible in order to revive the faith of their audiences.

In the spirit of the Counter-Reformation, missionaries preached against loans at extortionate rates of interest.[18] They openly defended the Inquisition, which had preserved Catholicism from heresy, even if a few innocent victims had unfortunately perished in the process, one preacher in Carpentras conceded.[19] There were further echoes of the seventeenth century in verbal attacks on Protestants in La Rochelle and Montpellier, by the notorious Abbé Guyon.[20] The administration was relieved that preachers did not dare renew these sermons of intolerance in the strongly Protestant areas of Nîmes and Alsace. The faithful were urged to boycott those who had not participated in the mission's work. Innkeepers and merchants like those at Briançon were pressured to conform or else face the desertion of their Catholic customers.[21]

Although the secular authorities issued regular reminders that preachers should avoid political controversy, these reminders were ignored or circumvented. Since the missions aimed to rescue French Catholics from the evils of the Revolution, they repeatedly attacked the Revolution and its sympathizers. Preachers all over France attacked the purchasers of *biens nationaux*.[22] They asked for the 'restitution' of church property lost, sold, or purloined during the French Revolution. Arguing that the sale of church property had been illegal, the missionaries wanted the beneficiaries to either give it back, or at least pay the church the difference between the devalued *assignat* price they had paid and the 'real' value of the property. A few purchasers with a guilty conscience were thus induced to make a donation to the mission.

The missionaries argued that sacraments administered by the constitutional clergy were invalid, and that a civil ceremony alone, conducted by a revolutionary administrator, did not constitute a legitimate marriage. They therefore offered to rebaptize and remarry those who had undergone such ceremonies in order to rectify their position in the eyes of the church. Thus at Tarascon in 1819, *L'Ami de la Religion* reported that 'a large number of sinners ran to the bathing pool' after discovering their sinful status.[23] Some supporters of the Revolution, however, could never be redeemed in this way, and they were refused the sacraments. There was a brief scandal in Arles in 1817 when the mission refused a religious burial to the ex-Jacobin Antonelle.[24]

The political propaganda of the Catholic missions was only thinly veiled. Soldiers of 'the old army,' for example, were denounced as brigands and cannibals, which was a reference to the Vendean War.[25] The missionaries conventionally preached fidelity to the king, but the message was reinforced by a reminder of the disasters which befell France following the abandonment of monarchist loyalties in 1793.[26] The communal *amende honorable* was one of the key rituals of the mission. It was made to coincide as closely as possible with the anniversary of the death of Louis XVI; at Marseille in 1820, it occurred precisely on 21 January.[27] In this way, the ceremony was manipulated to express collective repentance for the sins of the French Revolution.

Above all, the missionaries warned against the dangers of pernicious literature. In Marseille in 1820, the missionaries preached to a mainly female audience against Voltaire and Jean-Jacques, 'expressly prohibiting reading them.'[28] In Grenoble in 1818, the missionary's sermon was 'a vigorous attack on Jean-Jacques, Helvétius, and Voltaire, against whom were contrasted Massillon, Pascal, Bourdaloue.'[29] Meanwhile at Le Mans, missionaries from the Laval diocese preached against 'The reading of those corrupting books, which soil the imagination, corrupt the heart, and never fail to lead imprudent youths who enjoy reading them to the precipice.'[30] Such sermons against *mauvais livres* were the immediate prelude to book-burnings, and will be taken up again later.

The missionaries knew that women were often more receptive than men to their revivalist rhetoric, and they had different messages for male and female members of their congregations. They organized separate 'retreats' for men and for women. The young girls of the community were assembled in church and asked to swear that they would give up dancing.[31] Nothing was likely to infuriate the young men of the village more than this approach, especially when the women were not permitted to leave the church until they had taken an oath not to dance with them.

Sexual segregation, whether aimed against dancing or contraceptive practices, appeared socially divisive and met with the candid disapproval of the secular authorities. The prefect of Grenoble deplored its unfortunate effects when he reported that the assiduous attendance of women at the missionaries' activities was not a sign of piety but 'of exaltation, and exaltation is dangerous. Some were so moved by the preacher's tone that several almost totally lost their reason.'[32]

The idea was to frighten people: *L'Ami de la Religion* described one purpose of a mission as to 'frighten people about the consequences of their indifference to salvation.'[33] Theatrical scenes of self-abasement inspired public outbreaks of weeping and moaning amongst the congregations, according to witnesses. At Rennes and at Soissons, missionaries tore off their own surplices, declaring themselves unworthy, and prostrated themselves on the ground, until the audience begged them to continue.[34] The preacher's humility could be short-lived: some missionaries claimed to be sent from God, and sold their portraits to the people.[35] The bishop of Avignon reflected the upper clergy's distaste for such activities when he called the missionaries 'the cossacks of fanaticism.'[36]

The culmination of all successful missions was the *plantation de la croix*, at the end of a solemn procession. According to the prefect of the Var, 15,000 attended the erection of the mission cross in Toulon, in 1820.[37] Twenty thousand reportedly attended the final ceremony at Nantes in 1827, made up of townspeople and peasants from the surrounding countryside.[38] An even larger crowd of 40,000 attended a *plantation de la croix* in Avignon in 1819.[39] The cross was often made of oak, and it took a huge effort to raise and support it, not to mention carrying it to its various 'stations' on the way. It would sometime fall and break. In Tarascon in 1819, the mission cross was forty feet high; in Reims in 1821, it was fifty-six feet long, carried by 240 men.[40]

The missions coincided with the critical moments of the Christian year; Christmas was a good choice, but Lent was the preferred time. Missions frequently lasted from Lent until the end of Easter. When the missions arrived earlier than this, that is to say before the beginning of Lent, they risked a clash with the local carnival, which inevitably created conflicts, as we shall see. Lent traditionally began on Ash Wednesday with the burning of an effigy of carnival. Ashes and symbolic fires were a common part of both Christian and non-Christian rituals at this time of year, as Cholvy and Hilaire have indicated (without, however, connecting them to the burning of books).[41] Missions often began on the first Sunday in Lent, known as *dimanche des brandons* (Torch Sunday), another occasion when fires were lit. In many parts of France, fires were set under fruit trees at this time because it was thought this helped the crop. On Good Friday, in eastern France, it was an old custom to burn 'a Judas' or 'a Jew.' In these instances, as in the burning of books, fire was an agent of cleansing and rebirth.

The fires, however, could also be fires of punishment, like that meted out by God to the Cities of the Plain: hence one *Catéchisme anti-révolutionnaire*, published at Montpellier, advised on burning *mauvais livres*, especially those by the wicked and depraved Voltaire, whose eyes were 'full of fornication; Sodom would never have received him, and Paris crowned him!'[42]

The *auto-da-fé*s were thus carried out in a highly charged atmosphere, fuelled by the preachers' insistence on redeeming the guilt of France's recent revolutionary past. They engendered a mood of popular revivalism, which sometimes disgusted the prefects and disturbed the bishops. The missionaries adapted the spirit of Counter-Reformation proselytism to the context of postrevolutionary society. This description of the 'cossacks of fanaticism' remains unbalanced, however, without an outline of popular and administrative reactions to their activities.

Popular Anticlericalism

Contemporary reports agreed that the missions drew huge crowds, usually from the urban lower classes, together with peasants who would swell the urban population during the erection of the cross, the spiritual climax of the mission. On the other hand, witnesses sometimes noted the indifference of the middle classes. Later on, in 1827–8, missions reported more frequently that they had to overcome the 'coolness' (*froideur*) of local congregations. A certain sexual dimorphism, often noted by historians of religious behaviour, was also apparent: the missions aimed to appeal to young women, but the opposition to them tended to come from young men. Male youths were likely to suffer unemployment as the result of the arrival of a mission; and they were also threatened by the missions' attempts to stop girls' dancing.

The strongest resistance of all was encountered in Brest in 1819, when the mission was virtually expelled; and in Rouen in May 1826, when a missionary was assaulted and anticlerical protests continued for a month.[43] In Sablé (Sarthe), in 1819, the combined opposition of mayor and prefect induced the bishop of Le Mans to suspend the mission.[44] There were riots in Paris and arrests outside Eglise des Petits-Pères in April 1822, and more disturbances against missionaries occurred in November 1822 outside St Nicolas-des-Champs.

The attitude of the Catholic hierarchy to such missionary activity was subdued. Although the upper clergy was clearly committed to the struggle against *mauvais livres* and to the promotion of *bons livres*, this did not necessarily mean that it approved of public book-burnings. The local bishop was often crucial to the success of a mission: it could not proceed without his authority, and he could intervene to prevent undue harassment from hostile municipalities. In Brittany and Provence, the missionaries needed the cooperation of local clergy to ensure that sermons were delivered in local languages. The bishop and the clergy, however, risked being reduced to impotence as outsiders virtually took over their regular flock.[45] The bishop had to balance several interests: the susceptibilities of his priests, the success of the mission, and the need to cooperate with the local prefect to maintain public order. The prefect could ultimately determine the bishop's attitude, as when he prevailed upon the bishop of Le Mans to suspend the mission in Sablé already mentioned.

The arrival of a mission threatened to disrupt the economic life of urban communities. Missions tried to stop all festive activities and popular amusements. When they arrived at carnival time, the missionaries almost inevitably provoked hostility. In fact, they took pleasure in making theatres deserted, and closing down all profane pleasures, as they did for example at Coutances in February 1822.[46] Missions were therefore bad for business because they threatened the livelihood of many artisans and shopkeepers who expected to make money out of carnival (lemonade-sellers, *pâtissiers*, restaurateurs, ice-cream merchants, musicians, and cloth-trade workers saw their carnival trade evaporate). The arrival of a mission in La Rochelle at the end of January 1818 meant there would be no dances, no *soirées*, and no theatre.[47] In Marseille, the prefect predicted conflict at carnival time, because small shopkeepers stood to lose an expected profit, and 'people will resent their apostolic fervour.'[48]

Young males objected strongly to the prohibitions imposed by the missionaries, and anticlerical protest took the form of charivaris and other festivities common to such youth groups. At Montréjeau (Haute-Garonne), for example, a charivari was accompanied by shouts of 'Down with the Jesuits!'[49] In Brest in 1819, a charivari of about 600 people initiated the disturbances which led to the suspension of the mission by the bishop of Quimper and the rapid departure of the missionaries. This agitation was led by well-off people (*la classe aisée*) and naval officers. In Tain (Drôme), in February 1817, youths entered the square beating drums and dancing the farandole on *Dimanche des Brandons* while the sermon was in progress.[50]

Youths repeatedly set off firecrackers (*pétards*) and stink-bombs in church, hoping to interrupt the sermon by suffocating the preacher with their 'mephitic odours.' At Dieulefit (Drôme) in April 1821, several youths interrupted the missionaries' sermon with cries of 'Fire! Fire!' The congregation rushed to the door to find the doorway blocked by a pile of well-placed excrement. As they extricated themselves, they could see the culprits climb onto the pedestal of the mission cross and urinate upon it. The local gendarmerie obeyed a standard administrative reflex: they blamed the Protestants.[51] Women's dresses would be slashed with knives as they entered and left the church and cats, dead or alive, would be hurled into the congregation.[52] Men with blackened faces left posters and graffiti hostile to the missionaries in Dijon in 1825.[53] Whenever the missionaries arrived in town, young men demanded that Molière's *Tartuffe* be performed at the local theatre, as happened in Brest in 1826, when the abbé Guyon was hung in effigy.[54]

Considering the missionaries' bans on dancing, dancing itself could be seen as a form of popular protest. This was the case in Arrau (Hautes-Pyrénées), where the missionaries had unfortunately arrived at the time of the *tirage au sort*, when many young men from surrounding areas were in town to draw ballots to select conscripts. Mayor Coma of Arrau (who, unusually on this occasion, was fully backed by his prefect) responded defiantly by giving a mayoral *bal* to celebrate the *fête patronale* while the mission was in the town. He invited minstrels to stroll through the streets to advertise the event, and they did not fail to stop outside the missionaries' house to sing them a provocative 'serenade.' As a result of this conflict with the mayor, the mission finished early and there was no *plantation de la croix*.[55]

Although missionary processions were well attended, the missionaries often triggered popular anticlerical reflexes. Male youths felt threatened by restrictions on access to young females, and by unemployment and loss of business if the mission succeeded in stifling traditional carnival celebrations. Their responses were a mixture of the juvenile and the literary (as in the battle for *Tartuffe*). The charivari exposed the missionaries to collective ridicule and occasionally produced the expulsion of the mission. Protesters borrowed elements of public theatre, an arena in which the missionaries themselves were adept. The throwing of dead cats into predominantly female congregations seems a rich and allusive event to those trained by Robert Darnton in the historiographical study of feline symbolism.[56]

Such vulgar demonstrations of popular anticlericalism were ignored by the liberal press. In their coverage of the Catholic missions, liberal journals did not normally denounce book-burnings, either. What concerned them most of all was the deliberate use of the missions to promote legitimist propaganda, and their commercialization. Judging by the relative amount of space devoted to these issues by *Le Constitutionnel* and *La Chronique Religieuse*, the profitable sale of pious booklets and rosaries was more scandalous than book-burning.[57]

Voltaire, Rousseau, and *Les Mauvais Livres*

Voltaire and Rousseau were the two demons most frequently vilified by the Restoration missions. These two authors and their *philosophe* acolytes were held responsible for the evils of the French Revolution. In the mind of the Catholic missions, the world was clearly divided between Christian and diabolical influences. Since Voltaire and Rousseau had been engaged in a philosophical conspiracy against Christianity, their offensive literature had to be destroyed, to prevent contamination by the works of the devil. Moreover, their works had to be offered in sacrifice, to redeem the moral collapse of French society since 1789.

The polemic about Voltaire and Rousseau was aggravated by the publication of several editions of their complete works in the early years of the Restoration. In 1817 alone, four new editions of Voltaire's complete works were announced, as well as two editions of Rousseau's complete works. Two of these were in small duodecimo format, capable of reaching a wider audience than the more traditional in-octavo editions. Any possibility of the wider circulation of Voltairean literature angered *L'Ami de la Religion*, which asked rhetorically, 'Isn't there enough poison circulating already, and do we absolutely have to increase the dose?'[58] The addition of Condorcet's *Life of Voltaire* as a preface to *veuve* Perronneau's

50-volume duodecimo edition of Voltaire seemed to confirm the thesis of a philosophical conspiracy against religion.

These publishing initiatives were not in themselves responsible for the outbreaks of book-burning. As the table above showed, the series of book-burnings was under way early in 1817, well before the new editions of Voltaire had been put into circulation. It was even earlier, in January 1813, that Madame de Lamartine, mother of the poet, found copies of *Emile* and *La Nouvelle Héloïse* in her son Alphonse's bedroom. Alphonse was 23 at the time, but his mother resolved to burn his dangerous library.[59] The output of Parisian publishers, however, certainly fuelled a bitter polemic between Catholics and liberals. The message of 'Ecrasez l'infâme' (Crush the scum! – i.e., the clericals) seemed about to circulate everywhere, together with parodies of the Scriptures, outrages against Jesus Christ and the saints, and slanderous versions of church history. In 1817, the *vicaires-généraux* of the Paris diocese entered the fray, issuing a Lenten letter (*mandement*) condemning philosophical works.[60] The liberal press defended the *philosophes* against the clergy. Benjamin Constant's paper *Le Constitutionnel* responded to the *vicaires-généraux* with a satirical parody entitled *Muphti des Musulmans,* and argued that the Revolution was not the fault of Voltaire and Rousseau, but of the privileged classes.[61] A battle had now been joined that would lead to a series of book-burnings and last up to the 1830 Revolution.

Voltaire was portrayed as a *fanatique* of unbelief, moved by 'that impious intoxication' which inspired 'the philosophical conspiracy.'[62] The attack was soon extended to include a new edition of Helvétius, 'that lesser writer.'[63] Nor did Diderot escape, when Belin announced a new octavo edition of his works in 1818. Diderot, alleged *L'Ami de la Religion,* was a well-known cynic and materialist and an enemy of Christianity. Catholic propagandists loved to cite the *philosophes'* criticism of each other, and Voltaire's adverse comments on Helvétius and Diderot were gleefully presented as proof of the latter's depravity.[64]

On Quasimodo Sunday, 1822, the abbé Frayssinous delivered a lecture in Saint-Sulpice on *mauvais livres*. The distinguished status of the preacher (he was First Royal Chaplain), the importance of the location, and the presence of eminent personalities including the Duchesse de Berri testify to the importance accorded to the 'battle of the books' in the political and religious struggles of the Restoration. Frayssinous attacked authors, either unbelievers or worse, the impious, who spread the social poison of philosophical literature; he denounced the disseminators of the poison who were putting huge numbers of volumes on the market; he deplored the tastes of readers rashly tempted by dangerous books instead of enjoying the great works of Greece, Rome, and Bossuet. He outlined a world divided into two camps, each aligned under its own literary banner. In the mentality of Restoration Catholicism, religion was locked in a cosmic confrontation with unbelief. For Frayssinous, 'good and evil are the forces in play' (le bien et le mal sont comme en présence).[65]

France was thus seen as the theatre of a Manichean struggle between *bons livres* and *mauvais livres*. The Catholic Church made a concerted effort in the 1820s to establish Christian libraries which would act as distribution centres for *bons livres*. One consequence of the mission in Grenoble in 1822 was the foundation of a *bibliothèque chrétienne*, which lent Christian literature free of charge to workers and young readers. By 1824, its stock of lives of the saints, religious history, and Christian apologetics had expanded to 6,000 volumes, and it boasted 1,300 readers.[66]

This service was duplicated in Bordeaux by the Assocation des Bons Livres, established by the bishop of Bordeaux in 1820. Its aim was to take *mauvais livres* out of circulation, by buying them or exchanging them for more wholesome literature. The papal nuncio in Spain agreed to ask the pope to grant indulgences to encourage subscribers.[67] In Paris, the Société catholique des bons livres published its own library in small in-18o format, starting with Lhomond's *Histoire abrégée de la religion* (1824), immediately followed by Fénelon's *Oeuvres spirituelles*. Its prospectus declared:

> It is through books that society has been tainted; it is through books that we must make it whole ... People are spreading shameful and degrading doctrines; let us spread doctrines that are holy and sublime.[68]

At the end of its first year of activity, the Société had approximately 7,500 subscribers, but numbers declined thereafter to 6,400 in 1826, and 6,000 in 1827, but it claimed to have sent out 900,000 volumes by 1828.[69] Other libraries were established soon afterwards in Lille, Tours, Autun, and Vendôme, where the moving spirit was Abbé Donnet, the instigator of the book-burning at Romorantin in 1825.[70]

Perhaps the unprecedented vogue for complete editions of Voltaire in the 1820s helps to explain the violence of the Catholic campaign against *mauvais livres*. According to Gérard Cholvy, there were twelve complete editions of Voltaire published between 1817 and 1824. He estimated that a total of 1,598,000 copies of Voltaire were produced, as well as 492,000 copies of Rousseau.[71] Cholvy, however, took these figures uncritically from a ministerial report of 1825 entitled *Sur la multiplication des mauvais livres.*[72] This census of philosophical publications submitted to the Ministry of the Interior was motivated by the fear that the adoption of cheap and portable formats like the in-18o would give philosophical literature a wider and more popular readership, and that 'in a short time Voltaire will be in every household, from the pauper's attic to the rich man's study, in the merchant's shop and even in the peasant's cottage.'

There are ways of obtaining more accurate information than that deployed by Cholvy. If the notices of new publications in the *Bibliographie de France* are matched with the information provided by the statutory declarations of Parisian printers, we can obtain a clearer picture of Voltaire publication in the period, as well as of the print-runs of relevant titles. This method was profitably used in *Le Triomphe du Livre*, in which I placed the complete works of both Voltaire and Rousseau among the best-sellers of the Restoration (see chapter 2 above).[73] It appears from the simultaneous study of these two sources that the figures for the circulation of Voltaire's works cited above are close to the mark, if they are taken to include the circulation of his plays. Voltaire's theatrical works were republished in eleven editions under the Restoration, although they were far less noxious in legitimist eyes than, say, his *Dictionnaire philosophique.*

The figures given above for the circulation of volumes by Rousseau, however, almost certainly underestimate production figures for 1817–24. In both cases, the aggregate number of volumes, cited by the ministerial report for its shock value, is a very unhelpful way of charting the undeniable surge in Voltaire and Rousseau production. The gross aggregate, compiled without regard for the format adopted, fails to distinguish between different editions and their different target audiences. Fain's twelve-volume edition of the Kehl Voltaire, for example, published with a modest print-run of 1,600, cost twelve francs per volume, and was surely destined for a cultivated, discerning, and wealthy clientele. This was very different from the miniature (in-32o) editions of Voltaire's *contes* or his dramatic works appearing in the 1820s, and from the issue of his works in instalments, which were cheaper, more portable, and enjoyed larger print-runs.

A summary of the publication of Voltaire's complete works under the Bourbon Restoration is provided in table 4.2. Altogether, thirty-seven editions of Voltaire's 'oeuvres' or 'oeuvres complètes' can be traced. The print-runs of most of these editions did not exceed 2,000 copies. As the table shows, some uncertainty remains about the figures. The number of

TABLE 4.2
Publishing History of Voltaire's *Complete Works*, 1816–30

Date	Vols/Format	Publisher/Printer	Price	Tirage
1817–19 [Kehl]	13v in-8o	Fain/Desoër	12fr per vol.	1600
1817–20 [Beaumarchais]	35 to 43v in-12o	Poulet + Veuve Jeunhomme/ Plancher	3fr50 per vol	2000
1817–18	36 to 40v in-8o	Crapelet/Lefevre	6fr per vol	unknown
1817–23 [Kehl]	50 to 56v in-12o	Veuve Perronneau	3fr per vol	1500/2000
1819–24	66v in-8o	Crapelet + Renouard	450fr	1500
1820–5	70v in-8o	Crapelet + Didot aîné/Lefevre	315fr	1200
1820–3	60v in-18o	Carez (in Nancy)	96fr	unknown
1820–3	75v in-12o	Baudouin + Laurens/Touquet	?	4000/6000
1821–4	60v in-8o	Ve Jeunhomme/Esneaux et al	135fr	1700/2000
1821	? in-8o	F.Didot/Desoër	360fr	1500 ?
1822 ['chefs d'œuvres']	5v in-18o	Rignoux/Aillaud	?	2000
1823–6	70v in-8o	Dupont/Chassériau	350fr	2000/3000
1824–33	95v in-8o	Didot aîné/Dalibon	450fr	1200 ?
1825 ['oeuvres']	? in-8o	Didot aîné/Froment	?	2000 ?
1825–9 ['1st ed']	75v in-8o	Didot aîné/Baudouin	?	2350
1825–8 ['2nd ed']	75v in-8o	Rignoux/Baudouin	?	2000
1825–9 ['3rd ed']	75v in-8o	Rignoux/Baudouin	?	3000
1825–	66v in-8o	Crapelet/Salmon	?	unknown
1825 [instalments]	75v in-18o	Carez et al (in Nancy)	?	1500
1825–9 [instalments]	? in-8o	Didot aîné/Baudouin	140fr	3000
1825–7 [instalments]	? in-8o	Fournier/Bossange	150fr	3300
1826	30v in-18o	Renouard/Boucher	75fr	2000
1826–9 ['4th ed']	75v in-8o	Rignoux/Baudouin	?	2000
1826- [instalments]	75 or 80v in-32o	Rignoux/Baudouin	?	2000/5000
1827–9 ['5th ed']	75v in-8o	Rignoux/Baudouin	?	2000
1827	50v in-8o	Didot aîné/Lefevre	200fr	2250
1827	75v in-12o	Cosson/Garnery	?	unknown
1827	100v in-16o	Doyen	300fr	1000
1827	77v in-8o	F.Didot/Mangié	?	1000
1828	50v in-8o	Rignoux et al/Aubrée	?	2500/3000
1828–34	70v in-8o	F.Didot/Lefevre	315fr	2000
1829 ['oeuvres']	? in-24o	Rignoux/Baudouin	?	unknown
1829	75v in-18o	Pochard +Tremblay	1fr25 per vol	unknown
1829	50v in-12o	Tastu + Pinard	1fr60 per vol	1500/2000
1829–33	75v in-8o	Didot aîné/Baudouin	2fr25 per vol	1100
1829	70v in-8o	Didot aîné/Baudouin	?	2000

Total No of editions = 37

Total estimated print-run = between 63,000 and 78,000

volumes planned by a publisher often changed in the course of publication, depending on how sales were progressing. If sales slumped, the
series might be shortened and the print-run reduced. Several different
print-runs are given for some editions, because the publisher could not

TABLE 4.3
Publishing History of Rousseau's *Complete Works*, 1816–30

Date	Vols/Format	Publisher/Printer	Price	Tirage
1817	7 or 8v in-8o	Belin	56fr	1500
1817–8 [ed.Déterville]	18v in-8o	Didot ainé	90fr	1500
1818 [ed.Déterville]	18v in-12o	Didot jeune	63fr	unknown
1818–20	22v in-12o	Veuve Perronneau	70fr	2000
1818–19	20v in-18o	Crapelet	45fr	3000
1819–20	22v in-8o	Crapelet/Lefevre	6fr per vol.	1000
1820–3	20v in-8o	Didot ainé/Lequien	85fr	1200
1820–1 ['oeuvres']	8v in-12o	Baudouin/Touquet	15fr?	3000
1821 [ed.Touquet]	12v in-12o	Lenoë + Plassan	2fr25 per vol.	1500/2000
1822–6	24v in-18o	Eberhart	?	2000
1822–4 ['oeuvres']	20v in-18o	Fain/Desoër	60fr	2000
1823 ['oeuvres']	24v in-12o	Laurens ainé/Garnery	72fr	500/1000
1823–5	22v in-8o	Laguionie/Bossange	110fr	2000
1823–7	21v in-8o	Didot ainé/Lequien	84fr	unknown
1823	22v in-8o	Jacob (in Versailles)/Esneaux	88fr	1700
1823–4 ['oeuvres']	20v in-12o	Tremblay (in Senlis)/Garnery	?	unknown
1824 ['oeuvres']	5v in-18o	Carpentier/Ménard	?	unknown
1824–5 ['oeuvres']	21v in-18o	Fain/Desoër	63fr	3035
1824–7 ['oeuvres']	25v in-8o	Didot ainé/Dalibon	150fr	1500
1825 [instalments]	? in-8o	Didot ainé/Baudouin	50fr	3000
1825–6 [instalments]	? in-8o	Fournier/Verdière	62fr	unknown
1825– [illust]	25v in-8o	Doyen/Dalibon	125fr	2500
1826	25v in-8o	Rignoux/Baudouin	?	3000
1826–8	25v in-8o	Didot ainé/Feret	?	unknown
1826	21v in-8o	Rignoux/Emler	45fr	unknown
1827	28v in-8o	Rignoux + Fain/Baudouin	?	unknown
1829	25v in-18o	Pochard + Tremblay + Pinard	?	unknown
1829	16v in-8o	Renouard	2fr25 per vol.	2000
1830	16v in-12o	Tastu/Drevet	1fr60 per vol.	2000
1830	? in-8o	Rignoux + Doyen/Aubrée	?	2000/2650

Total No of editions = 31

Total estimated print-run = between 56,000 and 68,000

sustain a high initial print-run after the first few volumes had been issued. The table demonstrates that the production of Voltaire's complete works accelerated in the late 1820s, *after* the publication of the ministerial report mentioned above. It is from about 1825 onwards that small-format editions, either in-18o or in-32o, become more popular, and publishers began to publish Voltaire in more affordable instalments. The total print-run of Voltaire's complete works from 1816 to 1830 can be estimated at between 63,000 and 78,000 copies.[74]

The publication of Rousseau's complete works in the same period is tabulated in table 4.3. A total of thirty-one editions were produced according to the *Bibliographie de France*. The rhythm of their publication reached a climax in the middle years of the Restoration, with eight editions started between 1816 and 1820, but no fewer than fifteen editions launched between 1821 and 1825. Another eight editions appeared between 1826 and 1830. The total estimated print-run of Rousseau's complete works from 1816 to 1830 was between 56,000 and 68,000 copies, only slightly fewer than those of Voltaire. Just as the table for Voltaire's works does not include either his dramatic works, or isolated volumes of his histories or *contes*, so the table for Rousseau does not include editions of single titles. The most common of these was neither *Emile* nor the *Social Contract*, which most worried the legitimists, but his ever-popular *La Nouvelle Héloïse*, which appeared in seven editions in its own right between 1816 and 1830.

The production figures suggest that the panic expressed in the 1825 ministerial report was premature in the case of Voltaire publications, or too late, in the case of Rousseau editions. In 1825, when the report on *mauvais livres* was drafted, the rhythm of Voltaire production was accelerating, as he took an established place in the French literary canon. As far as the legitimists were concerned, the worst was yet to come in Voltaire's case. The rhythm of Rousseau editions, however, was different. In the mid-1820s, Rousseau production had already peaked. After this period, as the interest of the romantic movement in Jean-Jacques subsided, reeditions of his works assumed a more sedate rhythm.

Voltaire and Rousseau were not the only authors accused. There were, according to the ministerial report of 1825, 209,000 copies of other dangerous philosophical works to concern the government. These included works by Helvétius, Diderot, Raynal, Saint-Lambert, four editions of Condorcet's *Esquisse d'un tableau des progrès de l'esprit humain*, eight editions of Holbach's *Système de la nature*, another eight editions of Dupuis's *De l'Origine des Cultes*, and no fewer than eleven editions of Volney's *Ruines*. The author of the report was also keen to bring to the government's attention the publication of 128,000 volumes of Pigault-Lebrun's salacious novels by his dedicated publisher Barba. How, asked *L'Ami de la Religion*, can this torrent of cheap editions be resisted? Cleansing and sacrificial fire was one answer. In a song about the Catholic missions composed by Béranger and published in 1819 by *La Minerve*, the missionaries are themselves portrayed as agents of Satan. Béranger has them repeat the following chorus:

Eteignons les lumières,

Rallumons le feu.

Let's put out the lights,
Let's relight the fire.

Parisian publishers may have relished the publicity given to their productions by vocal clerical hostility. In 1826, Baudouin even advertised a
fireproof edition of Voltaire, suitably decorated with a phoenix ready
to rise from its own ashes.[75] The idea, however, that they were putting
a copy of Voltaire in every peasant's cottage was an exaggeration. Their
market was still principally bourgeois and urban, and print-runs very
rarely exceeded 2,000–3,000 copies in this period. On the eve of the
French Revolution, more than a half of France's male population was unable to read French, and female signature literacy was well below that of
men. Literacy was higher in France's more prosperous urban areas, and
highest of all in Paris, where two-thirds of the inhabitants of the popular
faubourg St Marcel could already read and write by 1792.[76] Outside the
capital, reading literacy was limited by gender, socio-professional status,
and the use of *patois* and non-French languages.

In these circumstances, there were social and cultural limits to Voltaire's potential readership in the Restoration. Although Voltaire and
Rousseau appeared in a range of different formats, entrenched publishing traditions were not overthrown until 1838, with the introduction of
Charpentier's in-18o or 'Jesus' format. Price structures began to change
substantially only when Charpentier dared to eliminate blank pages and
well-ventilated texts which had filled out several volumes, pointing the
way forward to a more compressed text, in small-format compact volumes. But this had not yet occurred in our period.

Voltaire's complete works were usually aimed at a wealthy, cultivated
readership. He was becoming a cultural icon. His works were a necessary
acquisition for a Parisian *haut-bourgeois* with cultural aspirations, or a
desire to advertise his commitment to philosophical ideas. Owning Voltaire perhaps also signified a reluctance on the part of the bourgeoisie to
espouse the extreme forms of clerical legitimism which found favour
under Charles X. Of course, some ultraroyalists were also customers for
Voltaire. Julien Sorel found an eight-volume set, sumptuously bound in
London, in the library of the Marquis de la Mole, to which the marquis'
daughter was denied access.[77] A more typical purchaser was probably the
Rémusat family of rich Parisian lawyers, steeped in classical culture.
Young Charles de Rémusat had reread the *Iliad* and knew Plutarch and

Virgil before he was ten years old. His mother read Voltaire to him to raise his spirits when he was sick, although Charles preferred the gayer vaudevilles which the housemaid gave him to read.[78] The Catholic missions hoped to reclaim a popular following, but they were fighting a losing battle for the mind of the notables.

The thesis that Voltaire and Rousseau caused the French Revolution today seems untenable. For one thing, the idea that the *philosophes* prepared the outbreak of the Revolution rests on too many assumptions about the responses of readers to their works.[79] Individual readers rework and reinterpret the texts they read, and they are quite capable of resisting the ideological assumptions of their reading. It is therefore very unlikely that reading Voltaire and Rousseau ever made anyone a revolutionary. Perhaps, to reverse the argument, readers turned to Voltaire and Rousseau because they were already sympathetic to their viewpoint. Considering the large-scale publication of Voltaire in the 1820s, and the importance attached to his writings in political life, one is tempted to suggest that Voltaire had far more to do with preparing 1830 than 1789.

Anatomy of an *Auto-da-fé*

The mission at Bourges, led by the diocesan mission of Laval, began on the first Sunday in Lent. The clergy 'did' a station of the cross at Notre Dame Church, and the presence of the mayor and the local authorities in the procession gave their activities the official stamp of approval. The abbé Lambert of Poitiers was entrusted with the opening sermon. The next day, religious instructions began. On Sunday 16 March, a ceremony of expiation was held, in memory of outrages committed against the Catholic Church during the French Revolution. On behalf of the whole town, 7,000 attended to make an *amende honorable*.

On the following Sunday 23 March, the abbé Lambert preached against *mauvais livres*. 'It was this speech,' it was reported, 'which convinced several of those present to make a sacrifice of their dangerous books.' Reports on the extent of the burnings ranged from between 100 to 800 books burned. 'Sacrificed' works included Voltaire's *La Pucelle*, which allegedly insulted Joan of Arc, and Parny's *Guerre des Dieux anciens et modernes* which, it was claimed, ridiculed all religions.[80] Penitences continued during Easter week, and on 15 April, Lambert preached again, this time on fidelity to the king. Local government and military officials who attended heard him emphasize the terrible consequences which followed forsaking loyalty to the monarchy in 1793. Baptismal vows were

renewed, and a service was held accompanied by a sermon, in the cemetery. On Friday 18 April, the mission cross was erected and blessed, after
a procession and another sermon by Abbé Lambert on the *glacis* of Saint-
Ursin. The whole ceremony took four hours. On 20 April, Sunday of the
Good Shepherd, 4,000 attended a mass to conclude the mission. Before
the missionaries left the town, houses were decorated with flags for the
procession of the Holy Sacrament. There was a farewell speech and a Te
Deum.

The details described here during the Bourges mission were reproduced with minor variations in many towns all over France during the
next decade, and there is no need to repeat them, except to establish the
extent of the practice of consigning books to the flames. After Bourges,
the Laval mission reached Nevers, a town with a strong revolutionary history. Nevers was the birthplace of the revolutionary terrorist Chaumette,
as well as a focus of Fouché's dechristianizing mission of 1793. Here the
missionaries organized another *auto-da-fé*: 'Many good books were distributed ... many dangerous works were sacrificed,' it was reported.[81]

Some weeks later, the Laval missionaries appeared in Vannes for a six-
week mission, starting in mid-September 1817. In Vannes, they were
assisted by some local priests who could preach in bas-breton. *L'Ami de la
Religion* triumphantly reported that 'several people abandoned the dangerous books which had caused their downfall or even the frivolous
books which could have been an obstacle to the impulsions of grace.'[82]
Already the condemnation of *mauvais livres* had widened considerably.
No longer content with the destruction of Voltairean and other philosophical works of the eighteenth century (*livres dangereux*), the missionaries now attacked literature that was merely 'frivolous.' This clearly
marked the escalation of the war on books.

Having learned what had occurred during the nearby missions at
Bourges and Nevers, the prefect of the Allier desperately petitioned the
government in Paris to prevent the missionaries from proceeding to his
headquarters in Moulins. He managed to postpone, if not to prevent,
the arrival of a mission in his *chef-lieu*, but many of his constituents made
the journey to Clermont to swell the processions there over Easter 1818.
The mission in Clermont, led by the abbé Rauzan, also destroyed 'the
pernicious books sacrificed,' as attested by two different sources.[83] The
book-burning at Clermont will make Paris book-sellers happy, joked *La
Minerve française*, quoting the author of a pamphlet entitled *Mission à
Clermont*.

The book-burning at Avignon early in 1819 was described and no doubt embellished by *La Minerve*'s reporter. Father E. took it on himself to excommunicate all those who owned any works of Voltaire, 'even if it was *La Henriade*,' commented the journalist. Owners of Rousseau were also 'excommunicated,' as were readers of Diderot, Condorcet, Helvé-tius, and *Lettres provinciales* (the last-mentioned phobia possibly betrayed a Jesuit preacher, the journalist guessed). This unidentified missionary boasted of having burned an entire library at Grenoble, consisting of about 10,000 volumes, received as part of an inheritance. 'In a single town [Grenoble],' he exclaimed, 'I had the consolation of burning a library worth 50,000 francs ... we were at it for a week; ah! How that made' the angels laugh and the demons weep.' Whether these were his own words or those of the journalist, they certainly captured something of the book-burner's wild ecstasy. His sermon had a powerful effect, because it persuaded one Avignonnaise to go straight home and set fire to her son's library. Then followed a story with a neat ending which the *Minerve*'s journalist may have invented:

> On leaving the sermon, he wrote, Madame de C ... B ... made haste to throw on the fire almost all the books which comprised her son's library; the chimney where this was done caught alight; on his return home the young man found his neighbours engaged in putting out the flames. 'Let the house burn down,' he said, 'my mother has a liking for fires.'[84]

The book-burning in Orange in November 1819 was closely linked with the mood of abject sorrow produced by the Missionnaires de France at the fête of the *amende honorable*. The congregation carried candles as a sign of repentance and, gathered in Orange cathedral, heard the missionary call on them in these words to forgive their enemies:

> 'Repeat, my brothers, repeat after me from the bottom of your hearts the precept which Jesus taught you at his death, shout it aloud with me: I forgive!'
> Tears were the only response.
> He urged them again in the same tone which melts the soul, and finally the whole crowd cried out, stifled by their tears ... 'yes, I forgive! I forgive!'
> But then there was no more weeping.
> Moaning, stifled shouts, interspersed voices, plaintive cries interrupted the preacher ...
> Then there were restitutions, pernicious books put into the hands of these working evangelists or consigned to the flames; marriages were blessed,

people who had until then been irreconcilable enemies saw each other, spoke to each other, forgave each other and embraced![85]

One paradox of book-burnings organized by Catholic missions was the ability of the preacher to justify acts of intolerance in the language of reconciliation and forgiveness.

The wave of book-burnings subsequently recorded in the pays de Loire was perpetrated partly by the diocesan clergy from Laval (whose zeal in the matter has already been noted), and partly by a group known as the Missionnaires de Saint-Martin, who originated in Tours, usually led by a *père* Gloriot. At Chinon in 1823, there were 'some bad books sacrificed,' and soon afterwards during Lent at Amboise, 'bad books were consigned to the flames.'[86]

At Vendôme in Lent 1824, the missionaries of Saint-Martin de Tours were now under the leadership of Abbé Donnet. As missionaries loved to do, Donnet quoted the *philosophes* in support of his arguments against *mauvais livres*. On this occasion he cited Rousseau's remark that 'no chaste girl has ever read novels.' According to his sermon, novels inspire wild fantasies, overheat the imagination, arouse the senses, and make everyday reality seem intolerable. Donnet was therefore attacking fiction as well as philosophical works, although he declaimed against Voltaire and Jean-Jacques, and cursed recent reprints of these authors. Then he commanded:

'Burn I say, surrender these dangerous books without mercy to the flames; the longer you delay, the more difficult the sacrifice will seem to you. And what thoughts could hold you back? The cruel legacy you would leave to your children? I am burning these books, a saint once said, so that I myself will not be destroyed by them. – Would you keep the dagger which would murder your son? ... Your library is the armoury where he searches for the murderous weapon.'[87]

Although we have no hard evidence that any books were actually burned at Vendôme, it is reasonable to assume that Donnet's incendiary rhetoric had an effect.

Donnet continued to indulge his passion for book-burning in Romorantin in the diocese of Blois, at the beginning of the following year. Two thousand volumes were put to the torch in the courtyard of the local *collège*, 'because the missionaries desired that they should all be gathered in this place, to serve as an example to the young students who were given the job of setting fire to this pile of books.'[88] At Richelieu in the diocese of Tours, the missionaries of Saint-Martin 'sacrificed' another thousand volumes, songs, and engravings in a fire around the mission cross.[89]

There were book-burnings in Brittany, too, as Ernest Renan's memoirs inform us. The incident he related at Tréguier in 1827, however, seems to have involved private burnings 'at home,' rather than a public bonfire. Renan recalled what his mother told him:

> The preacher gave such a fine sermon against dangerous books, that everyone burned all the volumes they had at home. The missionary had said that it was better to burn more rather than less, and that in any case they could all be dangerous in some circumstances. I did the same as all the others; but your father threw several on top of the tall wardrobe. 'Those ones are too nice,' he told me. They were *Don Quixote, Gil Blas, Le Diable Boiteux.*[90]

The campaign had escalated even further. Not content with attacking Voltaire, Rousseau and some risqué fiction, the missions now affirmed that all books were potentially dangerous. The original urge to outlaw Voltaire had grown into a general condemnation of literature as such.

The last verified incident occurred in 1828 at Chambon, a small town in the Limoges diocese on the eastern edge of the department of the Creuse. Here, at some time in June, 'more than 200 *mauvais livres* were thrown on the fire, and other effective signs of faith and repentance were shown.'[91] There is every reason to believe, however, that public book-burnings were much more frequent events than this short list suggests. Abbé Guyon, who became the Jesuit bête noire of the liberal press, was accused of making a regular habit of burning the complete works of Voltaire and Rousseau.[92] This was a familiar enough event to be the object of a satirical pamphlet published in 1818. The author, Châtelain, suggested that the missionaries brought along their own stock of books in order to stage-manage a good bonfire. Subscriptions to Voltaire's works were so expensive, he remarked, that no one in their right mind would hand them over to the missionaries.[93]

Expiation and Sacrifice

In this chapter I have argued for the importance of the 'battle of the books' in the cultural politics of Restoration France. Catholic ultraroyalists and liberals waged a polemical war over the value of eighteenth-century philosophical writings. Behind this campaign lay conflicting interpretations of the origins of the French Revolution itself. For the Catholic missions, 1789 had been prepared by a conspiracy of intellectuals, whose subversive writings now threatened to engulf French society in the form of cheaper, more accessible editions. For the liberal press, on the other hand, the Revolution had been brought about by royalist and clerical extremism, while the principle of the freedom of the press was one of its most precious achievements. The original ecclesiastical proscription of Voltaire and Rousseau was soon extended. These two were seen merely as the leaders in a conspiratorial web involving many subaltern philosophical writers. Thus not only Voltaire and Rousseau, but also their alleged disciples such as Helvétius, Diderot, D'Holbach, and Volney were condemned to burn. Then preachers started to anathematize novels, too, until almost all literature became suspect, except for the *bons livres* promoted by their own clerical organizations.

In addition, this chapter has attempted to outline some features of the disturbed *mentalité* of the Catholic missionaries. They viewed the world as an arena in which two warring factions went into battle against each other. One represented religion, God, and monarchy, while the other fought for impiety, the devil, and the Revolution. There could be no neutrals in this fight: those who did not follow the works of the mission were threatened with ostracism. They adopted a rhetoric calculated to induce fear in their audiences: fear of the hell and damnation which awaited those who had read impious literature, contracted allegedly illegitimate marriages, or bought church property. They were well aware that women tended to be more susceptible to their message than young males, particularly those from the middle classes. They segregated the sexes and pressured young girls into refusing to dance with male partners. Historians have sometimes discussed the sexual dimorphism in religious behaviour as though it was almost 'spontaneous.' It is clear, however, that it was manipulated and exploited by the preaching clergy. As has been shown, however, the missionaries did not have everything their own way. Popular and middle-class anticlericalism frequently thwarted their plans.

The book-burnings were the products of these two convergent forces. The polemical war about eighteenth-century literature combined with the emotional religiosity of the period proved a highly combustible mixture. The incidents of counter-revolutionary vandalism analysed correspond in several ways to the general features of book-burnings isolated by Gimeno Blay. First, the Restoration book-burnings were directed against specific individuals, although Voltaire and Rousseau were not the only targets. As we have seen, the purge soon escalated to include novels and other suspect works. Unlike victims such as Salman Rushdie or Tasleema Nasrin, however, the authors targeted were of course dead and out of reach.

Second, the book-burnings of Restoration France, like the other examples cited, were conceived with the aim of cleansing and purifying society by exterminating a source of corruption. The purpose was to combat and remove the sources of dangerous ideas which were poisoning society as a whole.

Third, the book-burners sought to neutralize or control the memory of the recent past. Antirevolutionary propaganda was an important part of the work of the Catholic missions. The difference here is that the fires were lit not to eradicate the historical memory of a political, denominational, or ethnic rival, as in the case of the burning of the National Library in Sarajevo. The book-burnings symbolized an attempt to erase and rewrite France's *own* past, to expunge the moral stain of the French Revolution.

Besides these comparisons, however, the French book-burnings of 1817–29 had characteristics of their own. The notion of expiation was particularly strong. Books were not burned but, in the rhetoric of the perpetrators, 'sacrificed' by their owners. There is a marked emphasis on sacrifice and repentance in the preaching of the book-burners. It is significant here that Lent was the favourite period of missionary activity, for the ethos of Lent is one of self-sacrifice and renunciation. The aim of the book-burners was to persuade their Catholic followers to give up their own contaminated books. They induced a feeling of guilt, and then suggested a way to redeem it: by throwing their own literature on the flames, Catholics could wipe out the guilt of the revolutionary past. This was quite different from the case of Don Quixote, who was asleep and unaware that his personal library was being destroyed. In Restoration France, the book-burnings were largely voluntary; it was important that the owners were fully conscious of what they were doing when they sacrificed their libraries to the fires of expiation.

Epilogue

On 29 July 1830, on the third Glorious Day of the July Revolution, an angry Parisian crowd converged on the archbishop's palace. Spurred on by a rumour that priests had been firing on Parisians from the windows of the *archévêché*, they broke in and ransacked the building. Furniture, paintings, and the contents of the palace library were thrown into the

Seine. Books and manuscripts could be seen floating through Paris for several hours afterwards.[94] This, no doubt, was an act of rage rather than good sense, but in the light of the 'battle of the books' which had disturbed the Restoration period, it was perhaps an appropriate gesture of popular revenge against the clerical regime. One wonders, however, whether drowning books in the river afforded anything comparable to the 'strange pleasure' of putting literature to the torch.

5 Literary Commemoration and the Uses of History: The Gutenberg Festival in Strasbourg, 1840

The invention of printing, Elizabeth Eisenstein tells us, was a revolutionary event with far-reaching consequences for the development of Western thought.[1] The current consensus, however, on the exact date when printing appeared, and on where it was invented, has developed over centuries of argument over disputed evidence. The consensus view favours the German city of Mainz as the place of origin, and the invention is, of course, conventionally attributed to Jean Genszfleisch, usually known as Johannes Gutenberg. In this domain, as in many other provinces of the history of technology, the myth of the individual creative genius is alive and well. Yet it has not always been so. Although, as we shall see, several late fifteenth-century texts named Gutenberg as the inventor, the emergence of the revolutionary hero is a comparatively recent phenomenon. When the bicentenary and tercentenary of the invention of printing were celebrated in Leipzig in 1640 and 1740 respectively, Fust and Schöffer were named as the inventors, together with their 'assistant' Gutenberg.[2] Only in the mid-eighteenth century did Gutenberg emerge as the primary protagonist, with the appearance of Köhler's *The Vindication of Johann Gutenberg* in 1741, and Schöpflin's crucial collection of documents on Gutenberg in Strasbourg in 1760.[3] From this moment on, the myth developed that Gutenberg's backers and colleagues Fust and Schöffer played only a minor role in the story. Representations of Gutenberg in the romantic era portrayed him as a misunderstood genius, dedicated to the cause of universal education, but dying in poverty after being cheated by the parasitical capitalists who exploited him. This, at least, was the theme of Lamartine's work on Gutenberg, which he wrote for Hachette's railway bookstalls.[4] A poem composed by Paul Lehr and printed in Strasbourg during the Gutenberg festival in 1840 attributed to Gutenberg alone the dissipation of ignorance and the spread of progress and liberty. These are the florid terms in which Lehr celebrated the myth of genius:

La Force aux bras de fer, la Stupide Ignorance
Enchaînaient à leur char les peuples et les rois;
Mais un homme paraît, radieux, il s'avance
Et de leur joug honteux les délivre à la fois.
Par son art merveilleux il sème la lumière,
Et les livres sacrés sont partout répandus.
La docte antiquité renaît de la poussière,
Et Gutenberg lui dit: 'Tu ne périras plus!'[5]

Brute force and stupid ignorance had chained peoples and kings to their chariot;
But one radiant man came forward to deliver them both from their shameful yoke.
His marvellous art spreads light and holy books are everywhere diffused.
Ancient learning is reborn from the dust,
And Gutenberg decrees: 'Never again will you perish!'

One is entitled to question this myth of the inventor-genius, or what my colleague, David Miller, calls 'The Eureka Factor.'[6] In this popular version of scientific progress, 'discoveries' are 'made' by individual geniuses who have sudden and unexpected brainwaves, rather than as outcomes of a cumulative process of learning. Thus alongside Archimedes and his bath and Newton and his apple we also class Gutenberg and movable type. One pamphlet of 1840 called Gutenberg, with enormous exaggeration, 'inventor of the book,' ignoring two millennia of book production before print.[7]

My main aim is to examine the Strasbourg Gutenberg festival of 1840, together with its immediate prelude and aftermath, to see how literary commemorations are manipulated for political or religious motives. The celebration of the 400th anniversary of Gutenberg's invention can tell us something about contemporary attitudes to print culture. It can also point to discrepancies between grandiose claims made for the invention of printing, and some more mundane realities of municipal and denominational politics under the July Monarchy.

The Gutenberg Myth

First, however, a brief sketch of the development of the Gutenberg myth is appropriate, before I focus on the Strasbourg festival itself. The main arguments surrounding Gutenberg's life and invention have already been well rehearsed by eminent specialists. These include Henri-Jean Martin, in the history of the beginnings of print which bears the name of its originator Lucien Febvre, the late East German scholar Albert Kapr who addressed a series of key questions about Gutenberg, and Guy Bechtel, author of the most definitive and magisterial study to date.[8] All have noted the fragmentary nature of the evidence which has allowed plenty of scope for speculation and imaginative mythologizing.

There have been four principal rivals for the city of origin: Mainz itself where, during the mid-1450s, Gutenberg may have been responsible for the 42-line Bible which is normally attributed to him; Strasbourg where we know he lived and worked for at least a decade between 1434 and 1444; Harlem where it was claimed Coster was the true inventor; and Avignon, where the invention was attributed to Waldvogel. In Strasbourg, Gutenberg worked as a jeweller, cutting precious stones, and producing mirrors to sell to pilgrims en route to Aachen. Here, perhaps, he experimented with combinations of metals he would later use to manufacture his moulds and type, or with the chemicals needed to produce the distinctively rich black ink of the 'Gutenberg Bible.' It is not known whether he actually printed anything in Strasbourg. Kapr believed he did, but, as Bechtel pointed out, if he did print in his Strasbourg years his entire output has disappeared.[9] Bechtel insists that the invention was a long drawn-out process. Gutenberg may have done experimental and preparatory work in Strasbourg, but the real fruit of his labours did not materialize until the Mainz years (that is to say, certainly after 1448 and probably after 1450, because except for briefly surfacing in Frankfurt, Gutenberg's whereabouts between 1444 and 1448 are unknown).

The first attributions of the invention did not appear until forty years later. In 1483, Matteo Palmieri attributed the origins of printing to Gutenberg in Mainz in 1440.[10] Then a Cologne chronicle of 1499 again named 1440 as the date of origin.[11] The origins of printing were situated in Strasbourg for the first time over half a century after the event, in 1505, by Jacob Wimpheling, in a work actually published in Strasbourg, which again dated the invention from 1440.[12] These early texts successfully invented and consecrated the date (1440) which would henceforth be celebrated as the beginnings of printing. They also lent authority to the claims of both Mainz and Strasbourg to be the host city. The significance of Strasbourg was enhanced when Schöpflin produced (again, in Strasbourg itself) his collection of new documents which threw some light on Gutenberg's business activities, as well as on the suit for breach of promise which was brought against him.[13]

Modern scholarship has reexamined some further myths, suggesting for example that Gutenberg was by no means a victim of financiers, but an active entrepreneur in his own right.[14] In addition, it now seems difficult to align Gutenberg with the development of the humanist culture of the Renaissance. As for many contemporary printers, his primary customer was the Catholic Church, which provided his bread and butter.[15] The nineteenth-century myths of Gutenberg sometimes appropriated him for Protestantism, or else represented him as a liberal progressive breaking through the choking fog of clerical bigotry. Gutenberg, however, was a jobbing printer for the ecclesiastical authorities. As Kapr argued, not only did he produce the 42-line Bible, but he also printed the papal indulgences which had been one of the main targets of Lutheran polemics.[16]

A final issue is that of the eastern origins of printing. The first mobile characters made in metal appeared in Korea, probably two centuries before 1440. Although Kapr speculates that Gutenberg may have been aware of this, there is no evidence to support the notion that he was influenced by Korean precedents. It is agreed in any case that Gutenberg rather than the Koreans made the first printing press, and Gutenberg's putative Korean connection played no role in nineteenth-century Gutenberg mythology.[17] On the contrary, it was the other way around. In 1840, as we shall see, Europe was thought to have used printing to spread its civilizing influence to the primitive (i.e., non-European) world. We must now turn to 1840 itself.

The Utopian Vision

The Gutenberg celebrations of 1840 were remarkable for their universalizing rhetoric, which was continually undercut by local and municipal priorities. In a one-act entertainment, produced to raise funds for the Gutenberg monument in Strasbourg in 1840, Gutenberg is blessed by the Genius of Civilization, who is lowered from the flies to sing a song in his praise. The allegory proceeded with the emancipation of humanity from slavery and its discovery, through the invention of printing, of the Truth.[18] In official nineteenth-century discourse, printing was the source of truth and freedom, an essential means of spreading enlightenment and civilization throughout the world. In his oft-quoted memoirs, for example, the self-taught stonemason Martin Nadaud regarded the printing press as a source of education, and a weapon against clerical obscurantism.[19] The prospectus issued in 1834 to drum up public donations for the Gutenberg monument attributed four centuries of progress to the invention of printing. 'Think only' it urged, 'of the renaissance of literature, of the Bible distributed to pious souls, of the publications of every kind appearing daily which shine endless waves of light across the entire globe.'[20] When the monument was eventually inaugurated in June 1840, Mayor Lichtenberger assured the crowd that the invention of printing was a blow against ignorance, feudalism, fanaticism, and slavery. The individual genius of Gutenberg had thus rescued the world from despotism.[21]

This ideology of the print revolution, as Adrian Johns points out, is a construction of the French Revolution.[22] For the French revolutionaries, print production separated modern thinking from the barbaric, 'Gothic,' and irrational Middle Ages. For them, modernity began with print, which had made possible the diffusion of those eighteenth-century philosophers that the French Revolution selected as its intellectual ancestors. In September 1792, the Prussian-born revolutionary Anacharsis Cloots had asked the French National Assembly to transfer Gutenberg's ashes to the Pantheon, where great republican heroes were honoured. Cloots praised Gutenberg as the first true revolutionary, without whom Voltaire and Rousseau would be unknown.[23] The Gutenberg monument in Strasbourg echoed the utopian discourse of the French Revolution, with its emphasis on the advance of reason and liberty, attributing to Gutenberg the role of standard-bearer for the emancipation of all humanity. Paradoxically, it did so just at the moment when mechanization was beginning to make Gutenberg's techniques obsolete.

The July Monarchy of Louis-Philippe (to consider the French context) presided over considerable unrest and a rapid increase in book and newspaper production. The regime had been spawned by the 1830 Revolution, and while the government played down its insurrectionary origins, it reigned through a period of turmoil. It survived popular risings in Lyon and Paris in the 1830s, an attempted legitimist coup in 1832, and a Bonapartist rising in 1836. In the midst of unrest, the ruling classes sought the peace and equilibrium of the *juste milieu* – the 'happy medium' between order and freedom. In 1840 itself, the regime tried to neutralize the threat of Bonapartism by transferring the remains of the ever-popular Emperor Napoleon from St Helena to Paris.

The early years of the July Monarchy were the golden age of political caricature. Using the new technique of lithography, Charles Philipon collected a talented stable of graphic artists, including Honoré Daumier, in the editorial offices of his two illustrated papers, the weekly *La Caricature* and the daily *Le Charivari*. *La Caricature*, which was the more political of the two, conducted a systematic character assassination of King Louis-Philippe, portraying him as a greedy manipulator. Daumier and Philipon drew Louis-Philippe in the shape of a pear. This was a stroke of artistic genius – a censor could hardly object to a drawing of a simple pear, but educated readers understood the joke. Thousands of graffiti pears appeared in Paris streets – a sign of the new power of visual satire. In French, *le poire* became slang for a mug or a dimwit, which lent extra force to this insulting image of the monarch. Other targets were the 'pot-bellies' (*les ventrus*), bloated and complacent members of parliament whose loyalty had been bought by the king, and Robert Macaire, a fictional rogue and sleazy con-man who was identified with Louis-Philippe. Although the circulation of these journals did not exceed 1400 copies, they were read in reading-rooms all over the capital, posted on walls, and exhibited in shop windows.[24] Both Philipon and Daumier faced short prison sentences from time to time, which gave their activities more publicity without deterring them one bit. Although the July Monarchy had declared the freedom of the press, a worried government banned political caricature in 1835, and *La Caricature* was forced to fold. The Gutenberg festival thus occurred in a context in which the liberal defence of press freedom was a vibrant political issue.

The statue stands today in the Place Gutenberg in central Strasbourg, complete with the pedestal of bronze reliefs by David d'Angers (as will be discussed, these were the subject of later contestation). It is about ten feet high, and depicts a bearded and pensive Gutenberg taking a page proof from a press, on which one reads the phrase 'Et la lumière fut!' (And there was light!) – a phrase which Cloots had used in 1792 (fig. 5.1). The frontal frieze depicts an array of great intellectuals who benefitted from Gutenberg's invention (fig. 5.2). In the most central position, nearest to the printing press itself, stands Descartes. Behind him on the viewer's right are Montesquieu, Leibniz, and Kant, while on the left are Shakespeare and Corneille. Voltaire can be spotted midway on the left, and Galileo about midway on the right. On the far left is Erasmus and on the far right Raphael. This is in fact a highly canonical representation of the great men of Western civilization, concentrating on the Renaissance, the Scientific Revolution, and the Enlightenment – almost a pictorial version of Elizabeth Eisenstein's thesis. The other figures in the background include Racine and Molière, Dürer, Poussin, Calderòn, Milton,

Fig. 5.1   The Gutenberg statue in Strasbourg.

Fig. 5.2   The Gutenberg Monument – the frontal frieze.

Cervantes, Rousseau, Lessing, Copernicus, Goëthe, Schiller, Hegel, Newton, and Spinoza.[25]

This was to prove the most controversial of the four reliefs. The other three illustrated the spread of printing to three continents, Africa, Asia, and the Americas. In the American panel, Franklin prints the Declaration of Independence in the company of Washington, Jefferson, Lafayette, and Bolivar (fig. 5.3). In the African panel, Europeans emancipate Africans from slavery with the help of the press. In the Asian panel, Europeans again distribute books and teach the natives, while Mehmet II of Egypt reads *Le Moniteur,* a Chinese mandarin reads Confucius, and an unidentified Indian deity is about to be overthrown. In this official Eurocentric vision, the West, armed with the printing press, liberates the East from tyranny and religious bigotry. Like the northern French festivals analysed by Stéphane Gerson, the inauguration of the Gutenberg monument in Strasbourg expressed a utopian and universalist vision. It carried a pedagogical message, and promoted a notion of secular progress in tune with the ideals of mid-nineteenth-century bourgeois society.[26]

Just as printing was linked here with eminent intellectuals from almost every part of Europe between the Renaissance and the eighteenth century, a group of present-day intellectuals was enlisted as patrons of the

Fig. 5.3   The Gutenberg Monument – the American panel.

monument. The committee of patrons included Arago, Guizot, Lamartine, the historian Mignet, the art critic Quatremère de Quincy, the printer Didot, and the publisher Würtz of Treuttel and Würtz, originally a Strasbourg house which had relocated to Paris. Donations were provided by the king, and the ministries of the Interior, Commerce, and Education. The sculptor David d'Angers gave his services to the nation for nothing. The pedestal and bronze reliefs, however, together with the metal fence to be placed around it, were expensive, and the local response to fund-raising was disappointing. The departmental council of the Bas-Rhin refused to contribute altogether, on the grounds that this was solely a municipal responsibility, and when the statue was inaugurated in 1840, only plaster casts of the bronze reliefs were in place.[27] This was not to be the only difficulty experienced in translating a commemoration of (it was claimed) world significance into a local French and Strasbourgeois context.

The Strasbourg Festival

The Strasbourg Gutenberg festival was a three-day marathon. My brief summary of it draws on two main sources. The first is the plan of events which was submitted for the approval of the prefect some weeks in advance. Since the Minister of the Interior also had to approve details such as the wording of all toasts proposed on the occasion, there is a file of official correspondence discussing and modifying the plan of festivities.[28] The second source is a long description of what occurred, printed in Paris in pamphlet form by Auguste Luchet, an enthusiastic local supporter of the event.[29]

On the first day, the city received foreign delegations to the festival, and then a procession marched from the town hall to the Marché aux Herbes, with musical accompaniment and a military escort. Prefect Sers insisted on a strong military presence to impress Prussian visitors.[30] The authorities shrewdly scheduled the inauguration of another statue, to the Napoleonic general Kléber, a week before the inauguration of the Gutenberg monument. This ensured that the town was full of soldiers and this would deter any potential disturbers of the peace.

The procession observed a strict social hierarchy. At its head were the political, military, and religious authorities. First came the members of municipal council, then judges of the local law-courts, justices of the peace, deans and professors of the university faculties, officers of the garrison, curés and pastors, schoolteachers, *avocats*, *notaires*, printers and students, and finally printing workers and apprentices.[31] Just as in the procession in eighteenth-century Montpellier analysed by Robert Darnton, urban society and its status hierarchy were here on display.[32] In eighteenth-century Montpellier, the social parade was dominated by the clergy, but nineteenth-century Strasbourg displayed the ranks of a wholly bourgeois society and its leading professions.

In the Marché aux Herbes, the audience saw a member of the organizing committee unveil the statue. The town bells were rung and a salute was fired. Next to the statue, a printing press had been set up, to produce the hymn of praise which would then be bound and distributed to all present. Mayor Lichtenberger gave the speech already mentioned above, and then the printer and municipal councillor Silbermann delivered a eulogy of Gutenberg. The sculptor David d'Angers was present but apparently too modest to come forward. In Luchet's overimaginative account, the artist wept with emotion privately.[33] In the evening there was a concert, the city was illuminated, and there was a firework display around the statue.

The second day of festivities was given over to a *cortège industriel*, followed by a banquet at the corn exchange (Halle aux Blés) attended by 600 in spite of rainy weather. The participants loyally toasted the health of the king.[34] This procession celebrated the trades and professions of the city. Each group dressed in its traditional costume. Prefect Sers, however, prohibited the butchers from wearing the revolutionary red bonnet. Instead, he ordered participants to wear 'tricolour caps in medieval style.'[35] Every trade had its own float, in a nineteenth-century rendering of ancient corporate pride. The printers' float, drawn by eight white horses, carried a completely reconstituted printshop. In a conscious revival of medievalism, the event celebrated the traditional and 'respectable' artisans of Strasbourg, to be distinguished from the unskilled cotton operatives of nearby industrial Mulhouse. Prefect Sers reported that he observed 'A rare example of a corporate spirit, preserved for fifty years in this city in spite of the new institutions proclaiming free enterprise.'[36] A collection was taken for the widows of printing workers. The third day was the day of the book trade professionals. There was an exhibition of the products of Alsace, featuring rare books, and the lucky winner of a 'loterie typographique' was drawn. The festival ended with a *bal public.*

Following Gerson's fine analysis of urban festivals in this period, we may conclude that the Strasbourg Gutenberg festival articulated a territorial identity, based on the city of Strasbourg in particular and the region of Alsace as a whole. It celebrated local traditions, but attempted to combine this with the commemoration of an event of universal importance – the invention of printing. It was an entirely secular festival, in which nothing offended the susceptibilities of Strasbourg's various religious communities (mainly Catholic and Lutheran, although the region's substantial Jewish population was conspicuous by its absence on this occasion). The festival had clear ideological aims: it instrumentalized Gutenberg to promote a secular view of progress, liberalism, and a free press; at the same time it evoked the tradition of the medieval guilds to present a vision of local society which was well ordered and harmonious. In addition, like every local fete, the Strasbourg Gutenberg festival attracted tourists and was good for business.

Local Meanings of a 'Universal' Message

If we examine the Gutenberg festival a little more closely, however, its grandiose universalist vision dissolves into a series of local conflicts. Although official discourse portrayed the invention of printing as a great boon to world civilization, and a source of progress and enlightenment, it could mean quite different things to local Strasbourg society. Rather than expressing the advance of humanity towards a secular utopia, the

Fig. 5.4   The Gutenberg Monument – a contemporary postcard.

Gutenberg festival reflected more mundane issues, and was interwoven with municipal rivalries, sectarian conflicts, and political divisions.

The origins of the festival were embedded, firstly, in Strasbourg's long-standing rivalry with the city of Mainz. Both claimed to be the site of Gutenberg's invention. In Strasbourg's version of the myth of origins, Gutenberg had been born in Mainz of a noble family, but moved to Strasbourg to escape religious persecution, and it was in Strasbourg that he first used his mobile characters, first of wood, later of metal. Gutenberg was portrayed as a dreamer, a misunderstood genius surrounded by idiots and greedy financiers from Mainz.[37] This was really a myth about the importance of the city, and its historical accuracy will not bear scrutiny. It did not explain Gutenberg's motives for changing residence, and there is little evidence that Gutenberg ever suffered religious persecution. It contrasted free Strasbourg with tyrannical Mainz, and by implication modern French liberties with German authoritarianism. This nationalist version of the myth ignored the minor detail that in 1440 Strasbourg was not yet part of France (the city became French in 1681). Nevertheless, the myth had its uses and it survives today (fig. 5.4).

Competition with Mainz thus fuelled the celebration. This is not just a city of beer and sauerkraut, Auguste Luchet protested, but also a city of literacy and freedom.[38] Since Mainz already had a Gutenberg statue, he added, Strasbourg should have one too. Mainz had already staged a similar three-day event to celebrate the 400th anniversary in 1837 and Strasbourg would not be outdone. The immediate context, therefore, was what Henri-Jean Martin called a 'war of plaques and statues,' waged between rival cities between 1823 and 1840.[39] Harlem had put up a statue to Coster in 1827, Mainz responded with one to Gutenberg in 1837, and Strasbourg had to compete. In 1835, the French government called the planned commemoration 'the greatest event in the annals of civilization, which has exerted such a powerful influence over the destinies of the world.' The fete would be 'more than a national or a European fete, it is the festival of all humanity.'[40] But rather than demonstrating this global character, the event was nourished by petty municipal rivalries.

Victor Hugo had added his considerable weight to the liberal dis-course on printing in his novel *Notre-Dame de Paris*, which he had con-tracted to produce for Gosselin in 1828, probably wrote during and just after the 1830 Revolution in Paris, and first published in 1831. In one of his dramatic and sustained antitheses, Hugo contrasted the influence of the clergy with the new domination of the printing press, referring to 'the terror and vertigo of the man of the cloth faced with Gutenberg's dazzling press' (l'épouvante et l'éblouissement de l'homme du sanc-tuaire devant la presse lumineuse de Gutenberg).[41] In Hugo's vision, the Catholic Church had for centuries spoken to a non-literate congre-gation through the visual medium of its architecture. Now the printing press would supplant the language of stone, heralding Protestantism and democracy. The main achievement of the printing press was therefore to undermine the falsehoods of Catholicism:

> It was the cry of the prophet who already senses the noise and ferment of liberated humanity, who sees a future in which intelligence erodes faith, opinion dethrones belief, the world makes Rome tremble ... that signified: the press will kill the church.[42]

Although Hugo never mentioned Gutenberg, he saw printing as the greatest event in history and 'la révolution mère,' the mother of revolu-tions.[43]

The discourse of liberalism and the anticlerical enlightenment, how-ever, seemed hollow in the light of sectarian divisions between Stras-bourg's Catholics and Lutherans. The Gutenberg festival occurred in a context of political and religious agitation in the southwestern states of Germany, the free cities, the Rhineland, and Saxony. Festivals like the Leipzig Schillerfest of 1841 were used as political rallying points, and religious disputes exacerbated political conflict. The so-called kneeling controversy erupted when Ludwig I of Bavaria demanded that his Protestant subjects should kneel as the annual Corpus Christi procession passed by. In Prussia, the monarchy's attempts to consolidate Lutheran and Calvinist organizations into a single state church were opposed by traditional Lutherans. The Protestant Lichtfreunde (Friends of Light) movement aimed primarily at religious reform but was also aligned with political radicalism. The idea of mixed marriage (i.e., between a Catholic and a Protestant) animated politics for years in Baden and Bavaria, as Dagmar Herzog has demonstrated.[44] In 1837, the archbishop of Köln was arrested in Prussia for opposing the law that children of mixed marriages should be educated in the faith of the father (but he was reinstated). In 1845, the Catholic archbishop of Baden took a public stand against mixed marriages per se. Meanwhile the Deutschkatholischer (German Catholic) movement criticized the Catholic hierarchy, attacked priestly celibacy, and pressed for a more humane approach towards marriage. The forces of liberalism and conservative Catholicism became increasingly polarized in Germany.

The year 1840 was a turning point in Prussia. The new king Frederick William IV authorized the Berlin celebrations of the invention of printing, which his predecessor Frederick William III had refused to allow. Here and elsewhere, the anniversary was an opportunity for a liberal show of strength, and for demonstrations against press censorship.[45] The campaign against censorship was briefly successful in 1848, and the book trade played a role in the 1848 Revolutions, just as the newspaper press had also done in the 1830 Revolutions. Robert Blum, for example, the German nationalist and radical executed in the Viennese Revolution of 1848, owned a Leipzig publishing company.

As fate would have it, on the evening before the Gutenberg festival, an almighty hailstorm hit Strasbourg. Windows were shattered and the stained glass of the Catholic cathedral was damaged. This was not auspicious. The real issue lay with the front panel of David d'Angers' bronze reliefs. In David's original version, Luther and Voltaire stood in very prominent positions, with Luther receiving a printed book from Gutenberg himself. On the Catholic side, Bossuet too occupied a prominent position in David's first design. Complaints from the Catholics of Strasbourg centred on the role of Luther in the foreground. The press protested and so did Raess, the *co-adjuteur* and future Catholic bishop of Strasbourg, who demanded the removal of Luther from the ranks of world geniuses.[46] In retaliation, the Lutherans complained about Bossuet's inclusion. The completion of the bronze reliefs had already been delayed by shortage of funds, but in 1842, these religious squabbles further threatened the completion of the project. In May 1840, the government had already warned Prefect Sers that Protestants might seek to disrupt the festivities. The Prefect predictably replied that Protestants were no more likely to be troublemakers than anyone else. In fact, Sers argued, their wealth and status made them natural pillars of social stability.[47] But neither the Prefect nor the government could completely contain sectarian conflict in this uniquely multireligious city.

The dispute was resolved by the sculptor David d'Angers who agreed to modify his design. He would remove Luther to appease the Catholic protests. David, however, would not let the Catholics have it all their own way: if Luther had to go, then he would efface Bossuet too from the ranks of great men in print. In their places, he added the more neutral figures of Erasmus and Montesquieu.[48] The pedestal was removed to a safe place in the municipal museum until the situation calmed down. The story of the Strasbourg bronze reliefs showed that the canon of Western thought was entirely contestable. The Enlightenment message of freedom and secular progress had come up against deep-seated religious loyalties seeking to manipulate the Gutenberg commemoration.

The Gutenberg festival attracted crowds from France, Germany, Switzerland, Scandinavia, and even Brazil, and it posed a police problem. Although the message of the Gutenberg commemoration was one of global fraternity, the influx of *étrangers* into Strasbourg was unwelcome and a threat to public order. The city, an individual named Cartier complained, 'is gradually becoming encumbered with a lot of strangers of sinister appearance, who are flowing in from the surrounding areas like filth in a sewer.'[49] Delegations of printing workers from Paris and Lyon were possible sources of dangerous subversive views, and to balance this threat, country mayors were brought into town to swell the ranks of loyalists.[50] German visitors also had to be heavily policed in case they included any conspirators of the Young Germany movement.[51] Swiss visitors and Polish exiles were also suspect, and at one point the Prefect was afraid that the archrevolutionary Blanqui would put in an appearance.[52] The playing of the Marseillaise also worried the authorities because of its enduring revolutionary connotations, but it could hardly be banned on this occasion: after all, it was originally a Strasbourg song! To the prefect's relief, the republican threat did not materialize. A radical banquet, held in the garden of the local liberal Lipp in opposition to the fete's official banquet, only mustered ninety-seven guests according to Prefect Sers – a very precise head count which suggests a police informer was among them.[53] The festival of brotherhood and emancipation had been enmeshed in the political struggles and fears of the constitutional monarchy.

The Gutenberg statue stands innocuously today in the Place Gutenberg, on its pedestal and bronze reliefs in their revised version. Three days per week, appropriately enough, it is surrounded by a second-hand book market. The episode of its inauguration illustrates many aspects of urban festivals outlined by Stéphane Gerson, demonstrating social harmony, expressing a local identity, and tinged with bourgeois anticlericalism. The episode and its conflicts also demonstrate the contradictions between the official rhetoric about the invention of printing, and the reality of local antagonisms. The utopian vision of progress and liberation masked a series of manoeuvres to control the meaning of the festival. Gutenberg was a tool to be exploited in local municipal rivalries and inter-denominational quarrels, and he could also appear as a threat to the political stability of the regime.

Readers

6 The Reading Experience of Worker-Autobiographers in Nineteenth-Century Europe

Historians of popular reading practices are often forced to study them indirectly, through the work of those intent on disciplining or moralizing the poor. In the nineteenth century, too, a mass of advice literature appeared as churches, educators, librarians, and philanthropists attempted to direct expanding working-class literacy into safe channels. The competing discourses about reading during the nineteenth century reveal plenty, incidentally, about the fears and neuroses of elites, but in the end they only tell one side of the story: they say little about what workers actually read. As Jonathan Rose urged in a provocative article, we must 'interrogate the audience' itself.[1] This chapter tries to do that, at least for a small group of autodidacts, and to offer some clues about readers' responses. The clues come from the accounts given by individual workers about their own reading experience. These sources enable us to envisage workers not just as a passive body of readers ready to be shaped and disciplined, but as active readers who attempted to construct a distinctive reading culture of their own.

The core of this discussion lies in the autobiographies of workers themselves. I have consulted twenty-two French autobiographies, and sixty-eight for Britain, which was a far more prolific source of worker-autobiographies. The bibliography compiled by David Vincent and his colleagues lists no fewer than 801 working-class autobiographies written in Britain between 1790 and 1900.[2] In fact, the 1866 edition of the Larousse Dictionary described autobiography as an English invention, still rare in France.[3] The autobiographies consulted span the period from the last years of the eighteenth century to 1914. Seventy-nine works consulted were written by men, only eleven by women. They were published either in book form, or in newspapers, or as a brief life history to introduce a collection of poems. Working-class autobiographers rarely failed to give a description of their reading, and some of them outlined the detailed reading programs which had guided them. In relating their reading, they traced their triumphant struggles to acquire a literary culture. They established authentic foundations for their own literary aspirations. The eager search for book knowledge was vital to the intellectual emancipation on which political action was based; it also provided the knowledge and discipline required for moral, rational self-improvement.[4]

Working-class autobiographers had quite distinctive and intensive methods of literary appropriation. Their literary culture was improvised, developed haphazardly outside the structure of educational institutions. In its respect for the literary canon, the reading of the autodidacts seems extremely deferential to the literary monuments of bourgeois culture. This ambiguous reverence for official culture lies at the heart of working-class *autodidaxie*. Yet it never prevented working-class readers from proclaiming their class identity or making clear where their fundamental class loyalties lay. They lay, in the vast majority of cases considered here, with the working-class roots from which they had sprung. From this angle, we can justifiably call their reading culture a culture of resistance.

The Pursuit of Knowledge under Difficulties

The process of cultural appropriation, according to Pierre Bourdieu, depends on the balance between an individual's economic capital, and his or her educational capital.[5] In other words, the cultural goods we consume and cherish are determined by our income level and the level of schooling we have attained. It follows from this that the autodidacts were doubly disinherited. They were both poor and lacking in educational qualifications. The autodidact, deficient in both inherited and acquired cultural capital, was forced to accumulate it through his or her own efforts, and by unorthodox means. Excluded from the kinds of cultural consumption enjoyed by the well-off, the autodidact inevitably became a usurper of cultural property. He or she was an interloper, who had been denied access to an envied cultural world. This situation provoked alternating feelings of dutiful submissiveness and belligerent resentment.

The 'Pursuit of Knowledge under Difficulties' was the title of Edward Craik's successful work of advice literature for self-improving British workers, first published in 1830 under the auspices of the Society for the

Diffusion of Useful Knowledge.[6] The title suggests the material handicaps which working-class readers had to overcome. The education of the autodidact was, by definition, intermittent and incomplete, constantly sacrificed to the family's economic needs. Erratic attendance made it difficult for teachers to impart learning as a cumulative process. Formal schooling was far less important for the apprentice reader than the informal networks of relatives, neighbours, priests, and benevolent employers who took time to assist the debutant reader. The home and the local community remained important sources of the educational process. Hannah Mitchell, a rare working-class suffragette, grew up on a farm in the Peak district in the 1870s and early 1880s. As we learn from her autobiography *The Hard Way Up*, she was taught to read by her father and uncle.[7] Then she herself taught her younger sisters to read. Hannah only had two weeks' schooling. The story of her reading apprenticeship is a good example of the importance of family transmission in the acquisition of literacy.

Self-taught workers had a love-hate relationship with formal education. They resented the fact that it remained the preserve of the rich and privileged. At the same time, they retained a strong belief in its value, and several autobiographers devoted considerable space to a discussion of their own education. Many were deprived even of the opportunity to learn to read. Perhaps the most harrowing tale of thwarted educational possibilities comes from the long-time illiterate, Norbert Truquin, the son of a northern French metal-worker. Born in the Somme in 1833, the young Truquin was put to work for a woolcarder in Amiens at the age of seven. For three years, Truquin led a brutalized existence, forced to sleep in a coal-hole under the stairs.[8] Truquin's release came in 1843 when his employer died, but this left Truquin unemployed, living by begging and then resorting to a series of itinerant jobs. At the age of thirteen, he could neither read nor write, but he had heard of the socialist writer Cabet, and he came to think of himself as a freethinker.[9] In one factory, he heard a fellow worker reading aloud from Cabet's *Voyage en Icarie*, but this worker was dismissed.[10] This incident testifies both to the importance of oral transmission in working-class reading, and to the fragility of any attempt to develop an independent reading culture in this period. Truquin had acquired strongly anticlerical opinions, but he still had had no opportunity to learn to read.

In 1855 Truquin was eking out a miserable existence in the silk sweatshops of Lyon. He discussed history and politics with fellow workers, and he heard the *Courrier de Lyon* read aloud, although he regarded it as a paper which continually slandered the working class.[11] Without any formal education or reading competence, Truquin had learned from direct experience about the exploitative nature of capitalism. In 1870 he was arrested for participation in the Lyon Commune. Once again, oral reading amongst his fellow workers continued Truquin's education. He persuaded other prisoners to read to him from Hernando Cortez's history of the conquest of Mexico.[12] Truquin had clearly developed a great interest in history, although historians, in his opinion, only wrote to praise the upper classes. The great philosophers were no better, Truquin decided after visiting the ancient sites of North Africa, for the great minds of antiquity cared nothing about the emancipation of the slaves who maintained their illustrious civilizations.[13]

Latin America now captured his attention. He was attracted by the promise of new, agrarian-based, social experiments. Still illiterate at the age of thirty-seven, he left in 1872 to help establish a socialist colony in Argentina. He returned briefly to France before his definitive emigration with his wife to Paraguay. His experience of Paraguay confirmed his anti-Jesuit opinions, but in all probability it was here that he eventually became literate. He finished his autobiography, *Mémoires et aventures d'un prolétaire*, in 1887, and it was published in the following year by Bouriand, a socialist publisher in Paris.

Norbert Truquin had spent much of his life trying to fight hunger and homelessness. No wonder that his autobiography, like many other workers' autobiographies, recorded such basic information as the price of bread and how much he earned. Such materialist concerns are a distinctive feature of working-class writing in the nineteenth century. In spite of his hardships and peregrinations, he had acquired a class-based culture, which was inspired by socialism and anticlericalism, and was well-versed in history. He asked questions, discussed issues with fellow workers, and responded critically to the literature that he listened to. His 'knowledge' developed out of his life experiences – physical hardships, two revolutions, and prison. Truquin had no roots and no craft-based training, and he suffered from his own illiteracy. He was deprived of an education, and his employers continued to prevent workers' access to culture. Nevertheless, he had by his mid-fifties acquired enough expertise to write his own autobiography, which concluded with a ringing call to social revolution.[14] Even in the most hostile of environments, a workers' literary culture could be formed.

However brief the experience of formal schooling, it nevertheless authorized some emphatically negative judgments from workers. They had, after all, obtained an education through their own efforts, and they were proud to have fashioned their own culture. It was natural that they should value the lessons of life and experience over classroom learning. For several of them, schools were purveyors of useless erudition and false knowledge. James Bezer, born in Spitalfields (East London) in 1816, complained about the ineffectiveness of the schools he attended. He claimed he was still unable to write, after fifteen years in Sunday school, where he had

> Six hours a week, certainly not ONE hour of useful knowledge; plenty of cant, and what my teachers used to call EXPLAINING difficult texts in the Bible, but little, very little else.

'My education was very meagre,' he wrote, 'I learnt more in Newgate [prison] than at my Sunday School' – a typical autodidactic rejection of institutionalized instruction, in favour of the 'hard knocks' school of life.[15] Yet later in life, after working as a shop assistant, a porter, and a beggar, he himself became a Sunday school teacher, before his emigration to Australia. The fact that a large number of working-class autodidacts did become teachers testifies to their deep-rooted concern for the cultural life of their own class.

The autodidacts pursued their desire for study and self-improvement with a determination that was sometimes obsessive. Indeed, it had to be, if they were to overcome the immense material handicaps that stood in their way. Sacrifice and ingenuity made up for the lack of money, light, space, and time to read. Gabriel Gauny, as a poor Parisian *gamin* in the *faubourg* St Marceau during the second decade of the century, even collected discarded wrapping paper used to pack seeds, sugar, or coffee. It was usually made of old books and newspaper, and provided him with an unlikely source of reading matter.[16] Gauny's difficult life as a child of the *faubourgs* did not prevent him from starting an apprenticeship as a carpenter, joining the Saint-Simonians, and developing a philosophical theory based on the palingenesis of souls. But this lay in the future. The publishing initiatives of the 1830s had reduced the price of novels without yet making them affordable to working-class readers. Another problem was the lack of light for reading. Windows were rare, and candles were expensive. In the 1830s and 1840s, oil-lamps were available, and after the 1850s, paraffin lamps were introduced. In many working-class households, however, the lamp might only be lit when all the family was present for the evening meal.

Working-class autodidacts embarked on the pursuit of knowledge with vast enthusiasm and little discrimination. They confessed to a ravenous appetite for literature of all sorts, which they admitted in retrospect was poorly directed. Only later did some of them organize their study into a pattern with fixed objectives. This indiscriminate and eclectic reading seems to have been a necessary initiation stage. The autodidact began by accumulating knowledge quite arbitrarily. He or she lacked the experience or education to classify his or her cultural acquisitions, or place them in a hierarchy of importance. Without the literary landmarks offered by formal schooling, the autodidacts were cultural usurpers, adopting independent and 'heretical' modes of cultural acquisition.[17] They looked back with mixed feelings on this stage of exploration and rapid, unsystematic consumption. The goal of self-improvement dictated a different kind of reading. Reading should have a clear purpose, and there was little room for casual browsing.

Autobiographers thus described an early stage of ignorance. At a certain point, however, the reader would be struck by the revelation that his or her reading had been desultory, indiscriminate, and poorly directed. He or she determined to pursue a more purposeful reading plan in future. This turning point has been effectively described by Nöé Richter as 'the conversion of the bad reader,' when the autodidact resolved to renounce his 'bad' reading habits.[18] At this point, the self-improving artisan or worker made his or her own reading time, and set his or her own program. A stern self-discipline and a careful economy of time were required. Moral, spiritual, and material improvement demanded neatness, sobriety, and moderation in all things. Self-denial was part of the *habitus* of the self-taught working-class reader. Nevertheless, self-imposed reading courses were sometimes so ambitious that they exacted a heavy price in terms of the reader's mental and physical energy. Teenage reading crises were not unusual, as the case of Thomas Cooper illustrates.

Cooper was a shoemaker and a Chartist, that is to say, a leading member of the radical working-class movement which held demonstrations and compiled petitions during the 1840s in favour of parliamentary reforms set out in the 'Charter.' As a teenager, he set out a reading program for himself, which aimed to absorb practically every moment of his waking life. He wrote:

> I thought it possible that by the time I reached the age of 24 I might be able
> to master the elements of Latin, Greek, Hebrew, and French; might get well
> through Euclid, and through a course of Algebra; might commit the entire

'Paradise Lost,' and seven of the best plays of Shakespeare to memory; and might read a large and solid course of history, and of religious evidences; and be well acquainted also with the current literature of the day.

I failed considerably, but I sped on joyfully while health and strength lasted ... Historical reading, or the grammar of some language, or translation, was my first employment on week-day mornings, whether I rose at three or four, until seven o'clock, when I sat down to the stall (i.e., the shoemaker's work-bench).

A book or a periodical in my hand while I breakfasted, gave me another half-hour's reading, or study of language, at from one to two o'clock, the time of dinner – usually eating my food with a spoon, after I had cut it in pieces, and having my eyes on a book all the time.

I sat at work till eight, and sometimes nine, at night; and, then, either read, or walked about our little room and committed *Hamlet* to memory, or the rhymes of some modern poet, until compelled to go to bed from sheer exhaustion.[19]

Cooper's program was intense, but kaleidoscopic. It embraced ancient and modern languages, mathematics, literature, and divinity. The program depended on allocating set reading tasks to every moment of a day that was rigidly regulated and segmented. His autobiography conveys in rich detail the importance of reading to the self-improving artisan. But Cooper's program could not be sustained for long. In 1827, at the age of twenty-one, he suffered a complete physical collapse, and he was confined to bed for several months.

Working-class readers improvised and borrowed from friends, neighbours, priests or schoolteachers. A collective effort could compensate for the lack of individual resources. As a soldier in Metz in 1846, Sebastien Commissaire joined with other members of his barracks to 'sub-let' two-day-old copies of progressive newspapers from a local bookseller.[20] In the Cheviot Hills, shepherds left books for each other in the crannies of stone boundary walls, to create an improvised ciculating library *en plein air*.[21] Family ties, professional or religious connections were sources of intellectual aid rooted in the working-class milieu itself. Working-class networks protected the autodidact's autonomy as a reader, and may have filtered his or her responses to the texts read. They ensured that he or she did not always respond predictably to the literary culture diffused by middle-class mediators.

Autodidacts, then, were condemned to improvise. They stole time to read, and they carved out moments of privacy from the continuous stream of demands from families or employment. By exploiting working-class networks or the generosity of relatives and assorted patrons, they manufactured their own culture. In spite of the need for middle-class patronage, 'self-culture' was still seen as a means to the independence and emancipation of labour. It is a paradox of *autodidaxie* that out of this very dependence on bourgeois help was to come self-reliance and the desire for emancipation. Only the successful autodidacts present us with these contradictions. The fate of those who tried the road to self-improvement, but failed, defeated by poverty or other pressures, can only be imagined.

Women Readers and Writers

As readers and writers, women had to contend with the barriers to education which handicapped all members of the working classes, but girls enjoyed more limited educational opportunities than boys. In France, the close association of Napoleon III's Second Empire with the Catholic Church brought some expansion of girls' primary schools after the Falloux Law of 1850. By 1866 the number of girls attending school was 93 per cent of the number of boys in school, most of them taught by nuns.[22] Schooling for girls, however, did not encourage further study beyond the requirements of the dutiful wife and the competent mother. The emphasis was rather on needlework, domestic economy and child care. The female version of Useful Knowledge consisted of the skills which would turn a girl into a competent housekeeper: sewing, mending clothes, baking, washing. These domestic subjects left little time in the day's curriculum for disciplines like history and geography.[23] The 1851 Census in England and Wales suggested that the education of working-class sons took precedence over girls' schooling.[24] Daughters were expected to stay at home to care for aged or sick family members. As a consequence, girls' truancy was not regarded as seriously as that of boys.

Hannah Mitchell, mentioned above, was acutely aware that her brothers enjoyed privileged status. She wrote resentfully:

> Sometimes the boys helped with rugmaking, or in cutting up wool or picking feathers for beds and pillows, but for them this was voluntary work; for the girls it was compulsory, and the fact that the boys could read if they wished filled my cup of bitterness to the brim.[25]

The point was further emphasized when the young Hannah was retained at home by her mother until her sister Ellen had finished her schooling: the farming household could not function unless one daughter stayed at home.

Such examples of women's struggles to develop their own literary culture may lead to the conclusion ·that working-class women laboured under a double burden: they suffered as workers and also as women. This, however, is to understate and at the same time to oversimplify their situation. The problems faced by women as readers and writers were multiple rather than dual. They encountered a complex network of constraints. In a patriarchal world, male authority operated in a variety of ways, and in each case, different forms of compromise and resistance were appropriate. As their autobiographies show, female readers negotiated their way forward in a world dominated in different degrees by husbands, fathers, lovers, male employers, priests, male fellow militants, and also male publishers. Female autobiographers found that the publishing industry did not welcome independent women authors. Women's autobiographical writing only saw the light of day through the intervention of a male intermediary. Marguerite Audoux, for example, the peasant orphan living in the enclosed rural world of the Sologne who wrote an autobiography in 1910, was 'discovered' and published on the recommendation of the writer Octave Mirbeau. Further examples will illustrate the extent of dependence which women readers and writers accepted, and the independence they achieved.

Suzanne Voilquin was a young socialist, living in Paris in the 1830s. She joined the Saint-Simonians, a group which stressed the social and moral role of women in a future society which would recognize the creative powers of both men and women. Nevertheless, Voilquin found that the male leaders of the movement were reluctant to recognize women militants as equals.[26] Voilquin found her greatest fulfilment in bringing children into the world. Her conception of maternity as moral guardianship survived experiences of personal loss which might have discouraged others. Her own mother, who has a strong presence in Voilquin's autobiography, gave birth to eight children, of whom four died. Voilquin herself had three miscarriages in her loveless marriage to Eugène before starting her successful career as a midwife in St Petersburg.

Voilquin's own life demonstrated her adherence to progressive views of female emancipation. She had rejected the notion of the permanent Christian marriage by separating from Eugène in 1833, and allowing him to leave for America with his lover. In the following year, she followed the Saint-Simonian leader Père Enfantin to Egypt. In spite of this,

Voilquin's relationship with the male hierarchy of Saint-Simonianism was full of friction. The issue of female equality was a very divisive one for the movement. As Grogan argues, Saint-Simonians were reluctant to recognize the woman's right to sexual freedom, and women played a subordinate role in the Saint-Simonian movement as a whole. One meeting which Voilquin relates with Enfantin may be revealing of the Saint-Simonians' difficulty in transcending traditional prejudices. As an unhappily married woman, she and Eugène had a confidential discussion session with Enfantin. When Voilquin 'confessed' that she had been seduced by a medical student in her youth, Enfantin was overcome by a wave of sympathy at this revelation. His first instinctive reaction was to embrace her *husband* to console him in his misfortune.

Women readers thus negotiated their intellectual progress in the face of male disapproval. The most influential figure of all was the father. As a mediator or controller of knowledge, a father could encourage or direct his daughter's interests. As a worker with his own intellectual or literary interests, he might provide a role model. As an oppressive moral guardian, he could drive his offspring into revolt. Marianne Farningham grew up in a Kent family dominated by her Baptist father who gave her a life-long affection for the Bible and an interest in Christian education. Her father, however, was 'the master and judge of the household' and his censorship of Marianne's reading habits frustrated her.[27] She read secretly at night, but her father discovered her. Having seen her geography notebooks, he told her that 'he did not think such knowledge would ever be of much use to me.' He refused to allow her to read at night, but she naturally disobeyed. Falling asleep over a book late one night, Marianne set the bedroom on fire.[28]

Marianne Farningham's teenage rebellion against patriarchal censorship challenged the moral ethos of Protestant Dissent in which she grew up. The influence of non-conformist Protestant sects was a defining feature of autodidact culture in Britain. Marianne recalled family Bible readings on Sunday evenings. She wrote: 'It seemed that every Sunday evening, before bedtime, we went to Bethlehem.'[29] Marianne's father's religious beliefs meant that the Bible was central to family life, and he acted as the family's moral guide and interpreter of it. Having signed the pledge (to abstain totally from alcohol), he helped Marianne to do the same. His opposition to Marianne's adventurous reading was typical of the scriptural basis of Protestant Dissent.

Just as this could constrain the reader's choices, however, so it could inspire a spirit of self-improvement. Thus Marianne Farningham's career as a reader continued with the help of an unlikely ally in the shape of her local Baptist minister. He lent her *Jane Eyre*, which awakened her romantic sensibilities and even enhanced them because she knew this reading was forbidden to her. *Jane Eyre*, Marianne wrote, 'haunted me for many nights afterwards. I had been taught that it was wicked to read novels, and this one marked my departure from the old limitation.' The unorthodox minister also allowed Marianne to borrow his Shakespeare, which greatly offended the older members of his congregation. Marianne wrote in her autobiography:

> One anxious lady begged me to let her burn it, as she was sure it was an offence in the sight of God, and several who heard of it advised me not to read it; but of course it brought me into a new world, and filled me with wonder and admiration.[30]

Her father's reaction was not recorded; perhaps Marianne had by now (at twenty years old) fully established her rights as an independent reader.

Parental censorship equally failed to crush Margaret Penn, who grew up in another non-conformist Protestant family in Lancashire during the early years of the twentieth century. Her father was a farm labourer who encouraged reading aloud as a means of controlling her reading. Margaret, who called herself Hilda, had great difficulty in expanding her reading beyond what was authorized, that is to say, the Bible and the books she won as Sunday school prizes. Hilda began to borrow fiction from her local Co-operative library, but her parents would only tolerate this if the local vicar approved the titles she read. They objected to all reading performed outside a supervised religious context. Hilda proceeded to devour a range of romantic and fictional literature, including *Robinson Crusoe*, the best-selling Victorian melodrama *East Lynne*, and Hardy's *Tess of the d'Urbervilles*, a book which became an emblem of independent womanhood at the end of the nineteenth century. Because Hilda's parents were illiterate, they demanded that she should read her books aloud.[31] Only in this way could they check that the contents of her reading were acceptable. Hilda could not oblige: she borrowed novels on a week's loan, which left little time for reading aloud before they had to be returned. Family tension mounted when Hilda became determined to leave home to go into employment. Her parents blamed her reading for her wilful departure to Manchester and an independent life as an apprentice dressmaker.

Hilda's novelettes, and the illicit thrill experienced by Marianne Farningham in her encounter with *Jane Eyre* remind us of prevalent stereo-
types of the female reader as a consumer of romantic fiction whose
imagination was liable to overheat. Solitary romance reading was considered dangerous for young girls, and even for married women, although
marriage entitled them to a little more licence. The dominant medical
discourse of the nineteenth century reinforced patriarchal assumptions
about the need to 'protect' women and adolescent girls from harmful
texts.[32] Women's reading ability, it was thought, was determined by phys-
iological factors. Women had a lower brain weight than men, and so
were considered less fit for intellectual pursuits. The shape of the female
brain in this view enhanced a woman's intuitive faculties but limited her
reasoning powers in comparison to those of men. There was a fear that
overworked female emotions would prove physically debilitating. High
levels of stimulation produced by novel reading could be harmful, caus-
ing hysteria and loss of fertility. It was very dangerous to extend the
female imagination too far.

Some women rejected traditional female roles, using their reading and
writing to introduce them into public life. Farningham, for example,
became a Christian journalist, while Mitchell was a suffragette, in a movement where working-class militants were rare, and between the wars she
became a municipal councillor in Manchester. Their careers ranged
from political agitation to a life in the service of God. They adopted different paths, but they all led these women into the public arena.

These themes are present in the rich autobiography of Adelheid
Popp, the Austrian Social Democrat, which clearly charts the author's
passage from a subjective and romantic reading model, to a style of reading which stimulated her political ideas and assisted her public role as a
party militant. Popp's work, prefaced by August Bebel, first appeared
anonymously in Munich in 1909, in a very impressive print-run of 30,000
copies.[33] Its success persuaded the author to come out into the open.
The autobiography was reedited under her name in 1922 and 1927, and
was translated into English and French.

Born in Vienna of Czech parentage, Popp was forced into a series of
unskilled jobs when her father's death made it imperative for her to become a wage earner. Like many autodidacts, she therefore had little formal education. In fact, her illiterate mother was opposed to compulsory
schooling. She was even sentenced to twelve days in prison because Adelheid had missed school. Popp's intellectual life was thus blighted by her
drunken and violent father, her stifled schooling, and parental opposi-

tion. Nevertheless, she borrowed fiction from acquaintances, and rented material from local booksellers. She read novels, broadsheets, and stories of brigands and unhappy queens, like Mary Queen of Scots and Isabella of Spain. At this stage of her life, Popp conformed to the sterotypical female reader as a consumer of romantic fiction and historical novels. On Sunday evenings in summer, she would retreat to the cemetery, where she could read instalments of Paul de Kock's novels undisturbed.

In her autobiography, she claimed she was the victim of sexual harrassment. On one occasion a male lodger approached her bed suspiciously as she slept. On another, a travelling salesman offered to put in a good word for her at the sandpaper factory where she was working, and she feared he would expect sexual favours in return. On each occasion, her mother told her to stop exaggerating, and blamed her anxiety on the effects of reading novels about romance and seduction. Too much escapist fiction, her mother was suggesting, had put absurd fantasies into Adelheid's head. As a result, when Adelheid was fifteen, her exasperated mother threw all her novels out of the house.

Looking back, she described this as a presocialist period, when she accepted all kinds of falsehoods. She had believed in miracles and gone on pilgrimages. She had accepted anti-Semitic propaganda uncritically and took an unhealthy interest in the life of the imperial family. Everything changed when a fellow worker introduced her to socialist ideas, and to the Social Democrat party. In 1890, at the age of twenty-one, Popp became a party member. She had experienced Nöé Richter's 'conversion of the bad reader' – a turning point at which the reader renounced his or her previously indiscriminate reading habits and resolved henceforth to read with more purpose and direction.[34]

Now began a new style of politically orientated reading. Unlike the private, withdrawn world of romance novels, read in solitude, Popp's new reading put her in touch with public life and encouraged her to start a new career. This began with her reading of the Social Democratic press. Every week she went to the Social Democrat offices to buy the party newspaper (probably *Zukunft*, The Future). She described this solemn occasion in almost symbolic terms. As if to emphasize the importance of her transformation, she would wear her best dress to appear at the party offices, just as she had once done, in a previous life, to attend church on Sunday. Popp borrowed books from the Workers' Association Library, she read Kautsky's weekly *Neue Zeit*, Lafargue, Lassalle, Engels on the English working class, and Liebknecht's *Knowledge is Power.*

Even so, it was not easy for Popp to imagine herself as a woman in a public, political role. When she read Social Democrat literature aloud at work, the clerical staff would say that she spoke 'like a man.' Politics was men's business and she was discouraged from meddling in it. When she attended her first public meeting, she was the only woman there. Nevertheless, she took enormous pride in her first public speech, as well as in her first published articles, knowing that her handwriting and spelling were defective. Reading, together with a generous dose of personal daring, launched Popp into a public career as a unionist and party militant. In 1892 she became editor of *Arbeiterinnen-Zeitung*, and after the First World War, she was elected to the Austrian National Assembly.

Adelheid Popp demonstrates the multiple handicaps under which working-class autodidacts laboured: hostile parents, a background of domestic violence, and the lack of formal education were among them. In addition, she encountered (but overcame) the exclusion of women from intellectual and public life. Her reading trajectory illustrates two faces of the working-class woman reader. At first, she was a very private reader of romantic and historical fiction. Her reading was subjective, solitary, and it nurtured sentimental fantasies which she later rejected. In her second reading phase, Popp read socialist philosophy, history, and party newspapers. She had undergone a profound reading metamorphosis. Her reading no longer led her to an interior world of romance, imagination, or religious devotion. Instead it introduced her to party meetings where she stood up to express the viewpoint of militant women. It led to trade unionism, journalism, periods of imprisonment, and election to parliament. Through her reading experience she had found a full-time career in the public arena.

The Uses and Abuses of Fiction

Working-class intellectuals had little patience with popular novels. They joined company with middle-class library reformers in urging workers to rise above the tide of pulp fiction which, by the end of the century, was engulfing lending libraries. The worker-intellectual Henri Tolain takes us further into the *habitus* of this emerging working-class intelligentsia.

Tolain was a Parisian bronze worker with Proudhonist sympathies who played a major role in founding the International in France. At first sight, his literary views showed a great respect for 'high' literary culture. In 1865, writing in the short-lived weekly *Tribune Ouvrière*, he regretted the banality and sensationalism of the popular novel. Pulp fiction, in his view, was a corrosive influence and an insidious poison, infiltrating the working household and sapping its sense of morality.[35] Tolain condemned novelists with no morality and no conception of justice. He criticized the rotten distortions inherent in the sensational novel. He did not shrink from condemning Goethe's *Werther* as a selfish, weepy lover, and Balzac's Madame Marneffe as a female monster. He severely criticized the novels of Eugène Sue. If we examine his ideas more closely, however, it is clear that he does not reject fiction outright. Tolain simply had his own agenda for the ideal novel. What he demanded from the genre was a clearer personal conviction on the author's part, and an awareness of social and political issues. What he valued in novels, and found wanting among popular contemporary writers, was precisely that sense of social justice and social realities which would make fiction meaningful and uplifting to working-class readers. Tolain cites Hugo's *Notre-Dame de Paris* as a novel with such ideals, and in spite of Madame Marneffe he grudgingly praised Balzac as a master of social observation. Everything else, however, was dross, nothing but overwrought sentiment and banality. The novel itself was not condemned, but Tolain expected novelists to be philosophers with principles and a message to impart.

Tolain, therefore, was a critical reader who had a clear agenda for his ideal working-class reader. But what did other autodidacts read in their dedicated pursuit of self-culture?[36] To some extent, they accepted advice to concentrate on utilitarian reading, together with a knowledge of uplifting canonical works. Many of them felt that purely recreational fiction was a waste of their time. Their responses to self-improving literature, however, were not uniform. Although they often read the same books, it is not always possible to predict what they thought of them. Workers conducted their own dialogue with the texts they acquired, and searched for answers to problems arising from their own experience of life and work.

Autodidacts shared similar preferences and similar evaluations of different literary genres. In the codes of practice they adopted, they unconsciously formed what Stanley Fish termed an 'interpretive community' of readers.[37] They developed common reading strategies, based on convergent assumptions about what constituted good literature. For the British autodidacts, their library reflected the heritage of radical Dissent. Bunyan, Milton, and Tom Paine formed a staple diet, to be supplemented perhaps by Cobbett, Ruskin, Carlyle, or by Chartist literature and the radical *Black Dwarf*. The classical literature of the seventeenth century was one common meeting point for French working-class readers, while

Rousseau was the dominant radical presence in the autodidact's library. The writing of Chateaubriand was another strong influence. The autodidacts read and responded individually but in spite of obvious divergences, they shared common interests and devoured the same imaginary library.

A few certainly used their reading in politics and economics to develop socialist ideas. Voltaire reinforced the anticlericalism of many militants, fuelled at the same time by a reading of Volney, Holbach, Meslier, or indeed of religious history itself, which could demonstrate the follies of the Crusades, the wars of religion, and the Inquisition. They devoured history, scientific works, and tried to master foreign languages. Louis-Arsène Meunier, the starving muslin weaver from the Perche, became an itinerant schoolteacher in the 1820s, but felt ridiculed by his social superiors for his ignorance of Latin, and so he taught himself Latin, with some assistance from a local lawyer. The phenomenal Meunier claimed that he read eight hours per day for six years, committing large sections of Rollin's *Ancient History* to memory. He had borrowed the work from a friend, and read it through twice within three weeks before returning the loan.[38]

Serious autodidacts, however, were not usually enthusiastic about fiction and recreational reading. Victorine Brocher, the militant *communarde* who was sentenced to death as a *pétroleuse*, recalled rather grimly that in her family 'we read progressive newspapers.'[39] Those who experienced a 'conversion' to more serious and purposeful reading looked back on fiction reading as a frivolous waste of time. When James Burn, the itinerant peddler, drew up a list of recommended books, he began with the categories of religion, history, the arts, and the sciences.[40] Only then did he turn to the humanities, and to the types of fiction to be avoided. Sentimental romances were better left on their shelves for all the useful knowledge they provided. They were 'full of language without meaning, and pretty flowers without fragrance!' They outraged common notions of probability, and above all, they lacked gravity. Only two novels were excluded from this class of useless fiction: Goldsmith's *Vicar of Wakefield* and Defoe's *Robinson Crusoe* had a moral content and were sufficiently 'true to nature' to qualify among Burn's recommended literature.

On the other hand, many working-class autobiographers, like Tolain, took a personal and selective approach to fiction. Hugo was especially remembered by the autobiographers, because he could be read as a social radical, and so was Dickens for his 'deep and abiding sympathy with the poor and suffering.'[41] Victorine Brocher clearly took time off from her progressive papers because she reported that she was inspired by *Les Misérables*, which she read in a *cabinet de lecture* in the mid-1860s, and reread annually thereafter.[42] She described it as a great work of social philosophy, well worth the one franc per day she paid to borrow it.

Women readers tended to place a higher value on fiction than did men. Similarly the Saint-Simonian militant Suzanne Voilquin enjoyed novels, chiefly those by female authors like Madame Cottin, Madame de Genlis, and Madame de Staël. 'These various works', she wrote, 'exalting love and reinforcing my natural inclinations, acted forcefully on my imagination and filled my heart with unknown desires.' But looking back later on her novel-reading, she tended to disqualify its legitimacy, writing, 'From these novels I drew false ideas about the realities of life.'[43]

Jonathan Rose's prolific study makes very clear the reverence which self-taught British workers showed towards the canonical texts of English literature.[44] They cited Shakespeare and the romantic poets. Lancashire construction workers could be encountered reciting Tennyson, while collective renditions of Handel's Hallelujah chorus would drown out the throbbing of the looms in a Blackburn cotton mill. Later, in the early twentieth century, they resisted modernism and preferred books by dead white males. The proletarian canon was a very conservative one.

Working-class readers, however, were not passive or subservient readers. They knew what they wanted from imaginative literature. They compared their fictional worlds to their own world and judged them according to their own standards of realism. They usually also demanded that novelists should be aware of social problems and social inequalities. What mattered most was the novelist's social conscience. Working-class readers respected the classics of bourgeois literary culture but measured them according to their own needs and standards. Many read works of liberal political economy simply in order to reject their principles in favour of socialism. They read novels, too, but made use of them to reinforce their notions of contemporary social injustices.

Workers as Writers

Workers were not just readers. They also wrote. If we are to fully measure their achievement in constructing an independent literary culture, we must also consider the phenomenon of workers as poets and, above all, as autobiographers. Working-class authors searched for the means to legitimize their writing efforts and, almost inevitably, they imitated literary figures from the world of high culture. Yet the derivative nature of their literary projects encountered sneers rather than applause. The unschooled worker who doffed his cap to the prestigious authors of the past had pretensions which the cultivated elite might regard as a mockery of the literary canon. Bourdieu accurately characterized the paradoxical situation of the autodidact in search of acceptance:

> The traditional kind of autodidact was fundamentally defined by a reverence towards high culture which was the result of his brutal and premature exclusion from it, and which led to an exalted and poorly directed devotion to it, inevitably perceived by the agents of official culture as a sort of caricatural homage.[45]

Several workers became published poets. Poetry was not the preserve of a distant, learned culture; it was produced and published by working-class writers. Their poetry, however, was often an extension of the oral culture which they inherited, and which survived in popular song. Chartist poets like Willie Thom drew on a local (Scottish) ballad tradition, and were not afraid to write in dialect, sometimes providing a glossary for the uninitiated. French worker-poets might prefer local languages which were closer to popular usage. The *coiffeur* Jasmin, for example, wrote in Occitan, looking ahead to the renaissance of regional languages which occurred in the mid-nineteenth century.[46] Poetry was closer than prose to popular oral tradition, and it found ready outlets in nineteenth-century newspapers.

Working-class autobiographies are another clear indication of a growing self-awareness, and mastery of the printed word. Without formal tuition, without ghost-writers and without literary credentials, a group of remarkable individuals set out to write their own stories. They wrote autobiographies for different purposes: to warn, to instruct, to record, to preach. Some were inspired by nostalgia, some by vanity, others by anger. They wrote at different times of their lives, some taking advantage of a prison sentence, others reflecting on their past in old age, others taking new stock of themselves as a result of a personal trauma, a few writing to reassess themselves, and resolve what we might now call a mid-life crisis. They adopted traditional literary conventions, but sometimes escaped those set formulas to express the more authentic voice of the 'unlettered' author. We must consider the literary strategies that dominated their autobiographies.

The commonest autobiographical idiom in the first half of the century, in Britain at least, was the spiritual autobiography. The ancestor of the genre is usually recognized as St Augustine, but for the writers who concern me, John Bunyan's *Pilgrim's Progress* was the strongest influence. The spiritual autobiography traditionally told a story of youthful depravity and moral degeneration. This usually induced a phase of suffering, loss of direction, and mental prostration and alienation, the nineteenth-century equivalent of the Augustinian fall and *peregrinatio*.[47] Then the autobiographer experienced a spiritual crisis, resolved by a sudden, dramatic conversion. Self-regeneration and moral self-improvement could now begin. Autobiographers in this tradition were principally concerned with the salvation of their soul, and their main subject was their private relationship with God. From seventeenth-century English Protestantism, and from the Bible itself, they inherited biblical language and metaphors with which to describe their own spiritual odysseys. They relied heavily on models of the exodus, a paradise lost, aimless wanderings in the wilderness, redemption, and finally the sight of the promised land to interpret their own misfortunes and revivals.[48] Their autobiographies are therefore full of references to Bunyan and the Bible, which operated as a kind of code, demonstrating their entry into an elite spiritual community.

The autobiography of James Hopkinson, the Nottingham cabinet-maker, relied on the idea of a spiritual conversion. James Hopkinson took up his pen in 1888, induced to reflect on his past by the shock of his wife's death, 'who I trust and believe is now before the throne and with the redeemed, who have washed their robes and made them white in the blood of the lamb.'[49] Hopkinson considered himself 'as a frail Barque launched on the ocean of time.' His account of childhood and the years of apprenticeship is a repentant confession of drinking and lying, and his own involvement in fights with other apprentices. Then, at the age of eighteen, Hopkinson experienced his conversion:

> I cannot tell, like some can, the exact time I found liberty. It appeared to me to be like the shining light, that shineth more and more unto the perfect day. However this I know that a very great change had come over me. And instead of desecrating the sabbath I began to enquire like Saul of Tarsus Lord what wilt thou have me to do. I soon found my work in the Sunday school, and as I loved it I soon began to make myself useful.[50]

The New Testament provided the classic metaphor of a sudden illumination, which changed the direction of Hopkinson's life journey, on his personal road to Damascus.

Later in the nineteenth century, this mode of writing expired. Auto-

biographies became more positivist and scientific. They referred to neither God nor the salvation of the soul, but saw personal development
rather in terms of the growth of the power of reason. A second popular
style adopted by autobiographers, after that of the spiritual traveller, was
that of the historian. Autobiographers like William Lovett consciously
assumed a responsibility for recording their own history. No-one else,
they knew, would provide the kind of working-class history they wanted
to leave behind them, and a few were well aware that no adequate history
of the Chartist movement had appeared by the end of the century. 'It is
extremely unlikely' wrote William Adams, 'that any competent and satis-
factory narrative of a stupendous national crisis will ever now be given to
the world.'[51] The 'stupendous national crisis' was, of course, Chartism,
and Adams set about to give its history, sketching its leading figures and
citing previous autobiographies of Chartists as he did so. Radicals like
him set out to balance the public record, giving their version of their
own role in British radicalism. At their worst, they offered little more
than anecdotes about the public celebrities they had known, as Linton
the engraver did, recounting his casual acquaintance with a string of
European revolutionaries, like Mazzini and Herzen.[52] At their best, they
offered a kind of alternative political history of the century, from the
Reform Bill agitation of 1830–2 to Bradlaugh in the 1880s.

A third autobiographical stance was to demonstrate a success story,
when success was to be measured in material terms. This, of course, was
quite compatible with the autobiography-as-spiritual-odyssey and with
the autobiography-as-alternative-history. Radical historians of their own
movements often finished their careers as successful journalists or teachers; they had escaped the necessity of grinding manual work. One function of the autobiography was to demonstrate how this was done. Like
the autobiography as spiritual odyssey, the autobiography as material
success story had a pedagogical purpose: it stood as an exemplum for the
next generation, teaching the path which led forward and upward, and
the virtues required to tread it successfully.

Thomas Burt, the Northumberland miner, advertised his success in his
subtitle: 'Pitman and Privy Councillor,' and his autobiography actually
concluded with Burt's election as Member of Parliament for Morpeth in
1876. John Hodge was a puddler at a Glasgow blast furnace who became
Lloyd George's Minister of Labour in 1917. His autobiography was entitled 'Workman's Cottage to Windsor Castle,' since he considered as the
pinnacle of his career an invitation to spend the night as a house guest of
the royal family. Titles and subtitles proclaimed the autobiographer's

achievement, as in William Cobbett's proud proclamation, 'The Progress of a Ploughboy to a Seat in Parliament.'[53]

In France, the best example in this category is the autobiography of Jacques Laffitte, which boasts of his successful *montée* to Paris, and his 'arrival' at his 'gilded mansion' on the fashionable Chaussée d'Antin. Laffitte was concerned to impress the reader with the author's overpowering sense of self-importance.[54] His vanity was characteristically male, expressing the pride of men whose sense of self-worth was intricately bound up with a public career and the exercise of political power. The autobiography of the self-made author was in this sense a highly gendered text.

It had a linear narrative structure, with the account leading on to greater and greater achievement, in spite of hardships encountered. It revealed little about the intimate, emotional or even the family life of the author. As Marianne Farningham, born in 1834 and the daughter of an artisan, discovered to her chagrin, this was an almost exclusively masculine genre. She wrote:

> My father gave us two monthly magazines published by the Sunday School Union, the *Teacher's Offering* and the *Child's Companion*. In one of them was a series of descriptive articles on men who had been poor boys, and risen to be rich and great. Every month I hoped to find the story of some poor ignorant GIRL, who, beginning life as handicapped as I, had yet been able to live a life of usefulness, if not of greatness. But I believe there was not a woman in the whole series.[55]

The woman's role was to support and comfort the so-called self-made man.

Working-class women writers came into their own, however, as authors in another popular genre, that of the militant's memoirs. Their interest lay not in material success, but in self-emancipation. The author's gradual radicalization and perceptions of the sources of oppression were the true subject of these autobiographies. In addition, their writing had a historical purpose – to tell the story of the century's revolutionary struggles from a true perspective, in other words, from the point of view of the protagonists and victims.

A good example is the autobiography of Victorine Brocher, published like so many militants' memoirs by François Maspéro. Brocher, who was an ambulance worker with the Paris Communards, wrote of a life whose emotional landmarks were connected to the men she cared for. Her life of political commitment and action was inseparable in her narrative from her relationship with her father, husband, and sons. She was the daughter of one Parisian cobbler, and became the wife of another. Her father had introduced her to Lamennais's writings, and her husband was linked to the International under the Second Empire. She was therefore connected to a male network which was both a professional network and a fraternity of committed republicans. Victorine's life as a militant, however, grew more bitter and intense as she found herself becoming indispensable to at least a part of that militant male network. She struggled to sustain an incapacitated (and possibly alcoholic) husband, and a partly crippled son. The passion in her autobiographical account derives not merely from her part in the Paris Commune, but also from the personal tragedies which punctuate her narrative. The deaths of her father and son in 1868 destroyed any lingering faith in Christianity: After the siege of Paris, another of her sons died. Her escape to Switzerland after she was condemned to death as a *pétroleuse* meant a sudden and permanent separation from her husband.

Her story centres almost exclusively on her experiences of 1848 and of the Paris Commune. It is a passionate account of the February Revolution and of the massacres of the *semaine sanglante*, when the Commune was suppressed. The author gives day-by-day accounts of these revolutions, culminating in the discovery that she had been sentenced to death as a *pétroleuse* (petrol bomber). Her narrative reflects the problems of material life with which nineteenth-century workers commonly struggled: the price of bread, the problem of finding shelter, and the levels of wages are often detailed. Victorine Brocher wrote exactly what she paid for butter and potatoes, and she described the illnesses and diet of her children, which was a vital concern in the siege of Paris, when she unwittingly found herself eating mouse paté.[56] Even if the style of working-class autobiographies was frequently derivative, they expressed specifically proletarian concerns. Frequently, and Brocher was no exception to the rule, this kind of autobiography took on a profoundly anticlerical or atheist animus, which spared neither Catholic nor Protestant.

Working-class writers were usually conscious of writing history for public consumption, but at the same time, writing an autobiography fulfilled an inner need. Autobiography was a step in the process of defining one's identity, both as an individual and as a member of a group or class. The act of writing itself brought greater self-knowledge and self-assertion. Philippe Lejeune described autobiography as principally the 'history of a personality,' and envisaged the autobiography as a pact which the writer makes with himself or herself.[57] The purpose of the pact, Lejeune argues, is to redeem a flawed destiny, and to rescue a personality which has doubted its own value.

The problem for these 'new writers' was to find a suitable language and style in which to 'make themselves.' Jacques-Etienne Bédé's editor, for example, lists the author's many grammatical mistakes, wrong use of tenses, incorrect agreements, and bad spelling.[58] Christopher Thomson, a ship's carpenter, apologized for 'the natural roughness of this book', and was 'well aware that to the critic, and to the refined in literature, his Book will appear a crude and faulty production.'[59] Their apologetic descriptions of their humble status and lack of qualifications for the job were ways of articulating a genuine difficulty. Charles Smith, the journeyman printer, was embarrassed by the weight of the classical literary tradition:

> I make no claims to literary talent and must crave the reader's indulgence for my want of literary tact ... So pardon, gentles all, and a plenary indulgence (if such a word may be mentioned in these papaphobic times), for all the sins I may fall into, and all the *lapsus pennae* which must occur now and then to one but little accustomed to trail the quill.[60]

After such affectation, the bluntness and brevity of J. Taylor, the Sunderland blacksmith, are refreshing. Taylor apologized for 'a blacksmith's hammer comes easier to my hand than a pen, and I doubt my ability to strike any literary sparks from the anvil of my life.'[61]

A few more experienced writers knew how to capitalize on confessions of modest talent. They insisted on their inadequacy as writers, and the lack of intrinsic interest contained in the story of their dull, working lives. W.E. Adams was a Chartist who became newspaper editor and a leading light in the English republican movement. He seemed to have lived anything but a humdrum existence. He composed his autobiography at the age of seventy, in Madeira, and it was published in 1901 in the *Newcastle Weekly Chronicle*, which he had himself edited for three decades. Nevertheless, he called himself a mere 'social atom,' and explained

> I call myself a social atom – a small speck on the surface of society. The term indicates my insignificance. I have mingled with no great people, been admitted to no great secrets, met with no great adventures, witnessed no great events, taken part in no great transactions. In a word, I am just an ordinary person.[62]

Autobiographers protested, with suspicious vehemence, that they only took up the pen because their friends had for some unknown reason insisted that they should.

They were untutored and unsophisticated writers, but however uneducated they were in a formal sense, working-class authors brought a great deal of cultural baggage to the task of writing. They had inherited or acquired a sense of correct literary tone, and they adopted linguistic or stylistic modes encountered in their own reading. They plundered their existing capital of images, metaphors, and narrative techniques for the style best suited to the expression of their own individual identity.

Self-taught writers were naturally self-conscious, and aware of the existence of a long literary tradition, which they had to adapt for their own ends. Bédé, who led a strike of Paris chair makers in 1820, wrote his life as a late eighteenth-century melodrama. In his autobiography, he continually addresses God or destiny in a romantic style reminiscent of Ducray-Duminil ('O dreadful fate!,' etc.). A carefully crafted mise en scène frames his father's death which opens the story. In a terrible thunderstorm, with thunder crashing, a heavy beam tragically fell on him in his mill. At the sight of this accident, his uncle swooned and 'almost lost his life.'[63] His narrative reads like a novel throughout. Bédé entitled it, in the style of Ducray, 'Etienne et Maria ou le triomphe de l'amitié' (Etienne and Maria or the Triumph of Friendship). He provided the triumphant ending which the genre demanded: in 1820, with the devoted support of his friend Maria, he was released from a prison sentence with a royal pardon. The denouement, however, has a final novelistic twist. Until the end, Bédé concealed the real identity of the beloved Maria who worked loyally for his release from jail. The reader learns that Maria is not, in fact, Bédé's wife, but the wife of a comrade Bicheux, to whom the work is dedicated, and whose real relationship with Bédé can only be surmised. Historians of labour have appreciated and exploited Bédé's work as a valuable source for early nineteenth-century labour struggles, but they have not always appreciated the narrative strategies and novelistic style which order the text.[64]

Autodidact writers struggled to find a narrative mode appropriate to their message and their abilities. English romantic poets and novelists had several conscious or unconscious imitators. Ellen Johnston, factory hand and daughter of a Glasgow stonemason, read many Walter Scott novels in the 1840s at the age of about thirteen, and gave herself the role of a Scott heroine. 'I fancied I was a heroine of the modern style,' she wrote, because 'by reading so many love adventures my brain was fired with wild imaginations.'[65] She identified herself with Scott's fictional heroines, and sustained herself with idealized images of courtship and married bliss. Scott provided the only means available to articulate female desire. She tells how she

> waited and watched the sun-set hour to meet my lover, and then with him wander by the banks of the sweet winding Clutha, where my muse has often been inspired when viewing the proud waving thistle bending to the breeze, or when the calm twilight hour was casting a halo of glory around the enchanting scene.[66]

The realities of factory and family life were far removed from these romantic images. Johnston's haunt was not the sweet-winding Clutha, but the rather less salubrious Paisley Canal. Instead of the lover who made her happy at the sunset hour, she met one partner who left her in 1852 not with a halo of glory, but with the burden of an illegitimate daughter. The harsh realities of the factory, the canal, and her tormenting stepfather are in stark contrast to the romance genre in which Johnston elaborated her own female identity.

Working-class writers were an articulate but inexperienced minority. A few wrote to demonstrate that they had achieved bourgeois respectability. Others wrote to educate others in a spirit of militant defiance. Their work was inevitably derivative, as they improvised a literary style and a narrative structure to announce their presence alongside the paragons of 'legitimate' culture.

Working-Class Intellectuals as Cultural Intermediaries

If worker-autobiographers had been called on to justify the fundamental purpose of their writings, they would probably have claimed that they were engaged in a struggle against popular ignorance – an ignorance which they knew perpetuated the enslavement of the working class. The ex-*communarde* Victorine Brocher wrote passionately in defence of education: 'Education, and more education ... only the ignorance of the people gives the ruling classes their power.'[67] Chris Thomson, the Yorkshire carpenter and strolling player, echoed the cry, differing only in assigning Dissenting preachers a constructive role in advancing the education of the masses:

> Until education shall teach a majority of the toiling artisans of England to become calm, sober, thinking and self-dependent men, uniting themselves into a deliberative league for the emancipation of labour, they will continue

to be at the mercy of the mammon-lovers, who thrive by their ignorance and division ... Brother Artisans, up then, with the banner of education![68]

Autodidact readers adopted some of the rhetoric of the eighteenth-century enlightenment to explain the importance of their reading. Reading was the herald of enlightenment for the itinerant worker James Burn, for instance, who wrote:

> I must confess that my most important information has been obtained from books ... The light of knowledge bursts upon some men like the rays of the sun just emerged from behind a dark cloud; while to others it gradually opens up its unfolding beauties like the dawning light of a spring morning.[69]

The metaphor was hardly original, but it suggested the liberating effect of reading on the autodidacts.

Their reading practices emerged from a common aesthetic of self-denial and earnestness. The social psychology or *habitus* of the self-taught worker, however, exhibited some characteristics (thrift, sobriety, respectability) of nineteenth-century bourgeois culture. Working-class readers distanced themselves from the crowd of fellow workers. Reading was a solitary activity, and individual working-class readers were often shunned by their fellow workers, or treated as peculiar antisocial recluses. The worker who read, Agricol Perdiguier recalled, was an object of ridicule (*un objet de raillerie*).[70] A few might have welcomed this ostracism, as it gave them more time and solitude to devote to reading. But individual readers had an uneasy relationship with fellow workers. Jean-Baptiste Arnaud described French *compagnons* as 'blind, credulous, worshippers of prejudice.'[71] Their reading opened up for them a world of middle-class culture and middle-class values, which accentuated the ambiguity of their position.

A distance opened up between the working reader and the ordinary worker, often filled with a poorly disguised antipathy. Even language barriers appeared between ambitious working-class intellectuals and their fellow workers. Laffitte, in order to facilitate his Parisian *embourgeoisement*, had got rid of his Bayonnais accent. For Perdiguier, as for Nadaud, learning French and discarding their local language (Provençal in Perdiguier's case) and pronunciation were part of their intellectual progress. Nadaud was for a long time a worker with his feet in two different worlds. As a regular seasonal migrant from the Creuse to the French capital, he was part Limousin, part Parisian, speaking with a natural Limousin accent which he gradually lost as his life centred more permanently on Paris. As an autodidact, he despised the apathy of his fellow masons, and yet was eager to do something for their education. He characterized the duality of his position as that of a revolutionary vanguard. 'In each occupation,' he wrote, 'groups formed amongst the proudest and most intelligent workers, who spurred on the masses and made them ashamed of their indolence and apathy.'[72] Nadaud identified himself with 'the proudest and most intelligent,' leading the rest out of ignorance and indifference. As a reader and an autodidact, he was detached from other workers, but at the same time he appointed himself their guide and leader.

Working-class intellectuals had a very keen sense that they were different. They knew they belonged to a small group more determined and more far-sighted than most other workers. They tended to adopt reading practices which reinforced their sense of distinction. My purpose, however, is not to argue that the nineteenth-century autodidact was on the road towards *embourgeoisement*. His or her predicament was far more complex than that rather simplistic term implies. The improvisation of a culture often followed middle-class models, but between what the autodidacts read and how they responded as readers there was scope for many possible outcomes. Some autodidacts certainly emerged from the working-class throng determined to distinguish themselves irrevocably from it, but few denied their class origins entirely. Gilland, the adamant locksmith of the *faubourg* St Antoine, declared, 'I love my position (mon état), I love my tools and even though I could have made a living from my pen, I would not have wanted to stop being a working locksmith.'[73]

The working-class intellectual did not share what he or she perceived as the laziness and prejudices of the majority of workers. At the same time, he or she did not necessarily share middle-class versions of respectability either. Autodidacts in general were cultural intermediaries, working-class activists with a broad knowledge and their own interpretation of a hallowed literary tradition.

Political radicalization was filtered through the values of an informal but distinct community of readers, with its own evaluation of the uses of fiction, poetry, history, or science. Print culture was vital to this politicization, although it also depended on oral transmission. The autodidacts are best seen as cultural intermediaries, standing between the learned culture, which became accessible to them, and their working-class roots, from which their education had partially detached them.

Theirs was a reading culture with which we are no longer in touch.

The cultural practices of the nineteenth-century autodidacts have been buried by a century of social change. Universal schooling made their improvised reading culture superfluous. The rise of new forms of leisure has made their intensive reading practices seem obsolete. A general process of acculturation has transformed all of us into consumers of culture and of commercialized entertainment rather than independent seekers after self-emancipation. The compulsive reading of nineteenth-century self-taught workers is a distant reminder of individual potential, when driven by a passionate desire for intellectual liberation.

7 Oral Culture and the Rural Community: The *Veillée d'Hiver*

The *veillée d'hiver*, or 'winter wake,' was an important part of the social and cultural life of village communities in many parts of Ancien Regime France. The common need for heat and light brought people together, in a private house, stable, or barn, on long, cold, winter evenings. Villagers would carry out various agricultural tasks, tell each other stories, and recite the local popular legends which have helped to make the *veillée* an institution of great interest to historians of popular culture. Historians as a whole have been dimly aware of the importance of the *veillée* as a medium for cultural transmission between older and younger generations, but they have sometimes lacked a very precise grasp of the principal functions and activities of the *veillée*.[1] It would be dangerous, for instance, to rely on the descriptions of the *veillée* given by Robert Mandrou, who interpreted them as vehicles for the dissemination of chapbooks and other texts of the Bibliothèque bleue. In 1964 he wrote:

> We must situate this public reading of the Bibliothèque bleue in the context of the *veillée*; someone could always be found who could read, even in the poorest village, either priest, sexton or returned soldier, and with the aid of a candle or the light of the fire, he could read aloud for everybody.[2]

This chapter, which presents a brief examination of the purpose and social function of the *veillée* in the nineteenth century, suggests why Mandrou's characterization is a misleading one.

It appears open to question on at least three points. First, Mandrou saw the *veillée* as an occasion for reading aloud within the group. The evidence suggests, however, that reading was an extremely rare event, although not an unknown one, in the *veillée d'hiver*. The storytelling of the *veillée* was usually quite independent of any written text, and was part of a traditional oral culture rather than a written culture, although it would be unwise to assume that the two were mutually exclusive. Second, Mandrou suggests in the above extract from his influential book that *veillées* were to be found in almost every French village: this was probably far from the case. Third, Mandrou implies that the village *curé* had an integral part to play in the cultural life of the *veillée*. This view overestimates the contacts possible between a cultured elite (the clergy) and a genuinely popular culture; it also overlooks the profound hostility with which the clergy often regarded popular amusements, and the activities of the *veillée*. The evidence for this hostility, and some of the reasons for it, will be reviewed here.

The sources used in this survey are principally nineteenth-century sources, deriving from a period when the *veillée* was in decline in many areas of the country, and when, consequently, folklorists and amateur ethnographers began to take an interest in recording the disappearing customs of their native province. The reasons for the *veillée*'s decline, incidentally, must also be addressed, and they may have some relation to debates on the modernization of nineteenth-century French society and culture.[3] With a few exceptions, our knowledge of the *veillée* in this period does not come directly from popular origins. The popular participants in the *veillée* shared an oral culture, and did not normally leave written records for posterity. Our picture of the *veillée* is filtered through diverse cultural intermediaries, such as the clergy, or individual memoir writers describing their childhood in the countryside.

The perspectives of these cultural intermediaries are of two kinds. One group, consisting of the clerical sources, wrote in terms of moral disapproval. A good example of this discourse of repression is provided by the replies to the questionnaire issued by Monseigneur Rendu to the curés of the diocese of Annecy (Savoie du Nord) in 1845.[4] The questionnaire was an attempt to investigate popular religious practices, customs, and superstitious beliefs in general, but the 122 replies published also give some useful information on the *veillées d'hiver*. There is little doubt that priests regarded the *veillée* as an opportunity, actual or potential, for dangerous popular licence, and the institution was, for the curé of Lullin in the province of Chablais, 'one of the great blights (*plaies*) on the mountain parishes.'[5] The *veillée* was an institution under constant suspicion and attack from social elites.

Individual memoirs make up a second, more diffuse group of sources. Their perspective is very often affectionate and nostalgic. This is true of the memoirs of Louise Michel, looking back on the attractions of a tranquil, provincial childhood, after a turbulent life of revolution and the hardships of exile in New Caledonia.[6]

An exceptionally rich source is Eugène Leroy's novel *Le Moulin du Frau*. As a tax collector in the Périgord, Leroy certainly qualifies as a 'cultural intermediary,' but he was one with an intimate acquaintance with the popular milieu, and the book is full of details of peasant life and culture. In fact, it is a veritable encyclopedia of Périgourdin folklore.[7] *Le Moulin du Frau* is of particular interest, because it places the history of peasant acculturation within a political context, that of the peasant revolutionary tradition and its survival throughout the nineteenth century. This is a tradition which sets the peasants against their priests and their corrupt, arrogant seigneurs, but only those who are literate, like the family of the main character, Hélie, feel involved in national republican politics. In *Le Moulin du Frau*, the *quarante-huitards* (veterans of the 1848 Revolution) look back with respect to the patriotic and revolutionary tradition of 1792, which is revived once again in the *revanchisme* of the 1870s, and in the new desire to expel the Prussians. It is no coincidence that Hélie's family is remarkable for both its literacy and its politicization in the republican camp. This fictional family, however, was exceptional: usually, the written word failed to penetrate the oral universe and 'bookless' sociability of the Périgourdin peasant. Only here, in a world of predominantly oral transmission, could the belief arise in 1848 that Lamartine ('La Martine') was the mistress of Ledru-Rollin, the social democrat candidate for the presidency of the Republic.[8]

The Working Community and the Campaign against Popular Culture

These varied sources suggest that the *veillée* had a very scattered geographical distribution. It was perhaps most common in the Midi, being found in Languedoc, Vence, the Périgord, and the Rouergue. But we cannot classify the *veillée* as an exclusively southern or Mediterranean form of rural sociability, for its existence was also reported in the Limousin, Savoy, the Mâconnais, the Allier, and the Haute-Marne. It is also found in the Mantois and parts of Brittany.[9] Communal life, however, was certainly richer in some places than in others, and it should not be assumed that the *veillée* was a regular or universal gathering. The inquiry of the Abbé Rendu, mentioned above, produced responses from 122 Savoyard villages. The existence of the *veillées* can only be deduced in about 50 per cent of these villages, and only definitely confirmed in a third of them at most.[10] Another episcopal inquiry in 1859 in the Versailles diocese revealed that the *veillée* survived in only 35 out of 107 parishes.[11] In these areas at least, only a minority of rural communities would hold a *veillée* by the middle of the nineteenth century.

The timing of the *veillées* did not differ greatly between regions. The *veillées* coincided with winter, and thus with a particular phase of the agricultural calendar. In Languedoc, the *veillée* or *velhador* might assemble between All Saints' Day and the following February or March.[12] In the Mâconnais, the *veillées* customarily began on St Michael's Day (29 September), or St Martin's Day (11 November), but they would invariably be over before the following Easter, when springtime and longer daylight hours imposed different daily rhythms on the rural population.[13] In other words, the *veillées* would not begin until after the wine harvest, and sometimes not until winter grain sowing was finished, too. St Martin's Day, when they sometimes began, was an important milestone on the agricultural calendar, being the date when annual leases began for *vignerons* and *métayers* (share croppers).

As this may suggest, the existence and duration of the *veillée* were deeply embedded in the seasonal variations within the annual cycle of an agrarian workforce. Various kinds of work, more or less agricultural in nature, were, as we shall see, central to the activities of every *veillée*. In the *veillées d'hiver*, however, work was combined with social intercourse, amusement, and the consumption of refreshments. The main 'program' of the *veillée* may be expressed schematically thus:

$$\rightarrow \text{ (light meal}$$
$$\text{WORK} >>>>>>> \text{STORIES} \rightarrow \text{ (games or dancing}$$
$$\rightarrow \text{ (courting rituals}$$

| 1 | 2 | 3 |

Not every *veillée* contained all these elements: in fact, only a few did so, but all invariably involved some kind of work undertaken collectively. This was a constant and central feature of the *veillée*. In addition, the *veillée* was almost universally the occasion for the recital of stories, usually well-known tales, developed or embroidered by a regular *conteur* or *conteuse* (for there was a recognized expertise involved), drawn from the collective memory of the rural community. More rarely, some food would be prepared, there might be singing or dancing and, in some cases, a visit by a group of young men from the village who came to court their girls. The *veillée* did not develop in these ways everywhere, and there were many regional variations in its form. Nevertheless, the above 'program' does roughly correspond to a chronological agenda: whereas 1 (work) and 2 (storytelling) may have been simultaneous, 3 (meal, dancing, courtship) came later, towards the end of the evening, which might not conclude until 11 pm, midnight, or even later.

The primary raison d'être of the winter *veillée* was the search for light and warmth, and the need to economize by sharing the expense of both. Thus the collective basis of the *veillée* was first demonstrated in the arrangements to provide adequate lighting. Until oil lamps made a regular appearance later in the nineteenth century, the expense of candles was assumed by the community as a whole. Later, the provision of oil became a duty falling to the leading participants in rotation.[14] Lighting was vital to the ambiance of the *soirée*. Childhood memories of the *veillée* rarely fail to evoke the thrill of listening to ghost stories by candlelight as dark and menacing shadows flickered against the walls. In many villages, it would be very rare for any persons to permit themselves the luxury of artificial lighting: their day began at sunrise and closed at sunset. Candlelight therefore made the winter *veillée* a very special occasion, and it is not surprising that its image was closely associated with the flickering central flame, suspended from the roof. Those who needed the light most, either because of their age, or the intricacy of their spinning or lacemaking, sat nearest to it. The central light thus imposed a certain hierarchy on the seating arrangements. The old women would occupy the circle nearest to the light, with the spinners behind them, and perhaps the knitters (*tricoteuses*) a little further way, while the men (if they were present at all) sat in semi-darkness towards the back of the room.[15]

The common need for warmth, as well as for light, brought the group together in the *veillée*. In cereal-growing country or pasture areas, the venue would commonly be a barn, stable, or cowshed. In periods of exceptional cold, the local inhabitants might even decide to spend the whole night sleeping in the stable. In the Mâconnais, during the Second World War, some villagers still remembered that this had happened in the winter of 1889–90.[16] In wine-growing areas, these facilities were not always readily available, and the venue of the *veillée* had to be improvised. In the Mâconnais again, as well as in the Haute-Marne, villagers would construct their own temporary shelters from wooden poles, straw, and clods of earth known as *escraignes* (Latin *scrinia*). In desperation, they might build *escraignes* in the nearest town (Tournus for example), against the wall of a church.[17] All the same, the *veillée* remained a forum of essentially rural sociability, even if extremes of cold occasionally forced it into an urban exile.

The *veillée* was a communal event, uniting a whole *quartier* or hamlet in collective work and celebration. The precise allocation of gender roles within the *veillée* will be discussed below but, as a general rule, no member of the village community was excluded. The *veillée* united both sexes and all ages. It was common for two or three dozen people to participate. Later, in the course of the nineteenth century, as the *veillée* declined, it lost this communal aspect, developing into a meeting of a small group of friends and relatives in a private house. The *veillée* lost its communal character, to become increasingly familial in structure.

The nature of the work carried out in the *veillée* has already been indicated. The women would make lace, spin thread, knit, or strip hemp, while the men would make straw hats, brushwood brooms, or turn wicker into baskets or poultry cages.[18] None of the sources consulted suggest that any of this activity had a commercial purpose; we must assume that the products resulting were for the consumption of the villagers themselves. In the southwest, cracking chestnuts and extracting their kernels were important tasks of the winter *veillée* and, in the Périgord, this work sometimes gave its name to the institution of the *veillée* itself – known as the *nougoliosous*.[19] On the Sabbath, work ceased, and no *veillée* would be held.[20]

While work proceeded, the *conteurs* of the community would be pressed into action, to give their versions of the stories through which rural society expressed its own cultural identity and elaborated its own conception of the world. Most popular of all were ghost stories, and tales of diabolical apparitions, monsters, and other incarnations of death which hunted lonely travellers at dark crossroads. Younger listeners were particularly sensitive to such stories – they themselves would soon be finding their own way home after the *veillée*, in pitch darkness.

Tales of ghosts, werewolves, and the exploits of great criminals like Mandrin were not the only subjects of conversation. Bougeâtre suggests that political discussion certainly intruded into nineteenth-century *veillées* in the Mantois, and reminiscences of the First Empire and the Napoleonic campaigns gradually permeated the collective memory of nineteenth-century village society.[21] In *Le Moulin du Frau*, the storyteller Gustou holds his audience spellbound with the story of a local *fait divers*: the murder, before the Revolution, of Father Autier by a local nobleman. The mutilated corpse was discovered accidentally one day, when somebody found a dog carrying the victim's disembodied hand. The victim was identified by his ring, still attached to one of his fingers.[22]

It is not easy to find evidence of reading aloud in the winter *veillées*, in spite of Mandrou's sweeping assertion to the contrary. The Toulouse ethnologist Daniel Fabre speculated that familiar texts may have been consulted by Languedoc storytellers to refresh their memories, but this is quite hypothetical.[23] Rendu's questionnaire in Savoy is illuminating: out of 122 replies, only one made a clear reference to the habit of reading within the *veillée*, and this was to a catechism.[24] In northern France, the audience may have been more literate. In Bougeâtre's study of the *veillée* in the Mantois and the Vexin, it appears that almanacs were occasionally present, and towards the end of the century, *Le Petit Journal* or *La Lanterne de Boquillon* may have been read.[25] These references indicate how easily the written word could be assimilated into what was principally an oral culture, but they are very rare. The tales of the *veillée* were not drawn from a corpus of written works; they emerged from the age-old collective memory of the rural community. The *conteurs* of this culture appropriated the book for their own purposes, just as Tahitians assimilated the missionaries' Bibles. They memorized the text, and then they 'read' it, even holding the book upside down as they 'recited' it.[26] As Piniès writes of the *veillée* in Languedoc, 'books aren't read, they are spoken, they are recited, they are murmured' and, contrary to the suggestions of Mandrou, what counted here was 'oral knowledge (*savoir oral*) and the storytellers' performances.'[27]

'Talking, working, enjoying yourself with friends, those are the three aspects of a successful *veillée*,' writes Béteille of the *veillée* in the Rouergue.[28] After work and storytelling, other forms of amusement might follow. Food and drink might be served, at least in those communities which could afford to provide some. Once again, the burden of contributing to this supper was assumed on a group basis. In the southwest, it was natural that the snack should be largely composed of chestnuts, sometimes accompanied by mulled wine. In the Mâcon area, grapes and cheese might be provided. In Eugène Leroy's *Le Moulin du Frau*, the *veillée* concluded at 11.30 pm with wine and beans.[29]

The consumption of alcohol is important, since it was a target for clerical attacks on the *veillée*. Dancing, too, when it followed, was unpopular with the clergy. Béteille mentions dancing and card-playing in Rouergat *veillées*, and singing, dancing, and the reading of the tarot could be found in the Mâconnais.[30] In the Mantois, a game of dominoes might be in progress, but this was very much a male occupation, soon to be absorbed by the local café or club.[31]

Before pursuing this discussion of the ludic or festive aspects of the *veillée*, a few remarks must be made about the sexual roles and division of labour within the winter *veillée*. So far, only the evening *veillée* has been mentioned. There were similar daytime gatherings in winter, but since the men would usually be out at work, they tended to be exclusively female affairs. Even in the evening *veillée* proper, women played a dominant role. The gatherings were usually organized by the women in Languedoc: it was they who made the communal lighting arrangements.[32] Louise Michel remembered women-only *veillées* in the Haute-Marne of her girlhood, and female *veillées* were not uncommon in Savoy.[33]

Within most *veillées*, there was a clear division of responsibilities between the sexes. As we have seen, most women sewed, knitted, or spun, while men were engaged in wickerwork. The area nearest the light was female space, the outer and darker areas were masculine preserves. In the Mantois, only the men would discuss politics, and only the men would play cards.[34] For these men, the *veillée* already contained the germ of a new form of sociability, a male sociability, based on the local bar (*cabaret*).

Dancing, of course, as in the Breton *fest-noz*, brought the sexes together, and this was surely one of the institution's greatest attractions for young people in a well-regulated community. Tiennon admitted disarmingly in his autobiography, *La Vie d'un Simple*, that the best part of the *veillée* was walking a girl home afterwards.[35] Courtship was subject to strict rituals and, in the *veillée*, it was inevitably conducted under the close surveillance of parents and elders. In the Mâconnais, for instance, a group of male adolescents might arrive to make a formal visit, and talk to the girls as they worked. This was known as the visit of 'les magnats,' i.e., eligible bachelors, and was regarded as an essential stage in the search for a wife or husband.[36] Male youth groups in search of more vigorous entertainment might descend on a *veillée* in a neighbouring hamlet, sometimes provoking a fight over local girls with their neighbours and rivals, on whose territory they were trespassing.[37] In *Le Moulin du Frau*, Hélie presents his future wife with a symbolic nut in the *veillée*, which she keeps in a love-knot in her handkerchief as a sign of acceptance of his suit.[38]

These courting rituals associated with the *veillée* were thus carried out openly, under the gaze of the community as a whole. For the clergy, however, this was not always sufficient guarantee of propriety. Constant ecclesiastical pressure was exerted on the popular *veillée* from the period of the Counter-Reformation into the nineteenth century. For the world of official culture, the *veillée* was a dangerously autonomous cultural event, where popular practices resisted middle-class supervision, and escaped the tutelage of the written word. The *veillée* was seen as a political and religious threat to the cultural domination of the local clergy, and to the dissemination of official values via the medium of print.

The *veillée* was taxed with immorality, the unrestrained consumption of liquor, free intercourse between the sexes, and the propagation of dangerous superstitions. But its real offence was probably to express the values of an autonomous peasant civilization, impervious to dominant ideological persuasions. In the parishes of the Haute-Savoie, priests reported to their bishop that the *veillées* were 'a general evil,' and 'an inveterate abuse against which we constantly rail and which we cannot succeed in eradicating entirely.' They condemned card playing, dancing, and drinking in the *veillée*; the curé of Sallenove gave this description of proceedings in his parish:

> In autumn a few families bring together the young people of both sexes in *veillées* running quite late into the night, and according to need, until 2 or 3 o'clock in the morning, to prepare hemp, after which they think nothing of letting them dance the rest of the night: a custom which is the root of great immorality.[39]

The nineteenth-century clerical opposition to the *veillée* might thus be interpreted as part of a continuing attack on popular culture by cultivated elites eager to assimilate popular practices into the values of an official culture, at first monarchical and absolutist, later clerico-Bonapartist.

The nineteenth-century clergy, then, frequently regarded the popular amusements of the *veillée d'hiver* as practices dangerous to public morality, and attempted to eliminate them altogether. As exception which goes to prove this rule is the case of the curé Deguiges, discussed by Froeschlé-Chopard and Bernos.[40] Deguiges was the priest of a small village near Vence in the early years of the eighteenth century. He did not share the attitude of his superiors, who held the *veillée* at a distance. Deguiges, on the contrary, tried to make contact with his parishioners, using the *veillée* as a medium through which he could introduce them to the French language, to books, and ultimately to a process of ideological and religious conversion. He lent his own books to female parishioners, and he participated in local *veillées*. Occasionally he would read to those present who were most religiously inclined (*dévotes*). This was exceptional, for reading, as we have seen, was not a normal practice in the *veillée*. Rather it was a practice the clergy might have *wished* to introduce into it, in order to discipline and 'moralize' the *veillée*. Deguiges's liberal attempt to forge a direct link between the culture of the educated and popular culture failed. He was rejected, we are told, both by his popular audience and by the clergy as a whole. He was suspected of indulging in witchcraft, and in sexual escapades with the female audience he managed to assemble. Here the clergy again used the *veillée*=orgy association, this time to discipline a deviant member of their own ranks. Rejected by his bishop, Deguiges was condemned for Jansenism in 1709. His case underlines the failure of the clergy to transform the *veillée* into a means for assimilating a non-francophone peasantry into a dominant culture.

The Decline of the *veillée*

As we have seen, Mandrou's interpretation of the *veillée* requires some revision. Reading aloud was not at all common in the *veillée*, although the clergy might have wished it had been. The *veillée*, rather, was part of a traditional popular culture which resisted the spread of the written word. The *veillée* should be seen as the expression of the solidarity of the rural community, sharing the physical requirements of heating and lighting, working in common, and combining work with cultural and recreational activities enjoyed collectively. The *veillée* was primarily a working gathering, whose life closely followed the seasonal rhythm of agricultural labour. The duration of the *veillée* was dictated by the annual calendar of sowing, harvesting, and *vendanges*. At the same time, the *veillée* represented a particular form of peasant sociability, a sociability centred around work. It was a sociability dominated by women, but one in which courtship might be initiated and promoted by young males, under the surveillance of the elders of the community. The *veillée* was thus an integral part of peasant civilization. It was a forum for collective celebration, and for the transmission of an oral culture, rooted in the ancient memories of the group. The *veillée* resisted attempts made by an elite culture both to assimilate it and to destroy it.

In the second half of the nineteenth century, however, the *veillée* was dying. In the Mâconnais, occasional *veillées* were reported, it is true, in the 1920s, but they died out as a regular institution between 1870 and 1914, the period when, Weber argues, cultural homogeneity was achieved in French society.[41] In the Mantois, the *veillée* barely survived 1870.[42] In northern Savoy, the *veillée* was dying out in many areas by the 1840s.[43]

Other forms of social life were replacing the *veillée*. The café and the bar (*cabaret*) became rival attractions, at least for the male population. Maurice Agulhon has seen the local bar as a complete antithesis of the peasant *veillée*.[44] While the *veillée* reflected the independent but closed world of the peasant, café society, with its discussion of newspapers, opened up broader horizons. The *veillée* united all ages and both sexes; café society tended to segregate adult males from the rest of the community. So we can postulate that it was the men who abandoned the *veillée* first, so that the institution became more exclusively female as it fell into decline. Whereas the *veillée* was integrated into an oral culture, the *cabaret* might offer an introduction to written culture, through the medium of French-language newspapers.

Of course, not everyone went assiduously to the local bar for entertainment. Those who stayed at home, however, were also contributing to the decline of the *veillée*. Work in the evening, telling stories to the young, enjoying supper and a song became increasingly domestic, rather than truly collective activities. The functions of the traditional *veillée* were displaced, moving from the barn or stable into private houses. The *veillée*, commented Gabriel Jeanton in 1920, 'has become more of a family affair.'[45] Together with the café and the newspaper, the family unit itself was a solvent of traditional communal ties. In *La Vie d'un Simple*, the young Tiennon remembered frequent *veillées* in his native Bourbonnais. But as an old man in the 1880s, he spent his evenings differently. He would sometimes buy a newspaper at the Bourbon fair, and would gather his grandchildren round him at home to read it aloud to him.[46]

Several reasons can be postulated for the decline of the *veillée d'hiver* in the nineteenth century. Pressure from the clergy was probably not a major factor in this decline. The cultured elite had been attempting to undermine popular culture for centuries, with only mixed success in this case, and it is hard to believe that clerical criticism suddenly became more influential in the nineteenth century. The spread of written culture, and the development of rival leisure attractions, like the bar and later the radio, inevitably helped to dissolve and then marginalize the oral culture of the traditional rural community.

This discussion of the chief functions of the *veillée* suggests that material factors must also be considered. The chief reason for the *veillée* was the need to economize on winter heat and light. The *veillée* died with the spread of cheaper means of domestic lighting and heating. When improvements in material standards made it possible for the peasants to acquire their own paraffin lamps, and to heat their own homes adequately, the *veillée* naturally ceased to be an urgent material necessity. We have seen, too, that the *veillée* was the occasion for carrying out various 'industrial' tasks, such as cracking nuts, stripping hemp, and spinning thread. It would be logical to assume that the *veillée* changed as the nature of this work altered. Mechanization, for instance, made some of the main activities of the *veillée* obsolete. The invention of hemp-scutching machines would remove one of its functions. The widespread availability of more consumer goods in the countryside would also undermine the kind of village subsistence production which went on in the *veillée*. The *veillée* died, it is suggested, for economic, as well as for cultural reasons, and the decline of domestic industry on traditional lines was at least partly responsible for its disappearance. With the *veillée* died not merely a handful of quaint old rural crafts, but a section of the entire and distinctive peasant culture of pre-industrial France.

8 Why We Need an Oral History of Reading

Historians of reading practices have often assumed that the only good reader is a dead one. Only after death, when books and possessions had been inventoried or sold at auction, did the reader seem to offer historians the kind of documentary sources which voracious computers could devour and exploit. Sources like the post-mortem inventories, however, can never tell us how many books had been removed from private libraries even before the inventory was drawn up, sometimes because they were particularly treasured by the deceased's family, or because they were in very bad condition, or because the auctioneer regarded them as being of no market value. Even when we can establish the presence of books in a household, we cannot know how many were bought or inherited, how many had actually been read and by whom, or how many had stood unread on the shelf.

In researching reading in the recent past, it is worth asking living readers and their families such questions. Of course, we cannot expect them to give us a complete account of all their past possessions, but unlike dead readers they can at least respond to the historian's questions. Just as written autobiographies reveal the reading experience of skilled workers in the nineteenth century (see chapter 6), so oral life stories provide special insights into reading practices in the twentieth. In interviewing elderly readers about the reading habits of their parents, historians have sometimes reached back even further to earlier, pre-1914 generations. These generations lived at a unique cultural conjuncture. They had already achieved a mastery of print culture at the end of the nineteenth century, and were only beginning to become familiar with radio and the cinema in the 1920s. They belonged to a transitional period between the world of the book and the world of electronic media. Australian interviewees recalled the popularity of the magic lantern, a pre-cinematic cultural form typical of this cultural turning point in which the brief supremacy of print was about to be undermined.

French historians have been far slower than their counterparts in English-speaking countries to tap the resources of oral testimony. The reasons for their reluctance are unclear, and this puzzle is especially paradoxical in light of the leading role played by French specialists in developing a history of memory.[1] In assessing the contribution of oral history to the history of reading, we must therefore make an excursion beyond France to include the most significant and influential models. This chapter therefore draws on four studies, two of them French, one American, and one Australian. The French studies are those of Anne-Marie Thiesse on peasants in the Ardèche during the Belle Epoque,[2] and the study conducted amongst Rouennais workers by Nathalie Ponsard.[3] The two other important studies are those by Janice Radway of romance readers in the American Midwest,[4] and the less sophisticated but wide-ranging study of Australian readers which I carried out with Lucy Taksa.[5] Both these latter studies demonstrate the value of the oral history of reading in quite distinctive ways, and their historiographical significance extends beyond their original contexts.

The oral history of reading can throw light on sections of the reading public which traditional approaches neglect. Oral history introduces readers from the margins of historiography, and it allows ordinary people a voice. Their 'voices' are never spontaneous or unmediated but are offered in response to an interviewer's question; nevertheless they are the voices of real readers from social groups who do not always speak for themselves. Nathalie Ponsard, for example, concentrated on two groups of about thirty workers each in St Etienne-du-Rouvray, an industrial suburb on the banks of the Seine near Rouen. Her study of paper-mill employees and railway workers shows us the reading habits and reading models of unionized and politically conscious working-class readers in the 1930s and beyond. Anne-Marie Thiesse interviewed one hundred respondents born between 1883 and 1900, some of them Parisian and some from the rural department of the Ardèche. Her study went on to analyse the content of popular literature itself, but not before she had presented the very valuable reading memories of some obscure peasant women, whom she called 'illiterate readers'. Janice Radway focused on a homogeneous group of women in her fictional Midwest town of Smithton, all assiduous consumers of romantic fiction of the Mills and Boon variety. The Australian study investigated the reading experiences of a much more heterogeneous cohort of sixty-one readers in the Sydney region. Unlike the tight-knit communities studied by Ponsard and Radway, these Australian informants had little in common save their relatively advanced age, but this allowed some social and cultural comparisons to be drawn. Bourgeois reading habits were contrasted with those of workers, city dwellers with country dwellers, men with women.

Towards a History of Reading as Cultural Practice

The (mainly German) exponents of Reception Theory launched their hunt for the reader in the literary text itself. Embedded in every piece of literature, in this argument, lies an 'implied reader,' or a 'hidden reader.'[6] Novels give the reader guidelines on which to base judgments, they raise his or her expectations and leave clues designed to mobilize the reader's imagination. On occasion, the eighteenth-century novel would address the reader directly. The text, in this theory, may open up several different interpretive possibilities for the reader, and it assumes his or her active participation. The presence of the reader, and the reader's expectations of a work of fiction, may thus be deduced from within the text. Oral history, however, is not interested in implied or putative readers; it seeks instead to interrogate actual readers. We are chiefly concerned here with real readers in specific historical circumstances.

All those who have practised oral history in a university environment know only too well that many historians instinctively privilege written or printed sources and are suspicious of oral testimonies. They expect oral history to 'verify' its own data by referring to documentary sources – which are the only ones considered credible. For such historians addicted to what Marc Bloch called the 'documentary fetish,' oral history occupies an inferior position in the hierarchy of historical sources. For other historians, oral history can offer interesting anecdotes to enliven dry and tedious narratives. Here, oral testimony plays a purely decorative role. From this perspective, the role of oral history is either to say insignificant things about important people, or else to say important things about insignificant people. It provides a stock of good stories which can be freely plundered.

As a research method, however, oral history has some specific characteristics. Oral historians study areas of the past which traditional historiography has obscured or marginalized, like the history of private life, of reading, or of child rearing. In spheres like these, the oral historian is working with data which can never be corroborated in documentary sources, for the simple reason that in these areas written sources just do not exist. Oral testimony may help us to construct a history of memory, and a history of representations. Consider Luisa Passerini's research into the Turin working class under Fascism, in which she tried to explain how her informants constructed their social identity as a group.[7] The women workers she interviewed saw themselves as rebels. They relished the chance to describe how their behaviour did not conform to the desired stereotype of the submissive wife, the devoted mother, and the docile worker. This image of the woman-as-rebel enabled them to resist the Fascist regime and, symbolically at least, to overthrow its value system. Only through an analysis of oral testimony could Passerini come to grips with the self-representations which had sustained the workers of Turin.

Public and private memories can sometimes reinforce, and sometimes contradict each other. Oral history presents many opportunities to examine the discrepancies between individual constructions of the past on one hand, and the official version on the other. Our task is to try to understand the relationship between these different memories. Like all historians of reading, oral historians would like to know not just what books were produced, and in what quantities, and who bought them (elusive information in itself) but also through how many hands a given text passed, and the status of books in the households which found some use for them.[8] A social history of the reading public must consider the act of reading as a cultural practice, and ask a series of questions about the history of the assimilation of literary culture. How were books received by their readers? In what circumstances did they read – alone, or in a group, silently or aloud, at home, at work, while sick, or in the bath, or on the train? Within what patterns of sociability did the act of reading occur in a given historical context? Were books read casually in the nonchalant way described by Richard Hoggart in *The Uses of Literacy*? Or were they read obsessively to satisfy an insistent and passionate curiosity, a desire for knowledge and emancipation? Were books revered, despised, or treated indifferently, and how did attitudes towards them differ among various social classes, religious denominations, men and women? Oral history can help us find some answers to all these questions.

My perspective here is not that of a traditional book historian but rather of a historian of reading practices. I especially value the autobiographical testimonies of individual readers. Autobiographies, both written and oral, provide new opportunities for the study of readers' experiences and attitudes to literature. Reading is an active process. The reader is not a mere receptacle, and never comes to a text empty-handed, without previously formed preferences and expectations. The reader brings to the text a literary culture which has developed over a lifetime, and mental habits rooted in his or her background or social class. In other words, readers' responses are connected to the cultural baggage they bring with them, which in turn depends on their level of formal education, their father's profession, and many other factors. Readers take what they choose from their texts, reworking them and interpreting them in the context of tastes or concepts already inherited or acquired.

Janice Radway interviewed romance readers in the American Midwest from a similar perspective. The women readers she questioned saw their romance reading not as an act of conformism which reinforced a patriarchal ideology but rather as a claim to female independence. For the romance readers of Smithton, the act of reading was in itself an assertion of the right to privacy, and a temporary refusal of their everlasting duties as wives, mothers, and housekeepers. Romance reading, Radway argued, was a mild protest against the emotional demands of husbands and children. She reminds us that 'commodities like mass-produced literary texts are selected, purchased, constructed and used by real people, with previously existing needs, desires, intentions and interpretive strategies.'[9]

Reading Communities

The literary critic Stanley Fish would probably be enormously surprised by the distance that cultural historians have since run with his original conception of the 'interpretive community.'[10] The notion of a reading community, however, has helped us to think about what readers have in common, in their choice of literature, in their reading strategies, and in their conception of what constitutes 'literature.' It also helps to understand aspects of the oral history studies under discussion here. Nathalie Ponsard's workers from St Etienne-du-Rouvray formed a close community of readers. What they had in common was first their union organization, which promoted certain reading models and educational priorities, and second the left-wing press which also promoted a specific discourse about reading.

The militant workers of the CGT (Confédération Générale du Travail) were communist inspired and had a very purposeful and utilitarian view of reading.[11] They read to inform themselves, and to fill in the gaps in their knowledge left by what they regarded as deficient schooling. In the rival Catholic trade union federation, the CDT, another group of workers formed a separate community whose reading was framed by their

Christian commitment. Here, for Ponsard, were two distinct reading communities within the same workforce – one Catholic and the other 'coco,' to use the familiar French slang for 'communist.'

These reading communities of workers responded with mixed reactions to the reading models proposed by their union and their weekly or fortnightly journals. The French Communist Party saw reading as a propaganda tool and an ideological weapon. Unlike the Catholic reading model which proposed a study of the Bible and the gospels, the communist reading model preferred realistic or historical novels. It recommended literature which embodied a criticism of capitalism and had a negative view of the United States. It promoted literature with a message of peace and decolonization, and it favoured fiction whose heroes were drawn from the working class.

Not all readers followed these precepts and, as a result, Ponsard's workers acquired a mixed literary culture. They devoured detective fiction, including that of Agatha Christie and Georges Simenon, and they read the adventure fiction of Jules Verne, although both Catholic and communist models frowned upon escapist literature. Above all, they became fascinated by the literature of the Second World War, stories of the Resistance and the battle of Stalingrad. This certainly would have pleased the CGT and its journal, *La Vie Ouvrière*. So too would the workers' penchant for approved writers such as Emile Zola and Jack London. For both these communities of readers, the press played a vital mediating role, and constantly encouraged personal reading as a personal duty.

Completely different reading models emerge in Protestant environments, as several studies indicate. The scarcity of books and reverence for print culture were two characteristics of the traditional world of reading identified by David Hall in Puritan New England in the eighteenth century.[12] Reading aloud in family groups was another frequent practice that was an aspect of traditional literacy. Reading, whether silent or verbalized, took place in a religious context, either for the purposes of the education of the young, or in the context of family piety. Books were so rare that the Bible might have been the only book read by some New England families. As a result, its pages were well-trodden territory, and its wisdom constantly evoked.

Rolf Engelsing found similar reading practices in his study of the bourgeoisie of the north German city of Bremen at the beginning of the nineteenth century.[13] He described their reading not as traditional, but as 'intensive.' Readers who often read and reread a small number of familiar texts had an intensive relationship with their books. These few steady sellers, the Bible among them, would be handed down from generation to generation. The memorization of favourite texts and their recitation 'by heart,' were part of this intensive style of reading.

A number of Australian interviewees had a close acquaintance with this lost mode of reading. They would have recognized some affinities between eighteenth-century Connecticut, nineteenth-century Bremen, and early twentieth-century Sydney. One important link between them was the strength of evangelical Protestantism. The presence of the family Bible, the practice of group reading in a religious context, and the respect which books inspired as material objects all evoke a world of reading we have lost.

The family Bible was a weighty and substantial possession. In the family of Mary Gilmore, the Australian poet of the 1920s, the Bible, handed down through at least six generations, was a 'priceless treasure,' preserved in a wrapping of flannel and silk, valued at thousands of pounds, but probably burned as rubbish by an ignorant aunt.[14] In the blank pages of the family Bible, as interviewees remembered it, were recorded births, marriages, and deaths and sometimes baptisms and confirmations as well. The family Bible registered and commemorated every landmark and rite of passage in the Christian life of succeeding generations. It was an assertion of family identity, an identity which could only be conceived within a Christian framework. It was a confident statement of family unity and continuity. Interviewees suggested that it was usually handed down through the female line, and transmission often occurred when their mother was married, after which the continuation of the lineage would depend on her.

Several informants recalled family Bible or prayer readings as a daily event; for others, it was a Sunday ritual. For Laura P., born in 1911, collective Bible reading was a central family institution. 'Reading the Bible,' she declared, 'was part of our life.' Her father, a classics graduate and a Sydney secondary school teacher, led family prayers, and if there were any guests for dinner they were included in the reading. After dinner, she recalled, the family would 'read around' the Bible; in other words, each member would take a verse in turn around the table.[15]

Group Bible reading had a privileged place among the prescribed duties of the Presbyterian sabbath. Mary Banks took a favourable view of the Presbyterian Sunday in her Queensland memoirs:

Our bush Sundays were happy in spite of the restrictions which hedged them round; we might not run, nor gather fruit, nor sing songs, nor read anything but books on religion or the magazines laid out on the verandah for Sunday reading.'[16]

The strength of Puritanism and strict sabbath observance were important elements in traditional reading practices in Australia, just as they had been in Germany and New England. Oral testimony confirms the survival of this distinctively Protestant reading model.

Gendered Reading Practices

Oral history investigations have illuminated the different reading practices of men and women by putting them into an everyday context. Radway's romance readers constituted an exclusively female community of readers, many of them married mothers in their twenties or thirties. For them, reading the romances of the Harlequin or Silhouette series was a daily need. They shared similar values when it came to the most desirable or undesirable qualities of the fictional romance heroine. They preferred her to be intelligent, with a sense of humour and independently minded. The heroine's initiative and resourcefulness appeared as part of her female identity, as it was part of the readers' fantasies.[17] These readers identified closely with the romantic heroine and in so doing they exhibited the kind of identificatory reading practices often associated with female readers. Even the distribution networks of romance novels targeted a female audience: the books were commonly available in supermarkets and shopping malls.

We can go further in comparing male and female reading practices if we consider what oral historians in various contexts have revealed about newspaper consumption. They agree that different family members read different sections of the newspaper and discard others. In the case of Thiesse's respondents, the father of the household would read the political news, while the women read the crime reports and the serialized novel.[18] The newspaper, in other words, was gendered territory.

Australian evidence from a more recent generation confirms this. Australian respondents remembered that women rarely bought a newspaper – this was a male responsibility. In fact, some women reported that they never read a daily newspaper regularly at all before their marriage.[19] Men had privileged access to the newspaper. Many respondents recalled that their father always read it first. When Mabel T. tried to jump the queue at the family breakfast table, she was prevented from getting to the newspaper by her mother and elder brother. Mabel indignantly told her interviewer: 'I didn't see why it should be given to him … why couldn't I read the paper, but he had to read the paper because he was a man, Oh, drive you mad, it drove me mad.'[20] While men were more interested in the sporting pages, women scanned the announcements of births, marriages, and deaths. The paper's thematic geography was sharply delineated along gender lines.

How Readers Represent Themselves

The oral narrative has its own structures and obeys its own rules. Oral autobiographies never follow the chronological narrative strategies adopted by written autobiographies – that is, they do not start at the beginning of the life, continue through the middle, and reach the end. Instead, oral autobiographies begin at what appears to be a random point, and resort to flashbacks, sometimes jumping ahead, repeating themselves, and indulging in unpredictable digressions. Memories become telescoped, and the historian must try to reestablish the interviewee's sense of chronology.

Memories are selective, but the selection may not always be gratuitous. Sigmund Freud and others taught us that 'lapses of memory' may conceal difficult or traumatic experiences that the subject does not wish to remember. Or perhaps the memory deletes whatever fails to conform with the image of oneself that the informant desires to present. If an interviewee cannot recall what books were present at home, perhaps this is significant. Perhaps books are forgotten because they are not regarded as important. In this case, amnesia constitutes evidence in its own right. The memory censors itself in significant ways.

There is a large subjective element in oral testimony. All autobiography, whether written or oral, is a form of fiction. When informants speak to the historian, they do not give a transparent view of lived experience, but one which is censored and reconstructed by the memory. The autobiography, John Murphy wrote, is very much the revised edition of one's own life.[21] The past is reworked for a particular purpose: to justify oneself, to make a claim on the interest and sympathy of the interviewer, or to find meaning and coherence in one's own personal experiences. Writing or speaking an autobiography is part of a process of discovering or manufacturing a personal identity.

The oral historian does not therefore expect interviewees to relate the verifiable truth about their reading practices, past or present. A clear gap emerges between actual reading practices and the image the reader wants to present. Ponsard calls this discrepancy the space (*décalage*) between discourse and practice.[22] The subjective factor in the evidence, however, is not a handicap but a resource. It gives precious clues about how interviewees represent themselves as readers. Almost all oral historians of reading report that they have encountered the familiar situation in which the interviewee modestly denies ever having being much of a reader, in spite of clear evidence to the contrary. This reluctance to admit reading habits is reported by Thiesse in the case of the peasant women of the Ardèche, and by Ponsard in her personal reflections on the practice of interviewing.[23] In Australia, too, we find echoes of the same familiar phrases: 'I never had time to read,' 'I never sat down idle,' and so on.

All these studies agree that this tendency to underestimate one's own reading is predominantly a female trait. Many women begin the conversation by telling us that they never had any time for reading, because there was always so much to be done in the house or on the farm, especially with children to bring up, and none of the electrical appliances which are supposed to make the job easier today. These denials can never be taken at face value. Further questioning often reveals that a considerable amount of reading was done, albeit of a fragmentary nature, whether of newspapers, magazines, or books themselves. Obviously housework did not necessarily occupy twenty-four hours of every day. There were moments of respite, for instance in the evening or on Sundays, when housewives could relax. There were always hiding places for reading, too, even if dire punishment awaited the clandestine reader.[24]

Why did women so vigorously deny their status as readers? They refused to grant their reading any cultural legitimacy. They insisted that they only read 'stupid tripe.'[25] Madame Z. told Nathalie Ponsard that she had six children which made reading impossible and, even in her parents' house, reading would only be permitted on Sunday afternoons.[26] Reading was condemned as an idle pursuit which offended against a rather demanding work ethic. It further clashed with the desired self-image of a conscientious housewife and mother. So women often represented themselves as readers in a most unflattering light. They despised their own cultural competence. They accepted a conventional view that their reading was inferior in comparison to the reading of serious and edifying literary classics, which they had been taught to regard as worthwhile. In Australia, they accepted the values of bourgeois or official literary culture, which held up such paragons as Dickens, Shakespeare, and the other monuments of English literature.[27] In France, they hardly considered the *romans-feuilleton* (which they loved) as literature. As for their knowledge of legitimate culture, they knew Hugo because they had read him at school, they knew Jules Verne because he was often handed out as school prizes, and they knew Zola because he was on the Catholic Index of forbidden books.[28]

Problems of Oral History

What distinguishes oral history from other forms of historical analysis is the active role of the interviewer. Oral testimony is not produced spontaneously. It is recorded in response to specific questions framed and posed by the interviewer. The evidence emerges from a process of interaction in which the interviewer has an important role. His or her social status, gender, and religious or ethnic origins may influence the answers elicited from an interviewee, depending on the kind of historical problem being addressed. So the interviewer is intimately implicated in the process of data production. The dynamic nature of the relationship means that the presence and influence of the interviewer ought to be recognized, and not effaced in an attempt to demonstrate some spurious objectivity. Thus when Anne-Marie Thiesse reproduced her interviewees' testimony in edited form, as an uninterrupted narrative, she unfortunately disguised the hidden text of the interviewer's questions. She gave her evidence a coherence it probably did not originally possess and a spontaneity which was illusory.[29] The interviewee cannot hide, or pretend to be a completely detached and neutral observer. He or she is directly engaged in the negotiation which creates the oral evidence.

Personal interaction becomes a vital component of evidence collection, and the interviewers in question report moments of complete blockage and embarrassed silence as they struggle to find the appropriate strategies and vocabulary to set the memory in motion. Equally, they report occasions when they are overwhelmed by their informer's verbosity, and swamped by an individual life story running out of control, which they somehow need to bring back to the topic without showing disrespect.[30] Older interviewees sometimes feel uncomfortable when questioned about their educational history by highly educated, university-trained historians. Australian interviewees had usually left school at the age of fourteen, which was the norm at the beginning of the twentieth century. The stigma of illiteracy was still powerful, and questions about their parents' ability to read and write could provoke a very defensive reaction.

The way the oral historian formulates his or her 'sample' is also a significant factor in the end result. Projects often begin with a few significant personal contacts who introduce others, and they in turn put the investigator in touch with further informants. In this way, as with Ponsard's group of interviewees, more interviewees are recruited in a kind of snowballing process. At a later stage, more purposeful sampling may be necessary to correct inherent biases in the group of interviewees. There are some advantages in taking all comers – the Australian study discussed here gathered together a very heterogeneous group in terms of social status and some comparisons were possible between lower- and middle-class practices. The future probably lies, however, with the kind of highly focused studies carried out by Radway, Thiesse, and Ponsard. When the interview group is more homogeneous, some generalizations are better grounded in the evidence, and reading communities, as we have seen, may emerge more clearly. The oral archive is unique, but the investigator must constantly reflect on the methods by which it is compiled.

An Improvised Culture

Some years ago, a well-known international brewery ran a series of TV commercials which claimed that its beer 'reaches the parts other beers don't reach.' This statement was accompanied by a fanciful diagram showing the beer gradually percolating to all extremities of the drinker's anatomy. In a sense, the value of the oral history of reading lies in its ability to go where other sources cannot venture. It does so by coming face to face with living readers, and in setting their reading practices in the context of everyday life and work. A few more brief examples will conclude the argument.

In digging below the surface, we discover a large reading public which never bought books, and which only rarely borrowed them. Respondents describe improvised personal libraries, made up of a wide range of reading matter, given as presents by friends or family, or school prize books and scrapbooks. Thiesse's women readers would read the *feuilleton* in their newspaper aloud to friends or relatives, and this was an important part of the social network of the neighbourhood. Readers would cut out the *feuilleton* episodes and sew or paste them together to form an improvised, continuous novel. Some daily papers even offered a cheap binder to assist such readers.[31] According to one woman, born in the Auvergne in 1896,

Me, I used to cut out the serials from *Le Moniteur* and sew them together,
and I exchanged them with other girls whose parents took *La Croix*. They
were love stories, the *Moniteur*'s serials weren't particularly socialist. My
father never read the serial. Oh noo![32]

Here was an improvised reading culture in which consumers created
their own literature and formed a close female network of readers and
borrowers.

The importance of reading aloud is made very clear in oral testimony,
and the love of reciting aloud was shared by many members of what I
have called the 'poetry generation' of 1914.[33] This was perhaps the last
generation for whom poetry had such an influence on the collective discourse that shaped a common experience. The 'literariness' of the First
World War emphasized by Paul Fussell was not confined to the well-educated officer corps – it was shared by a much wider audience, too.[34] This
was an audience which not only read poetry, but also recited it and wrote
it. The *Times* of London, for example, received about 100 poems per day
on patriotic themes in August 1914. Julius Bab estimated that 50,000 war
poems were written daily in Germany at the same time.[35] In Australia,
too, the veneration of canonical English literature often took a verbal
form. Ena P.'s mother quoted 'great slabs of Shakespeare.' 'Mother,' said
Kathleen T., born in 1902 and another survivor of the poetry generation,
'used to quote Tennyson by the mile.'[36]

Oral testimony provides evidence of reading attitudes historians have
only speculated about. Readers emerge, for instance, with a fine sense of
book-consciousness and an appreciation of the book as a physical object.
They appreciated the quality of book-bindings. To quote Kathleen T.
again:

> We collected small editions on very fine Indian paper of Dickens … *Little
> Dorrit* had a beautiful leather cover … Later on I bought the whole edition,
> lovely green books with gold lettering on it.
> I've kept a mass of books … They were all beautiful big books with lovely
> bindings and good thick covers, you know, not like a lot of the ones these
> days that are so flimsy and that. Of course they didn't cost the earth like the
> good ones cost these days'[37]

Even the humblest readers had a code of practice to enforce respect for
the book. Books, they said, should not be torn or scribbled on, and one

should never put a book down with the covers open. In Australia, above all, library books should never be left out in the sun.[38]

Without oral evidence, therefore, collected from actual readers, our study of book history stops short at the point of sale. The statistics of production and distribution are silent on questions about the usage of books by purchasers and borrowers. Oral testimony reveals hidden networks of readers, whether based on a neighbourhood, a religious community, a trade union, or a workplace. It shows us the everyday reading practices through which living readers appropriate their texts. It lays bare, lastly, the myths and attitudes which determine how ordinary people represent their own reading.

Writers

9 Reading Practices, Writing Practices: Intimate Writings in Nineteenth-Century France

Nineteenth-century readers were also prolific writers of letters, private journals, and diaries. Historians of reading practices and literary appropriation, however, have been slow to analyse the history of writing, and to see its close connections with the world of reading. This is changing. Love letters, family correspondence, and *journaux intimes* have come under scrutiny as evidence of reading and writing practices, and as indicators of the multiple uses of personal writing in the past. The nineteenth century, which provides some impressive examples of personal writing, is a rich field for an investigation into the functions of writing in bourgeois society. This chapter considers the importance and some of the many purposes of *écritures intimes* or, as Dutch and German scholars prefer to call them, 'ego-documents.'[1]

Letter-Writing and the Private Journal

Current approaches focus not on the contents of private correspondence but on letters as cultural artefacts.[2] They analyse the geography of letter writing and reception, the frequency of letter writing, and its relationship to the map of literacy, as well as the various uses of the letter in nineteenth-century France. They do not treat correspondence as a set of 'documents,' to be plundered for what they reveal about the details of daily life. Instead, what is important is their existence, and what that existence may tell us about the act of writing as a cultural practice, and what writing meant to those who practised it.

Family archives, like the 3000 letters of the Duméril-Mertzdorff family spanning a continuous period from 1795 to 1933, are accumulated by complicated processes of selection and destruction, and surviving letters offer only fragmentary and vestigial versions of individual experiences and family relationships.[3] Writers often asked that their letters be burned. George Sand, for instance, was a letter burner, who asked correspondents to burn her letters to them. For no doubt different reasons, Colette's surviving brother Achille unfortunately destroyed 2000 letters written by Colette.[4] Surviving letters must be treated with prudence, after considering all the decisions, interventions, and accidents responsible for their survival.

Correspondence is a highly coded form of writing, obeying generally accepted conventions, applying and adapting unspoken formulas. In addition, we must focus on the practices which generate letters, to ask these questions: What are the situations, conditions, and networks of sociability that bring them into existence and allow them to survive? What are the rules and shared rituals that determine their form? In attempting to unravel the social grammar of private writing, we can delineate the role of personal writings in the cultural exchanges of the past. At the same time we may elucidate the social relationships which letters express, hold together, and perpetuate.

The principal sources for such a project are to some extent self-evident. They include, first and foremost, the archaeological evidence provided by the letters themselves, the criss-crossed correspondence of nineteenth-century lovers, eager to fill every space on the page, the letters of friends, cousins, and acquaintances, the black-edged letters of death, the announcements of pregnancies, miscarriages, births, weddings, illnesses, and accidents. They include more ephemeral communications, as far as they have survived, such as the Valentine cards and the mountain of postcards produced since the early years of the twentieth century. They include even the imaginary letters, never sent, which Annabella Boswell, for one, nevertheless copied into her 'letter-book' as a young girl.[5]

Private writing often mixes various genres, and personal letters must be situated within the multiple relationships connecting different forms of *écriture intime*. Private letters may relate to, contradict, or overlap with personal diaries. Lucile Le Verrier, for instance, writing in the 1860s, maintained several different and parallel forms of personal writing. She had her agenda or diary, her *journal intime*, and also her private correspondence. All three levels had their own distinct purpose, and their distinct degrees of privacy, but they were closely intertwined. In her journal, for example, Lucile commented on the agenda, and she also copied both incoming and outgoing correspondence into it. At these moments when one genre merges into another, the style changes. The journal starts to sound as though it is written in the style of a personal letter. But Lucile herself defined the separate functions of her own writing:

> As for things that happen from moment to moment I write them in a diary. Then when I want to write some thoughts which are too fully developed for my diary, and too secret for my correspondence, I will insert them here.[6]

Personal diaries take many different forms; sometimes they are an accumulation of short notes recorded at odd moments, like the ideas Stendhal scribbled on his braces, and in other cases they are more reflective and the result of considerable recopying and editing by the author.[7] Diaries and correspondence therefore plagiarize each other. When Alexis de Tocqueville sent family letters home during his visit to the United States, he asked for them to be saved: he would later use them as notes for his book *Democracy in America*.[8] Labels such as *écritures intimes* or ego-documents conveniently blur the distinctions between literary genres, but genre definitions are not a major concern for the cultural historian.

Like personal correspondence, private journals do not often survive. The emotional scene in which Samuel Pepys tore up his wife's journal is well-known, mainly because the great diarist himself recorded it. Sometimes diarists make a point of periodically destroying their own journal, as in the case of one Parisian woman who responded to an inquiry by Philippe Lejeune.[9] Personal journals are a hybrid genre and they display varying degrees of privacy and secrecy. Some writers used codes to make sure intruders could not decipher their innermost thoughts: in his Charenton journal, for example, De Sade signalled a sexual experience by the symbol Ø; while Victor Hugo's troubled daughter Adèle disguised her thoughts in a form of *verlan*, a code in which letters, syllables, and entire words are inverted (*verlan* = an inversion of 'à l'envers' or backwards).[10] But the personal diary was not always private. It was customary in the nineteenth century for husbands to read their wives' diaries, and sometimes write entries in them, as Percy Shelley did for his wife Mary. According to some theorists, the author does not write for himself or herself alone. The writer of a journal always consciously or subconsciously addresses a real or imaginary reader, perhaps the ideal mother or a dead friend. Diaries may thus contain an element of posturing, and in Lynn Bloom's phrase, there may be 'an audience hovering on the edge of the page.'[11]

Literary specialists are fascinated by the *journal intime*, but their approaches tend to be overschematic and their literary preferences too
canonical. Michèle Leleu, for example, constructed a typology of private
journals, dividing their authors into four main types: the *sentimentaux*,
introverted, timid and full of melancholy, who love solitude and are
responsible for the greatest number of *journaux intimes*; the *nerveux*, anxious and restless like Stendhal or Byron; the *passionnés*, proud and active
in the world like Tolstoy; and the *colériques*, like George Sand, who wrote
a diary for three weeks in a rage at being rejected by Alfred de Musset.[12]
This analysis is at times very illuminating, but it offers a very static view of
the writers' psychological make-up. Leleu's analysis, moreover, like that
of other critics, concentrates on the personal psychology of famous
writers, like Amiel, Gide, or Kierkegaard, whose personal diaries tend to
dominate the critical literature. Simonet-Tenant's more recent overview
similarly rounds up the usual suspects, although feminist scholarship has
now ensured that writers like Marie Bashkirtseff are included.[13]

Feminist scholars have analysed personal diaries in order to retrieve
and validate women's voices, and to argue that women's journal writing
deserves better than to be classified as a minor literary genre. Even so,
their approach remains selective and canonical.[14] Clearly, gender differences may determine both writing practices and also writing content, the
nature and structure of personal narratives. According to J.-P. Albert,
twice as many French women keep a private journal as do men, and their
writing practices differ markedly.[15] Most female writers abandon their
diary before the age of twenty, whereas journal writing for men is far
more likely to be an activity of adulthood and middle age. The *journal
intime* was a place where notions of female subjectivity could be defined.
In some cases, the journal was a refuge for a woman's stifled emotions, a
withdrawal into a private space where she allowed herself to express the
feelings (erotic, resentful, disloyal) she dared not utter publicly.

Literary specialists have usually interpreted the private journal as an
instrument in the formation of a personal identity, and often their focus
is on the growth of female individuality in a patriarchal environment
which made this problematic. This is a very partial reading of the private
journal, which may have many purposes besides identity construction.
When Philippe Lejeune advertised in 1988 in the *Magazine littéraire* for
journal writers willing to talk about their journals, he received a wide
range of responses. In a special index he listed sixteen different functions of the diary, provided by over forty writers who answered his invitation. They show that developing a personal identity is only one part of
the story. Here are Lejeune's index headings in full:

The Functions of the Journal
- recording the present and fixing it in one's memory
- the desire to leave behind a trace of oneself
- to be read later by one's children
- to guide one's life
- for prayer and spiritual examination
- to comfort oneself by expressing oneself
- to clarify things by expressing them
- to accompany psychological therapy
- to embellish or dramatize one's life
- to escape from oneself and communicate with others
- to make loneliness tolerable
- to avoid anxiety (one gets anxious if one doesn't write)
- as a collective function (writing as a member of a group)
- as a tool of one's profession
- for the pleasure of writing
- for writing practice

As we can see, several of Lejeune's correspondents did not necessarily see their journal as intimate, and they envisaged other readers of their work in the present or future. Some wrote for pleasure. Others were afraid of death and the cruel passage of time, and they wanted to capture something of their life on paper while they could still do so.

This is of course a group of diarists of various ages writing in the 1980s, and it may have little relevance to the nineteenth century. It is a small group of just over forty diarists and it cannot be in any way either representative or exhaustive. It suggests, however, that we should consider private diaries in terms of multiple functions. There are travel diaries, dream journals, philosophical journals (Kierkegaard again). There are adolescent diaries which may have a masturbatory function.[16] There are working journals, like those kept by the painter Ingres, or by Dostoevsky, who conducted a private written discussion of *The Idiot* in parallel to his work on the novel itself. A history of cultural practices, however, must shift the focus away from these canonized authors and eminent artists.

Personal Correspondence, the Private and the Public

Personal or intimate correspondence only formed a small proportion of the mounting body of letters mailed in the nineteenth century. A random sample of 608 letters in the Musée de la Poste, dating from between 1830 and 1864, suggests that only 15 per cent of letters sent from Paris were personal, and this includes many formal announcements of births, marriages, and deaths.[17] Of the 158 million postal items franked in France in 1849, personal as opposed to business correspondence accounted for little more than 10 per cent of the total.[18] Although the volume of postal items went on rising, there is no reason to suppose that the proportion of personal letters increased.

The history of postal services provides an essential context for this study. In 1849, following the British example of the Penny Post, France introduced a postal rate of 20 centimes, fixed regardless of distance and payable in advance. This encouraged the use of letter mail, even if for many years writers often declined to prepay, believing the post office would take better care of their letters if there was money to be collected on delivery. The Paris basin dominated the geography of French letter writing. With little over 3 per cent of the nation's population, Paris received 27 per cent of France's mail, according to the postal inquiry of 1847.[19] The Seine, Saône, Loire, and Rhône valleys were well integrated into the network of postal communication in the nineteenth century, as was the Mediterranean coast. In contrast, Alsace and the Nord used the mail less frequently, while Brittany, the Pyrenees, the Massif Central, and the Alps were predictably areas which sent little mail, received little except from migrants, and waited longest for it to arrive.[20]

International comparisons put French letter writing into perspective beside the prolific epistolary culture of English-speaking countries. In 1891, the average number of letters generated per capita in France was just nineteen. This was considerably fewer than the fifty-two letters posted per inhabitant in New South Wales, according to the Postmaster-General's estimates at the end of the century, and even further behind Britain, where, by 1900, the postal service provided sixty deliveries of letters and postcards per capita, surely the highest rate anywhere in the world.[21]

We are accustomed to think of personal correspondence as a very intimate medium of written communication. The notion of correspondence, however, as a private dialogue between absent individuals is not always appropriate, given the collective nature of much letter writing, and attempts by parents and husbands to supervise it. In 1790, the French Revolutionary National Assembly, keen to defend individual rights, decreed the inviolable confidentiality of correspondence. Such measures prevented postal workers from reading mail, and they were based on emerging ideas about private property, which made letters the property of their addressee.[22] Nevertheless, prefects could intercept and confiscate mail until the Third Republic. French fathers claimed a right of surveillance over the correspondence of their wives and children, but this right was increasingly contested in the wife's case at the end of the century. We may speculate that many women destroyed their letters in order to avoid detection by male family members.

Courting rituals and family solidarities often prevented love letters from being privately written or received. The letters written in 1844, by the courting couple analysed by Saint-Laurent, were all overseen by the girl's mother, and they had to pass through her hands.[23] Personal intimacies could only be exchanged within the demands of existing group and family networks. In the Mertzdorff correspondence, there are shared letters with multiple authors, all family members adding a little in their own handwriting, as well as letters which are dictated to a third party, letters addressed to several recipients at once, and letters designed to be copied and passed on to other members of the group. We know that even letters between the Mertzdorff spouses were read aloud on receipt *en famille*, because on one occasion Charles specifically wrote a paragraph to his wife Eugénie asking that it should NOT be read out.[24] Among the lower classes, the concept of individual privacy was probably even less respected. Among the artisans of the Compagnie du Devoir, solidarity between fellow journeymen insisted that all mail should be opened in public.[25] In many rural areas of France, the postman's job was not only to deliver the mail, but to read it out aloud.

Love Letters and the 'Epistolary Pact'

Cécile Dauphin and her colleagues have analysed the codes and rituals that determine personal correspondence.[26] Correspondence, Dauphin reminds us, fills an absence, and constitutes a ritual of separation. It is further based on the mutual exchange of pleasure given by the letters, and of sacrifices undergone to write and send them. In addition, letter writing follows certain norms. Transposing the thoughts of Philippe Lejeune on the 'autobiographical pact,' which the writer of an autobiography makes with himself or herself, Dauphin and her colleagues postulate the 'epistolary pact,' a contract to which the correspondents tacitly subscribe.

Sometimes the pact between correspondents was extremely bizarre. Consider the thirteen-year correspondence maintained by the composer Tchaikovsky with Baroness Nadejda Von Meck, a rich widow enamoured of his music. She was his patron, providing him with rented Italian villas and the use of her chateau in the Ukraine.[27] The baroness dictated the terms of their epistolary pact: not only was absolute secrecy to be maintained, but she also insisted that the correspondents were never to meet. Even when they lodged a few blocks away from each other in Florence, the baroness wrote to inform Tchaikovsky of her movements so that he could avoid encountering her. This correspondence, based on the deliberate perpetuation of distance between the writers, was also predicated on silence and deceit. Tchaikovsky certainly never revealed his sexual preferences for young boys to his romantic admirer. If the baroness was forced to confront the composer's homosexuality, her largesse as well as her pen would dry up (when she was later told the truth, this is exactly what happened). She never knew that he was travelling through Italy in the company of Kotek, the seventeen-year-old peasant violinist.

Like all personal letters, love letters have tactical objectives. They carry rhetorical ploys to provoke certain feelings, and manipulate the reader's emotions, as Madame de Merteuil in Laclos's *Liaisons Dangereuses* well knew.[28] Love letters may paradoxically strive for spontaneity, they may affect a kind of planned disorder in the author's thoughts, but too much contrivance appears suspect. Writers of love letters calculate how their messages will be received. They enunciate their desire in fear of how the reader will react – a fear which Cornille called 'the anguish of reception.'[29] In Roland Barthes's oft-cited analysis, all love letters are variations on a single theme, and on five words: 'I am thinking of you.' When unpacked, this statement usually contains its opposite: I forget you, because otherwise my life would grind to a halt, but then I remember you again. Or alternatively, the love letter's essence is summed up thus: I have nothing to say to you, except that you are the one to whom I want to say nothing.[30]

The length of letters was a delicate point of negotiation, which formed part of the unspoken contract between the writers. The 'epistolary pact' demanded that a long letter should receive a letter of equal length. Most commonly, writers used a folded sheet, giving them four pages to fill. Often they overflowed into the cross-writing characteristic of letter-writing in the period between friends, lovers, and close relatives. If time and inspiration were available, the writer took another sheet to add another four pages.

Specific forms of address and farewell define the tone of the relationship, encouraging familiarity or establishing distance. The spouses of the Mertzdorff family addressed each other as 'mon bon petit mari' (my good little husband) or 'ma chère petite femme' (my dear little wife).

Charles called his wife 'ma chère amie.'[31] The final formula, which late nineteenth-century etiquette manuals prescribed in minute detail, was perhaps the most important part of any letter. In Léon Gambetta's secret correspondence with his lover Léonie Léon, which generated 6,000 letters over ten years before the politician's death in 1882, the couple were rather more amorous than Charles Mertzdorff. Gambetta called Léonie his 'gracieuse et tendre nini' or his 'chère mignonne adorée' (dear adored darling).[32] But when Charles Mertzdorff called his wife 'his dear friend,' he was suggesting a partnership based on equality. In the Gambetta-Léon correspondence, as Susan Foley points out, Gambetta called Léonie 'tu,' while she addressed him with the more respectful 'vous,' implying a more unequal relationship between the senior republican politician and his lover.[33]

This should not disguise the fact that personal contact in the nineteenth century tended to become, in its written forms, more expressive and more effusive. In spite of Léonie's reserve, *tutoiement* became normal and appropriate, and words of affection could expand into hyperbolic extremes, offering 'a thousand tendernesses' (mille tendresses) or 'a million kisses' (un million de baisers), or into phrases like this one from a disappointed lover cited by Grassi: 'Your long silence has quite tortured me; you have apparently forgotten the colour of my imagination.[34]

Many authors of love letters fantasized about their happiness in a future home. As well as this *lieu de rêve*, the love letter also has its shared memories, its *lieu mémoratif*, where the lovers first met and declared their feelings for each other.[35] Personal anniversaries are recorded and celebrated by corresponding lovers. A certain fetishism is also apparent in the exchange of personal objects like locks of hair, a ritual sometimes reproduced today when photographs are enclosed. The love letter itself may become a fetish object, reread, kissed, carried on one's person. All these strategies were common elements of the reception and practice of intimate writing.

Family Networks

Correspondence kept families together, defined their internal dynamics and guaranteed the cohesion of the familial community. In the 3,000 letters spanning 140 years which formed the Mertzdorff correspondence, about half of the letters were exchanged between parents and children. About 10 per cent were letters between spouses, who normally corresponded with each other daily when temporarily separated by a business trip, a holiday, or exceptional events like war or the siege of Paris. Another 10 per cent of letters were written or received by brothers and sisters, and another ten per cent were between girlfriends (who were often cousins).[36] A similar pattern is found in the family correspondence of a middle-class couple from Anjou between 1868 and 1920. In this family, spouses wrote to each other daily, mothers and daughters twice a week, and sisters wrote to each other weekly.[37] A dense fabric of relationships was strengthened and perpetuated by regular and energetic letter-writing.

The rhythm was dutifully maintained over generations. The Anjou family would take an hour to write just before or just after the midday meal.[38] In the Mertzdorff family, as described by Cécile Dauphin and her colleagues, women would write in bed or when they were about to be undressed or dressed.[39] In other words, women would establish an intimate décor for the act of writing, while men would retreat to the study.

Examples of sustained correspondence thus reveal the family network in its dynamic operations and the rythms of reciprocal exchange. Such continuous correspondence always contains its own metalanguage – that is, it talks about itself, about what letters have been received and who has written to whom, and it comments on the speed or slowness of the postal service and on the length (desired or actual) of the letters written by one's dutiful correspondent. In the Mertzdorff correspondence, three quarters of letters by women and nine tenths of letters by men discuss such matters.[40] In this way they reflect upon the workings of the activity which holds the family together.

The language may be discreet, but this can be explained by the fact that the real recipient is not the private individual but the family itself. Some family letters had multiple authors, while others had many addressees and were destined for circulation amongst a group of relatives. Some letters were copied for this purpose and shared by several readers. Letters between spouses were read aloud. In fact, so public was a family correspondence that it is sometimes difficult to think of it as a form of *écriture intime*. In the Mertzdorff family, Caroline thanked her friend in February 1858 for writing a less intimate letter than before, because her latest letter could be 'shown and read *in familias* which produced the best effect in the world.'[41] Of course there were strict limits to the publicity of correspondence: collective rituals like reading family letters were designed to exclude as much as to include. They defined the family group by shielding it from intruders from the outside world. Family letters would discuss health, social visits, forthcoming marriages and births, occasionally local politics, and the maidservant problem. They would never discuss romance or open up about family dramas, and they rarely mentioned anything happening outside the family.

The *journal intime* and the Dutiful Daughter

For young Catholic girls, writing a diary was considered an important part of their religious education. In their spiritual diaries, they spoke to God, recorded comments on their edifying reading, and conducted a daily examination of their innermost thoughts and moral conduct. For Eugénie de Guérin, who wrote one of the best-known models of a spiritual diary, her journal was an instrument of redemption and a way of mourning her brother.[42] For Eugénie and others like her, the process of journal writing involved an intense process of self-reflection. As Béatrice Didier has suggested, we might see the nineteenth-century journal as a secularized version of this obligatory *examen de conscience*, playing a confessional role, and containing self-criticism which once might have been voiced in prayer or to a priest.[43]

Journal writing was thus an essential instrument in the moral education of young girls. They were often given diaries as presents to encourage them to use them for this purpose. A tutor, usually their mother, watched over the activity, insisting on regular entries and probably reading over what the young girl had written. This supervision was particularly intense in the period leading up to First Communion, an important moment of spiritual initiation.[44]

For poor Marie Lenéru, her childhood journal started on her mother's orders in the period leading up to her confirmation. In her own account she began it at age eleven very reluctantly:

> It's mother who forced me to do my journal, because as for me, I didn't really want to at all; it's mother who bought my notebook and so now it's really fun ... I will keep writing my journal all my life.[45]

Marie dutifully recorded her school marks, her homework and even the lies she told her mother about having finished it. She used the journal to list her faults and to confess her lies, her laziness, and her pride, and the fact that she didn't pay attention properly in church. Marie read the journal back to her mother, who reprimanded her if she had not written enough. At the same time, Marie shared it with her friend and cousin Fernande, two years older than herself. Marie and Fernande wrote their journals side by side, and it was later Fernande who scrupulously edited Marie's journal for publication.[46]

She found the journal an enormous burden. There were lapses when it was set aside, and new resolutions were frequently made to take it up again:

> My journal is boring me so much (m'assomme tellement) that I don't have the strength to do it and Fernande is writing it while I dictate ... I do think I am telling fewer lies, but on the other hand I don't know if I am getting any less lazy (entry of 6 January 1887).

In 1889, eye problems caused a six-month interruption to her writing. Tragically, at the age of fourteen she started to go deaf, and was to rely on sign language for the rest of her life. When she resumed her journal in 1893, at the age of eighteen, it was with a sense of desperation and profound disorientation caused by her disabilities. She wrote on but, as we shall see, for motives quite different from the early spiritual training which had first pushed her into keeping a childhood journal.

The *journal intime* and the Anguished Adolescent

Studies of contemporary French adolescents tell us that they feel an absolutely imperative need to write. According to Marie-Claude Penloup, 'children and adolescents need writing in order to function just as their bodies need an active nervous system.'[47] The Rouennais students she interviewed wrote lists, songs, jokes, and stories and devoted hours to leisure-time copying, even to the extent of copying out entire novels. The majority of such writers were female.

We can find nineteenth-century adolescent girls for whom writing was also an ontological necessity. Philippe Lejeune reports that the prenuptial years of fifteen to twenty are the optimum age for journal writers.[48] A sense of vulnerability or a period of severe emotional stress were often reasons for starting a diary. Coming to terms with marriage itself was a major theme in the diaries of many middle-class adolescent girls, and self-writing helped to prepare them for the ordeal. After the wedding, maintaining a private journal could seem quite incompatible with married life. The common destruction of private diaries at marriage suggests they were, particularly for girls, a rite of passage between adolescence and maturity. In Caroline Brame's journal, for example, the young author attempted to come to terms with the anguish of her impending marriage.[49] Caroline was the daughter of a high-ranking public servant living in the *faubourg* St Germain in the early 1860s, and keen to make an advantageous marriage. Not only had she seen how the marriages of her friends decimated her network of female companions, but now she herself faced an arranged marriage to the man she knew only as Monsieur Ernest. Caroline was probably in love with Albert Dumont, the brother of a friend, but her family ordained that her husband would be Ernest Orville, ten years her elder, whom she did marry less than three months after being introduced to him. The diary, interrupted by Caroline's marriage, was a way of both expressing and controlling her personal feelings and frustrations. It signified her realization that there were some emotions she was duty-bound to keep to herself. For Caroline, her *journal intime* was a means of controlling her 'egoism,' whenever it came into conflict with her allotted destiny.[50] Like so many female teenage diarists before and since, she had toyed with the idea of entering a convent before accepting her marriage.

The destruction of a personal journal might paradoxically illustrate how necessary it was for the process of individual growth. A journal would be terminated or destroyed at a moment when it had served its original purpose and a new phase of life was about to begin. Lucile Le Verrier, born into an upper middle-class family in the Second Empire, looked back on her own diary in order to reject it, and so to measure the personal progress she had made. Just three months after her wedding, she referred disparagingly to her old 'journal de jeune fille' which she now considered obsolete. She had used it, like so many others, to discuss the proposals of marriage she received, to contemplate entering a convent, and to talk about her growing happiness with her future husband, the architect Lucien Magne. After marriage she continued a sporadic journal, but she began it by marking her distance from her former single self: 'Today,' Lucile wrote, 'MADAME made her appearance in her journal' (entry of 16 May 1874). In 1878, Lucile made a final entry in her diary, which reviewed her past life (she was then thirty-five):

My name is Lucile Magne, I have an adored husband who is perfect, beautiful children, I live in a vast and well-furnished apartment, I am very happy, I ask God only to give me back my health. But when I think of Lucile Le Verrier, who would never leave her mother for a single day without sorrow, who used to live at the Observatory ... It seems to me that I am thinking of another person who used to interest me and who has disappeared (entry of 27 September 1878).

Lucile's diary registered her maturity and the development of her personal identity through marriage and motherhood. She achieved this growth by repeatedly distancing herself from her former life as a child and an unmarried woman. At the same time, in trying to cast off her former persona, she was expressing a sense of the fragmentation of her own self.

For Marie Lenéru, deaf and suffering from defective eyesight, the marriage market did not beckon. Isolated from her surroundings by her diabilities, she needed her new diary to express all her bitterness, to break out of her perpetual sadness and forge a new sense of individuality. She called herself a martyr, turning to God and cursing her suffering in what she called her 'Jansenist' phase (by which she meant she was metaphorically flagellating herself). In 1900, she looked back at her notebooks and entitled them 'the collection of my mental migraines' (entry of 13 March 1900). 'I must,' she wrote, 'give myself some proof that I exist. I am dropping off to sleep in a life which is not my own' (entry of 8 December 1893). In her diary, she struggled to find a new path for herself. 'The life of a happy woman has passed me by,' she wrote at twenty-two. 'I have to invent another one in which these awful years can have their place' (entry of 10 January 1898). Convinced of her own talent and imagination, she turned to study and eventually began a writing career.

Writing had been essential for Marie Lenéru to find her way through her suffering and adversity. But this is far from a cosy story of the triumph of the human spirit over hardship and disappointment. On the contrary, Marie Lenéru wrote with a bitterness and lacerating cynicism that make for harrowing reading. Her anguished journal nevertheless demonstrates the function of writing as self-discovery. As she herself put it:

> Writing is for me a veritable reading of myself, in which I often find much more unexpected things than I would even in a original book. But what I read didn't exist before, I just include it as I discover it. So one must write to live, to become oneself (entry of 7 December 1899).

These two examples of Caroline Brame and Marie Lenéru may give the impression that anguished adolescent journals are the special domain of rich well-educated Catholic girls. If so, the impression is largely correct. But we may achieve some perspective and balance by briefly citing a final counterexample: that of the journal of the young and lonely Pyrenean shepherd, Jean-Pierre Baylac.[51]

Before his death from pleurisy in 1920 at the age of only twenty, Baylac filled sixty handwritten notebooks, containing about 20,000 pages in all. He commented on his reading, which included Michelet, Proudhon, Lamartine, and the popular novelist Ponson du Terrail, all borrowed from the local schoolteacher's library. The journal contained all his adolescent longings, masturbations, sexual desire and experiences, jealousies, sex with sheep on his lonely hillside (he called it *le crime*), and magical invocations. He recorded the punishments he inflicted on himself when he gave in to sexual temptations. He covered the front page with melancholy mottos: 'Naître, pleurer, aimer, lutter, chanter, souffrir, et mourir' (Be born, weep, love, struggle, sing, suffer, and die), and 'Le génie ne fleurit que sur la terre des douleurs' (Genius only flourishes in the soil of grief). Baylac was eaten up by love, desire, and guilt. In spite of his humble status, he had mastered the power of writing for the most intimate purposes.

Dangers and Temptations of the *journal intime*

The uses of personal writings were many and various. They might constitute a form of psychotherapy. They might aid a mourning process, as in the case of Eugénie de Guérin, or assist anger management, as in the case of George Sand, already cited, when De Musset had left her. They offered pious exercises for the young and obedient. They pacified the prenuptial angst of young women about to enter unknown sexual territory in a marriage not of their own choosing. At the same time, they had their dangers and their temptations.

They could simply become too absorbing. Take the Swiss diarist Amiel (1821–81). Amiel's obsession with his personal journal was quite extreme but indicative of the author's inability to take any action to exert an influence on his own life. Amiel's massive journal filled 174 quarto notebooks. For over a century, it presented any publisher with an insurmountable challenge, although a complete edition started to appear in the 1970s, and a selection has even been produced in a pocket edition.[52] Amiel's journal expressed his inability to integrate either as a marriage partner or otherwise. It signified his (possibly homosexual) passivity and failure. The journal, however, did not merely reflect these problems, but it also contributed to them. The journal itself became such an obsession that it was a cause of Amiel's failure to connect with social realities. Like many journalists, Amiel recorded not only the date of his entries, but also the precise time. On 26 August 1868, for example, he wrote in his journal at

0730, and again later that morning at 0900. He resumed his journal entry the same afternoon at 1530, and wrote further entries at 1800 and yet again at 2200.[53] The journal itself, indispensable and all-absorbing, obstructed a solution to Amiel's powerlessness.

We have seen the power of correspondence to reinforce family solidarity. Private writings, however, could in some circumstances produce family conflict. As a retreat into private space and time, intimate writing could threaten a marriage in a situation where one partner grew jealous of the other's absorption in a personal journal. The family of the celebrated Russian novelist Leo Tolstoy, during the last years of his life, gives a spectacular indication of the power of the personal journal to erode family unity. Leo Nikolayevich's personal journal, which was at the root of the tension, was begun when he was eighteen and continued until 1910, when he was eighty-two, except for a long break during his first years of marriage.[54] As an aging but already legendary literary figure, Leo was in a position where almost anything he wrote could prove one day valuable, as part of his legacy and part also of his collected works. The issue of who would inherit the ordinary writings of the maestro's old age interested many members of his personal circle. Tolstoy kept a private journal, which his wife Sonya was aware of, but marital tension was aggravated when Leo made provision for his friend Chertkov to dispose of the journal after his death. Sonya regarded this as a personal slight, if not an act of infidelity to her. Considering Leo's distinguished reputation, the fate of his diary was an important issue for his estate and for the family's reputation. In retaliation, Sonya started her own diary:

> I am consumed by curiosity about what my husband writes in his journal. His journals these days are works in the sense that people will read them to study his thoughts and draw conclusions about them … My journal is a sincere *cri de coeur,* and the true description of everything that happens between us.

She fired a pistol at Chertkov's portrait and threw the portrait down the toilet. Soon, a veritable war of journals erupted in the Tolstoy household. Sasha, Sonya's daughter, started *her* own journal, arousing her mother's suspicions that she was making critical comments about her.

This was not all. Not only was everybody in the house apparently writing a journal, but Leo Nikolayevich was actually writing two of them. One was his private journal already mentioned. But there was yet another which he kept hidden in his boots so that his wife could not find it. Three people, four journals – all of which were weapons in the power struggle being played out in the Tolstoy household, which knew that its domestic life would soon be exposed to the scrutiny of posterity. It is hard to find a more extravagant example than this of the central importance of personal writing in the nineteenth century.

Finally, intimate writings carry within them a temptation of a far more benign variety – one which is really a quality – namely, what Penloup has called the 'literary temptation.'[55] Little-known authors of intimate journals are often assumed to be 'non-experts,' untutored writers completely unaware of the poetic functions of language. Marie Lenéru, who was very self-conscious about her style, contradicts this assumption. She was very aware of her literary peers, and constantly distanced herself from other writers in the genre, like Eugénie de Guérin and Amiel, turning more frequently to Marie Bashkirtseff as a literary model. Data collected from contemporary French adolescents also suggest that intimate writers had literary inclinations. In fact, private diaries often exhibit formal literary characteristics: alliteration, rhyme, balance, and the insertion of unusual words are among them. Writing clearly gave these teenagers pleasure. Even for the most humble authors, it seems, writing has some non-utilitarian value. Writing was seen as something which had to be polished and improved, as a struggle with words, a construction with materials carefully chosen or borrowed. The act of writing imposed its own little rituals and sensual satisfactions, as this forty-year-old French schoolteacher told Philippe Lejeune:

> Every morning, I come back to my diary.
> A rendez-vous I can't miss. A pleasure I can't miss, which gives me heart to continue working at it.
> Before I even open it, I caress the cover – one that I have chosen for its consistency and colour. My fingers linger over the threadbare areas, over the stains, those marks of time.
> Then I play it like an accordion, which opens and closes, with its fan of gaudily-coloured pages.[56]

Writing, then, is a physical pleasure, and an absolute necessity, as testimony and as an unavoidable means of existence.

10 French Soldiers and Their Correspondence: Towards a History of Writing Practices in the First World War

All the allied belligerents in the First World War developed techniques of postal censorship for limiting information leaks by their own troops. The British censors, followed after 1917 by the American censors, entrusted considerable responsibility for preliminary surveillance to junior officers at the front. British and American soldiers could bypass their superior officers if they wished by sending their outgoing correspondence in special coloured envelopes to a central censorship body. Such a decentralized system would never have satisfied the French High Command, which elaborated by far the most systematic control of both military and civilian correspondence in the war zones. The organization and diligence of French censors have created a valuable legacy for the historian of writing practices. They produced the voluminous records of the Commission de Contrôle Postal, preserved in the military archives in the Château de Vincennes. This substantial archival corpus must be examined in conjunction with wartime correspondence already published, and a certain number of literary works by ex-soldiers which illuminate the epistolary culture of the trenches. Together such documents can help to answer a few of the questions which scholars are asking about *écritures ordinaires* in general, and about private correspondence in particular. Soldiers' correspondence invites an analysis of the nature and purpose of letter writing, the rules and expectations that guided it, and the implicit social grammar that letter writing obeyed.[1]

The enormous archive of soldiers' correspondence has of course already been studied by historians of the First World War. Jean-Jacques Becker, to take one eminent example, used this source among many in his overview of French society during the war.[2] Usually, however, the correspondence has been studied as a guide to fluctuating morale on the western front, and as evidence of the anxieties which gave rise to the mutinies of 1917. This was the purpose of Annick Cochet's very thorough thesis on the correspondence between the end of 1915 and March 1917.[3] David Englander searched the correspondence for signs of revolutionary socialist sympathies, as indeed did the Postal Control Commission itself, to conclude (perhaps a little too readily) that socialist ideas had made little headway in the army, even if the vocabulary of protest often borrowed from the rhetoric of the left.[4] Guy Pedroncini produced the standard history of the 1917 mutinies, demonstrating that they were geographically limited to the section of the front between Soissons and Auberive, where most of the terrible fighting for the Chemin des Dames had occurred, and that 'only' about 40,000 troops were involved, mainly in the Sixth Army. There were just forty-five executions, and apparently no long-term consequences.[5] Even if, at Togny-aux-Boeufs for example, a small group unfurled a red flag and sung the Internationale, the essence of the 1917 mutinies remained simply a spontaneous refusal to fight. Revisionist historians now question whether a 'mutiny' ever happened at all.[6]

There is no need to go over this well-trodden ground again. My main interest in the correspondence is less with its content, which absorbed the interest of the historians mentioned above, and more with what it tells us about the nature and history of letter writing itself. I do not intend to use soldiers' letters, as others have done, to carry out a kind of historical opinion poll on the mood of the trenches, to measure the growing malaise, chart the spread of fatalistic indifference, or dissect the elaboration of a discourse of sacrifice, as John Horne characterizes the soldiers' representations of their struggle.[7] My focus is on letters as letters, their frequency, their destinations, their form, their conventions and formulas, all the unwritten codes to which they are subject. I am interested at the same time in the function and purpose of letter writing, and why, at a time of newly acquired mass literacy, so many in the trenches experienced the urgent need to write.

Private letters have traditionally been valued for their spontaneity and their ability to convey personal experience more authentically than official or administrative records. In this vein, Patrick O'Farrell found letters of Irish migrants to Australia to be personal, direct, and authentic, offering testimony about 'what being a migrant meant.'[8] Personal correspondence must be treated with more suspicion than this. In the nineteenth century, for one thing, the boundaries between private and public correspondence were often very blurred. Personal correspondence often implied a wide audience. Letters might have several authors, all writing their own messages. Others related family news to be read aloud or passed between various family members. Among the lower classes, letters were often intended to be opened in public and read aloud. They might be considered as a form of general newsletter from an emigrant or soldier to his village community as a whole. Soldiers' letters were very likely to be single-authored but they could be directed to a whole group of readers. This was overwhelmingly the case in the correspondence of Joseph Bourniquet, who wrote collective letters to his family finishing thus and making sure no-one would feel left out:

> Kiss the children for me Berthe Theresia Geneviève Lili Claudine Anna Mélie Clement Marius. I kiss you all not forgetting those little scamps Louisa Joséphine I will get my own back on them. Say *bonjour* to Montsarrat. *Au revoir* Isauline, from your husband.[9]

Bourniquet appears to hold the record for a collective letter here, with thirteen named recipients.

In addition, correspondence remains a highly ritualized and codified form of communication. In the First World War, and very likely in other contexts too, soldiers' correspondence is remarkable not for its authentic personal revelations, but for its reticence and the banality of its formulaic descriptions. Its purpose was not to reveal the truth so much as to disguise it.

As well as this interest in authenticity and disguise, soldiers' letters raise a second set of questions, relating to the issue of national integration, around which there has been a considerable historiographical debate. What was remarkable about the French victory in the First World War was that, in spite of France's social and political divisions, and in spite of the enormous toll of casualties, the front nevertheless held firm. This triumph of patriotism has been attributed to the successful work of the Third Republic in inculcating a sense of national unity, now fully identified with republican values. French endurance on the western front was in this view built on the nation-forming work of the Third Republic, especially through its new school system. The letters of the soldiers themselves can illuminate this link between the solidity of the front and the integrative work of republican pedagogy.

Epistolary Bulimia

The most impressive feature of the correspondence is the sheer volume of writing that occurred on the French front. The years of 1914–18 engendered 'a sudden and irrepressible bulimia' of letter writing, an absolutely diluvian outpouring which defied all attempts at administrative control.[10] This was all the more surprising considering the very recent acquisition of mass literacy in rural France. It was the norm for every soldier to send a letter daily, not counting the enormously popular postcards, whether illustrated or of the official military kind. In 1915 the military post was handling four million letters daily.[11] Consider the surviving correspondence of Jean Robin, a soldier from Nice, who spent 104 days at the front in 1915. In this period, he sent 390 letters or cards, and received 256. In other words, every day, Robin sent three or four letters and got two or three replies.[12] The epistolary dialogue was vital – sometimes to ensure it continued soldiers would leave space blank at the end of their message for the recipient to reply. 'E.A.,' a Protestant flour-mill worker in his forties from the Cévennes, exchanged letters twice a week throughout the war with his wife in the pages of an exercise book. His wife wrote in violet ink, and he replied in pencil on the same paper.[13]

Writing, in other words, was fundamental to life at the front regardless of whether or not the writer was familiar with the act of writing or with written French. One day without a letter, and André Kahn was talking already of suffering an 'epistolary famine.'[14] No wonder that censors reported in alarm 'an intensive use of correspondence,' or that 'soldiers are not content just to write to their family, they are writing to everybody.'[15] They wrote on hospital beds, after delousing, in the forest, in barns, on guard duty, huddled under a blanket, by the light of a bicycle lamp or a candle impaled on the end of a bayonet, seizing every occasion. If there was no paper available, they wrote on butcher paper or newspaper. The handwriting didn't matter – one postal censor complained that the handwriting of German prisoners of war was superior to that of desperate French soldiers.[16] Illiteracy was no handicap either: for a few favours a third party could be enlisted to write one's letter.[17] The war thus spawned a massive and possibly unique corpus of popular literature which could not be contained.

The Soldiers' 'Godmothers'

If a soldier did not have a correspondent, then one had to be found for him. This was the purpose of the 'marraines de guerre' (wartime godmothers), whose task it was to assume the role of maternal pen-friend to a lonely individual, write to him, raise his morale and fighting spirit, and give him regular solace in the form of food parcels. A few soldiers were of course delighted to have such an unexpected source of support from well-meaning women and exploited the possibilities to the full. When one British soldier put an advertisement asking for similar assistance in a London newspaper, responses intercepted by the War Office showed that he would have received in reply 4003 letters, 45 magazines, 5050 cigarettes, and ten shillings in silver.[18] Soldiers made the most of civilian sympathy. Some convalescents were known to correspond with six or seven 'marraines' at a time, and to get food parcels from all of them.[19]

The urge to correspond could be manipulated in both directions. The system of 'marraines de guerre' was adopted by enterprising prostitutes in search of customers. Some advertised their qualities as correspondents in Parisian magazines like *La Vie parisienne* or *Fantasio* which ran a special column headed 'Le Flirt au Front.'[20] There were also the train 'marraines,' who picked up soldiers on the leave trains heading to Paris. The British army provided the French with a long black list of undesirable 'marraines de guerre', who described themselves as actresses, dancers, the Lulus, Lilys, and Georgettes who took advantage of the extraordinarily good business opportunities opened up by the war. It is not clear that French authorities did anything with this list – it seems that the British knew more about French prostitution that the French did, or cared to.[21]

However genuinely sympathetic these female correspondents were, their correspondence was subject to close surveillance. According to the postal censors at Pontarlier near the Swiss border, correspondence with professional prostitutes or other romantic and frustrated women was hardly likely to maintain the *poilu*'s 'virile courage.'[22] 'Marraines' writing from outside France were seen as possible espionage agents, planted by the enemy to gather intelligence. To prevent any leaking of military information, all their correspondence was intercepted and confiscated until the end of the war.[23] In fact before long writing to any foreign 'marraine' was banned.[24]

Censorship

Attempts by the postal censors to stem the flow of correspondence were to no avail. To appreciate the task of the censors, however, we must clarify their objectives. The operations of the Postal Control Commission have been analysed by others, and here only a brief summary is necessary.[25] The initial concern of the postal censors was to prevent soldiers from revealing information about troop movements which could be used by the enemy. Soldiers were instructed not to send picture postcards revealing where their unit was stationed. Illustrated postcards, it was feared, might also point out good bombing targets to the enemy. These instructions fell on deaf ears. A stream of cards was sent, telling the family back home which village the soldier had arrived in, and even marking his billet on the view. Repeated admonitions and threats of punishment indicate the failures of the administration to control this form of communication.[26] Regulation field postcards were introduced, and the Ministry of the Interior rather hopefully ordered that only two such cards would be issued to every soldier each month.[27] In March 1916 soldiers were ordered to write no more than twenty words on their cards home, but again this was wishful thinking.[28]

Eventually, the administration of censorship developed new aims, and at the same time its organization became more sophisticated. First, it was realized that soldiers' letters were an excellent source of intelligence for the French military command itself and could be used to take soundings of soldiers' morale. As a result, an extensive apparatus for analysing and summarizing mail was put into place by the beginning of 1916, which went far beyond the postal controls organized by the British and American armies. Censors read and wrote voluminous reports on soldiers' correspondence under various headings, such as hygiene, optimism and discouragement, antimilitaristic sentiments, opinions about the enemy, opinions about the allies, relations with the home front, and so on. By 1916, the random inspections of mail first imposed by Joffre had developed into something far more systematic. A sampling system was established: Postal Control Commissions attached to each army read a sample of 500 letters per regiment, taking each regiment in turn, ensuring that every regiment came under review once a month.[29] They produced long weekly reports for the Quartier-Général. Every reader was expected to read and analyse at least 250 letters per day. In some armies, they were reading up to 400 letters per day.[30] Jean-Noël Jeanneney estimated that the postal censors actually read between 1/40th and 1/80th of the total sent. Annick Cochet thought the proportion was much higher, about 14 per cent, but this was based on the unsubstantiated assumption that only 60 per cent of soldiers wrote letters.[31] In 1917 censors' reports became more formalized because they were required to give statistical percentages reflecting the balance of positive or negative opinions on certain issues, like the possibility of victory.

By now, the nature of the sources should be a little clearer. The censorship archive only rarely permits us to read an entire letter in its original form. There are two boxes of original intercepted letters, usually irredeemably revolutionary or antimilitarist in opinion, as well as subversive songs, pacifist tracts, Russian newspapers, and confiscated correspondence on the Stockholm Congress of 1917.[32] For the most part, I rely on the indirect sources of the censors' reports. Fortunately, they are full, and at least for 1916, eloquent and sympathetic – so eloquent, in fact, that reporters were officially rebuked in 1917 for submitting analyses which were too 'picturesque,' and full of superfluous phrases rather than the bare facts. Reports, however, in which censors dared to express themselves prove to be far more interesting than those which followed official formulas.[33] They include many citations, sometimes very extensive ones. Without their digests and extracts this study would be impossible. In addition, Postal Control was not just concerned with mail sent *from* the front. The Commissions also had jurisdiction over incoming civilian mail, and over all mail posted in civilian post offices in the war zone. This is a boon for the historian, since it means we also have reports on and examples of letters from the home front – we are not restricted to examining one-way traffic only. Most of my analysis is based on the records of the 2nd and 7th Armies, which are of consistently good quality.

What criteria did the censors adopt? Picture postcards with views of the front were simply destroyed.[34] Passages of correspondence considered too revealing would be blacked out (*caviardé*) in blue or black ink, a reasonably effective process when most letters were written in pencil. Clearly subversive items could be confiscated, but there was little point in taking action about millions of messages expressing fatigue, disgust, or wishes for an early end to the war. If all soldiers' complaints were considered suspect, no mail would have got through at all. Usually only a handful of letters from each regiment's sample required some form of censorship. Mention of the 1917 mutinies was not allowed, nor was any criticism of officers. Details of French losses could not be transmitted. Letters from home telling soldiers about strikes in Paris and elsewhere were also intercepted.[35] Letters from home could not speak about the effects of the 1918 air raids on Paris, producing a bizarre reversal of roles in which the soldiers at the front were protected from bad news about casualties at home.[36] Chemical laboratories were set up to search for invisible ink. When an offensive was being prepared, all mail issuing from the front was temporarily subject to a systematic delay of three or four days.[37]

Correspondents knew that their mail was under surveillance. They wrote letters they expected the censors to read, attacking the censors as idle pen-pushers with cushy jobs (*embusqués*). They tended to exaggerate the efficiency of the censors, and looked for ways of resisting it. They posted mail in civilian centres behind the lines, hoping thus to evade the censor, but quite mistakenly, since Postal Control included the whole war zone within its jurisdiction. In 1916 one third of the mail posted in civilian post offices in the war zone came from soldiers trying to evade censorship.[38] Some tried in vain to disguise information about their whereabouts, like Julien D., who wrote home: 'After two days' march we have arrived at our destination in a camp three kilometres from V., the name of a village where Kellermann once won a famous battle.' Every French schoolboy would know this was Valmy, site of the first victory of the French revolutionary armies in 1792, and Julien D. wasn't fooling anyone.[39] They wrote on the inside of the envelope, they used number codes, or they failed to sign their name or to give their address.[40] It was perhaps characteristic that the French should feminize the watchful eye of 'Big Brother' as 'Dame Censure,' Dame Censorship, or in trench slang, 'cette vieille raseuse.' But this suggested a nosy neighbour rather than a systematic intrusion. Dame Censure made some writers very careful, like this soldier writing to his uncle in the United States in 1918: 'The Russians have really done the dirty on us, and we are going to suffer the consequences. I won't say any more: Dame Censorship is there.'[41] This discretion, however, seems quite different from the reticence caused by an inability to communicate the brutalities of trench warfare to loved ones. Other writers defied the censors, and even included special messages for the censor. 'They can open my letter I don't give a damn. I say what I think and that's all there is to it,' wrote a soldier to his sister in 1917.[42] And an anonymous but more emphatic soldier in the 2nd Army wrote 'When they get tired of sticking their nose in my letters, they can come and stick it up my arse.'[43]

Laconic Writing

Perhaps, then, the censor's presence, and the threat of a week or two in confinement as punishment for epistolary indiscretions, may have restrained some soldiers. Yet this does not adequately explain the 'laconic' nature of most of the correspondence. There were other forces at work which imposed reticence. Ephraïm Grenadou explained in his memoirs: 'On leave I used to get letters from my friends from time to time, saying "Have fun while you can. Here things are going badly." I didn't like that kind of mail; I was afraid my parents might read it. When I used to write to them, I never told them things were going badly.'[44] There were things one preferred not to write, in order to maintain the essentially consoling and comforting nature of the letter from the front.

As a result, soldiers' writing leaves us with an overwhelming sense of banality. The letters of the Savoyard soldier Delphin Quey are a good example of the emptiness and silences of soldiers' correspondence. They offer a nearly complete set of family exchanges during the war years. Delphin's letters always opened with a standard report on the state of his health, and went on to discuss letters received from home, postal delays, parcels received, and parcels desired. He would repeat the same formulas over and over again: 'I am in good health as ever I hope all the family is the same,' or to close: 'Nothing more of interest at present. Your son who is thinking of you.' There are no intimacies, and few expressions of feeling, even though Delphin's elder brother Joseph had been killed in action in 1914. The main concerns expressed in Delphin Quey's letters are personal health and the price of mules, goats, sheep, and horses.[45]

Maurice Genevoix, a realist novelist of the war, was a highly educated graduate of the Ecole Normale, who wrote with a literary detachment which was impossible for most peasant writers. In his *Sous Verdun*, he captured the paradox of trench writing – the experience of dire urgency to write and to receive, combined with the impossibility of saying anything but empty, borrowed phrases. Here is a passage dated 1916:

> I carefully sharpened my pencil, and, using my reading lamp (*liseur*) as my desk, I hastily scribble a few scraps of messages. Just a couple of words: 'Bonne santé; bon espoir.' I don't want to let myself say what's in my heart. And when would I say it? When I could repeat again and again: 'Write to me. I have had nothing from you since I've been fighting. I feel alone, and it's very hard ...' They write to me every day, I know. Why deceive them, why make them suffer? I must wait, wait, forcing myself to preserve the confidence I need, and which up to now has never deserted me. And my pencil runs, quickly, rewriting the banal words which are nevertheless the words they expect: 'Bonne santé, bon espoir.'[46]

Or take this two-faced diary entry from a soldier at Verdun:

> 12 July. Valley of Death. Greenflies in large quantities on the corpses and the earth impregnated with the stench of decomposition ... rations limited to bread and grog ... They gave us a few cards with ready-printed phrases. I only sent one to my parents, in which I told them we were doing alright, it was a pleasant spot and I hoped to spend more time here.[47]

As Annick Cochet puts it, the soldiers made many sacrifices, including the sacrifice of their own sincerity. What they reported to civilians was the civilians' war: their own war was a secret.[48]

There is no mistaking the desperate need to write and to receive letters. Soldiers were extraordinarily sensitive to postal delays. They checked the dates of mailing and receipt closely, and complained immediately if they felt there had been an unreasonable delay. They accused the authorities of insensitivity or of conspiracy. They seemed to expect the postal service to run as efficiently, if not more efficiently, in wartime as it did in peace. After the postal administration succeeded in channelling all soldiers' mail though a central sorting office in Paris, in fact letters from the front were received in southern cities within only two or three days of posting.[49] Soldiers' fears were not entirely groundless: if major troop movements were under way, their mail was indeed subjected to a *retard systematique* (systematic delay).

Soldiers without mail became desperate, as with this rather pathetic message from Bruno P. in March 1918:

> Somewhere on the Belgian front, there is a son-in-law who watches every morning for the postman to come, and he is so happy when he is given something from Algiers. There's no need to mention the name of this watcher, it's me, and the rarity of ships no doubt makes his waiting pointless. But he doesn't despair and he tells himself 'It will be tomorrow.' Tomorrow is the 4th. Will he be right this time? I hope so. What about you?[50]

The letters such men wrote and received contained absolutely essential platitudes. Marie F. thus wrote to her husband in 1915: 'I am writing not very interesting things to you, but I wanted to write to you and well, I must put something.'[51] Anything would do. 'Quelques lignes seulement' ran another typical letter, 'Just a few lines, to give you a sign of life.'[52] They wrote, and expected to receive, comforting repetitions of laconic formulas, which conveyed very little of their experience. Julien D. cheekily suggested that he should copy a circular letter with a standard message, leaving the date blank, to send home at regular intervals.[53] Rosa Roumiguières invited her correspondent to dispense with words altogether. 'I'd be happy with a single line, a single word,' she wrote in August 1914, 'even with just an envelope with nothing inside, but write to me often.'[54]

The task of consoling those at home could provoke outbursts of irritation, as in this letter from a soldier to his wife in Paris in 1916:

My dear Marguerite ... I urge you not to get so scared like that, things haven't been as calm as this for me until now, I know I am far from rue Brézin but what can you do, *c'est la guerre*, you mustn't take fright like that for no reason, I received your photo, your face looks like *papier mâché*, I can't see what's responsible for your chagrin, just look around and see how many other women are in exactly the same boat as you are, you tell me to reply if I'm still alive, well I'm sure *you* won't have given an order to have me killed.[55]

Usually such bad temper emerges in letters to wives rather than parents, but it reveals something about the expectations which the recipient invested in the correspondence.

The importance of the letter was not what it said, but the mere fact of its existence. It was quite literally a sign of life, brought into existence by the fear of silence, a silence which was unbearable to contemplate. For those at the front, silence or some irregularity in mail deliveries could cause panic and fear of infidelity. F.G., in oral testimony, was frightened by a change in tone in letters from his wife and was in a state of high anxiety about her loyalty. In fact his wife had been briefly incapacitated by the 'Spanish' influenza.[56] For those at home, silence had even worse connotations, and relatives lived in fear of the black-edged envelope with its awful announcement, or perhaps even worse, receiving their own letter, returned unopened from the front, franked with the sinister official message: Le Destinataire n'a pu être atteint en temps utile (The Recipient could not be usefully contacted).[57]

The Body

The censors were well aware that most of what they read was designed to say nothing. 'Nine letters out of ten say nothing, except that they long to see wife, children, home, the farm or the workshop again,' wrote one exhausted reader of the correspondence of the 8th Infantry Division, which included many peasants from the Mayenne and the Sarthe.[58] Another from the 2nd Army commented, 'It has to be said that the space devoted to very intimate questions is ultimately fairly limited.'[59] If soldiers were not prepared to write about what troubled their spirit, they made up for it by writing about their bodies. Health concerns were paramount. They wrote of what they had to eat, and what they had to drink (the supply of cheap wine or *pinard* was absolutely vital for morale, especially among southern soldiers). They wrote about the state of their bodies, the heat and the cold, the infections that ravaged them (commonly mumps, scurvy, typhoid, measles). They wrote about washing themselves in urine, and the number of times they used the latrines while victims of violent diarrhoea. They wrote about the difficulty of achieving erections on an exiguous diet.[60] They wrote about all the creatures that crawled over them, and the rats as big as rabbits that nibbled them while they slept. Some Parisians amused the censor by writing that they had been spending time getting to know 'our allies,' meaning the fleas, lice, and insects which irrevocably accompanied them.[61] Alcoholism and syphilis were perhaps the only two taboos in this litany of ailments.

Nostalgie du Pays or Dreaming of My Village

Along with this heightened body-consciousness, peasant letters are also concerned with the state of the farm back home. The peasant holding emerges clearly as a family business partnership, in which the wife naturally took control in the husband's absence. But this did not prevent the husband issuing instructions on planting and harvesting from the front. Their letters were full of advice and questions about market prices, and lists of tasks to be done. 'You've got it,' wrote one detailing a work roster to his wife, 'First the bulls, then the lucerne patch, then the garden. You've got six days' work there.'[62] 'Tell me how much the wine weighs,' ran a typical letter, 'how much you have made, and what prices are on offer,' and a postal censor commented with amazement, 'You would think these were good farmers striking deals for their produce on the village square, just as they would in peacetime.'[63] Grenadou dreamed of getting back to the fields: 'All through the war,' he said, 'I dreamed at night that I was in Saint-Loup. I dreamed I was harvesting, I dreamed I was at the plough.'[64] The peasant soldiers who made up at least 45 per cent of the army retained an umbilical cord with the land and with home. They remained instinctively concerned that the land should still be cared for. Nothing demoralized them more than the devastation of France's best northern farmland, or the destruction of the Alsatian vineyards. For the southern peasant, this scarring of a wonderfully fertile landscape represented the true obscenity of the war.

Quoi de neuf au pays? What's new in the village? was a standard phrase and a major concern in soldiers' letters. Does this nostalgia for the village or *le pays* denote a narrow focus, an absence of political awareness, a lack of integration in national politics? Or does it signify a very peasant version of patriotism, which consisted above all, of the defence of the ter-

ritory? Soldiers' correspondence may allow us some insight into the continuing debate about national integration, and the process, as Eugen
Weber described it, of making peasants into Frenchmen.[65]

Learning the Language of Patriotism

There were many reasons why France's peasant army 'held' on the western front, whereas the armies of Austria-Hungary disintegrated, and
Russia's collapsed in Revolution. In spite of invasion and enormous casualties, the troops saw through the winter of 1917 because they knew there
had been a good harvest. They were reassured, too, by rising prices
for agricultural produce during the war years, as Becker has demonstrated.[66] In addition, it is often argued, the work of national integration
had been effective. The inculcation of national and republican values in
the new government schools of the 1880s and 1890s bore fruit in the
'patriotic resignation' which endured the war. School manuals had
brought about a silent revolution, legitimizing national values, as well as
unifying classes and regions in a common cause and a shared heritage.

No doubt the sheer volume of correspondence considered here is in
itself evidence in support of this thesis. The language of contempt for the
enemy, the 'Boches,' who were vermin, beasts, bandits, and pirates, suggested that the classroom lessons of *revanchisme* had indeed been well
absorbed. The work of national unification, however, was as yet imperfect, and certain fault lines within the nation remained visible in the soldiers' correspondence. I will concentrate on the problem of regionalism.

The linguistic test of national unity was fundamental, and the correspondence was overwhelmingly and significantly written in French.
There are a few letters in patois or regional languages. There are some
illiterate letters, composed by third parties, or read to the addressees by
third parties at their destination.[67] Considering the linguistic diversity of
French society a mere half century before this, however, their number is
not significant. There were letters in bizarre French which linguists
believe were literal translations of Occitan or Catalan expressions, a sign
that writers were still thinking in their native language as they struggled
to compose in French.[68] Government schools had apparently produced
a hybrid or counterfeit French, in which expressions in local languages
still surfaced. When southerners wanted to express strong emotions, they
might revert completely to their spoken tongue, offering for instance
'oun gros poutou' (a big kiss in Catalan).

This, however, is not the whole story. Although almost all correspondents wrote in the national language, they could produce a highly individualized form of written French. There were letters, for example, both from the front and from home, composed in wildly aberrant grammar and spelling, betraying authors who had little or no familiarity with the act of writing. There were many examples of untutored phonetic spelling, in which for example 'dysenterie' became 'descenterie,' and some writers imaginatively invented the new psychological condition of 'anxiétude' (anxiosity).[69] Partly literate southerners wished 'Vive la pé et la fint au plus taux' (= Vive la paix et la fin au plus tôt/ Long live peace and the end as soon as possible).[70] Louis Lemaire's wife wrote a stream of invective quite oblivious of spelling conventions and almost completely liberated from the burden of punctuation:

> Vraiment il faut que ceux qu'il fond durée la guerre [= *ceux qui font durer la guerre*] que ce sois des vrais bourreaux ... c'est féneant la c'est buveur de sang bande de cochon de salop ci il serait dans les tranchées va cela la guerre finiré plus vite je ne comprend même pas comment les hommes y reste encore [for this phrase the letter was confiscated] ... Je m'ennuie à mourir quelle putain guerre.[71]

> (The ones who are stretching this war out are real executioners ... it's slack it's bloodthirsty bunch of pigs load of trash if they were in the trenches then the war would finish sooner I can't understand how people can still be there ... I am sick to death what a motherfucking war.)

Louise wrote entirely phonetically, but she had absorbed the talk of the trenches and was quoting doses of it back to her husband. Many peasant soldiers were as unaccustomed to receiving letters as they were to writing them; Firmin Bouille, the Catalan winegrower, was astonished to receive a letter from his mother for the first time in his life and thus did not recognize her handwriting. He replied addressing his mother respectfully by the formal 'vous.'[72]

Le Problème du Midi, le Problème du Nord

France's regional differences still persisted. Marc Bloch recalled encountering some very depressed recruits from the interior of Brittany who knew no French and could hardly speak to each other, so divergent were their dialects.[73] Prejudices against Bretons and Corsicans, antagonism between northerners and *les gens du Midi* can be found throughout the correspondence. Another reason not to exaggerate the success of nation forming is the persistent myth of southern cowardice, which first surfaced in Parisian newspaper articles as early as August 1914.[74] Accusations of cowardice were initially directed at the Provençal troops in the 15th Corps who had retreated under murderous fire in Lorraine, but this persistent myth was soon to question the patriotism of all southerners. Behind the myth perhaps lay the southwest's reputation as the 'Midi rouge,' reinforced by the winegrowers' revolt of 1907. This uprising had been firmly suppressed by Clemenceau, who himself contributed to the cowardice legend in an article in *L'Homme Libre* in 1914. Northerners felt that they bore a disproportionate burden. It was, after all, their region and their homes which had been invaded and occupied, and they expected a greater degree of commitment and urgency from southerners and allies alike in the task of liberating them.

Southerners, for their part, felt very keenly the isolation and disorientation of men transplanted into a different linguistic and cultural setting. Even in death, they would finish as an anonymous cross on an eastern hillside, without the consoling prospect of re-integration into their native village. Meanwhile, they endured insults and hostility from northerners. André Khan was furious with them as he wrote in May 1915: 'Our advance has been halted by the slackness of the southern army corps to our right. Ah! These accursed southerners! I would stick a machine gun up their arse to stop them shivering with fear and make them give their life for France.'[75] Needless to say, there is no substantial evidence for allegations of southern cowardice; they correspond to ancient and deep-rooted antagonisms.

As well as this alleged *problème du Midi*, there was also a less predictable *problème du Nord*, as Richard Cobb perversely argued.[76] The Nord and the Pas-de-Calais experienced two invasions (in 1914 and 1940), two occupations, in relatively quick succession, throwing German soldiers and administrators together with the poor working-class families of Lille and Roubaix for long periods. In the first occupation, these departments experienced four years of complete administrative separation from the rest of the country. This reinforced their sense of communal identity and regional separateness. They regarded themselves as the most vulnerable and patriotic inhabitants of the country, and yet Parisians and southerners regarded them with suspicion as 'les Boches du Nord,' 'contaminated' by German occupation. In 1914–18, German personnel became relatively well integrated in these French cities, and many formed enduring personal and sexual relationships with their hosts. These relationships inevitably produced Franco-German offspring. Thus, Cobb goes on, when the German army returned in 1940, men from the same regiments went in search of the French women they had lived with just over twenty years previously. There some of them may have discovered that they had been fighting against their own sons.

Conclusion

Leaving aside the potentially Oedipal dimensions of the conflicts, let us return to the corpus of letters. This brief presentation of the censored correspondence can only suggest the intermittent commentary that emerges on the Weber thesis, which claimed that national and republican unity was shaped in the school curriculum of the Third Republic, and hardened by the test of 1914–18. If historians are going to emphasise armies as nation-building institutions, perhaps they should take some notice of what soldiers are actually writing about this. Although the nation 'held' in the First World War, strains and conflicts nevertheless remained in the form of persistent regional loyalties and prejudices.

My principal purpose, however, has been to suggest the dangers of making too many assumptions about the value of personal correspondence itself. For one thing, nineteenth- and early twentieth-century letter writing was not as personal as it appears: it was often a relatively public practice, involving several writers and multiple recipients, not to mention the active surveillance of parents, husbands, fathers, and the military censor. For another thing, letters are a highly ritualized form of communication in which much rides on the choice of formulaic modes of address and signing off, and in which unspoken codes of reciprocity need to be unravelled. The military correspondence of the First World War is notable for its plethoric quantity, and for its mostly platitudinous contents. The 'laconic writing' of soldiers' letters was designed to blur as much as to reveal the reality of the trenches and long, intense, inescapable immersion in violence. Their purpose was rather one of consolation or reassurance – to achieve this they only had to exist. The soldiers' correspondence of the First World War, finally, raises some important issues about historical sources, especially posing questions about their transparency and their silences, and questions of authenticity and disguise.

Appendix: Calculating Bestsellers in Early Nineteenth-Century France

As indicated in chapter 2, the lists of bestsellers were calculated by matching up two sources – the editions announced in the *Bibliographie de la France* and the printers' declarations in series F.18 of the Archives Nationales.

The *Bibliographie de la France* records legal deposits, and gives details of titles, authors, format, and often the price of books published. Occasionally, too, the editor Pillet added an invaluable comment, indicating the number of editions previously published, and in doing so he sometimes exposed the extravagant claims made by publishers. Between 1810 and 1813, the *Bibliographie* also gave the print-runs, but after 1813 this precious information was unfortunately omitted. The defects of the *Bibliographie* as a source for book history were suggested in the 1820s by Philarète Chasles, and succinctly exposed by David Bellos.[1] It contained many double entries, which separately listed different volumes of the same work, and even different issues of the same periodical. These potential sources of confusion must be taken into account when calculating the total number of titles produced. In times of political upheaval, furthermore, there was always a tendency to underreport.

Two categories of titles seem to have been especially victims of under-reporting in the *Bibliographie*. Publications in very small format (in-32o) suffer from omission. For example, whereas the general catalogue of the Bibliothèque Nationale lists sixteen of these miniature editions of *Robinson Crusoe* published by Dauthereau between 1827 and 1849, none of them appear in the official *Bibliographie de la France*. Looking on the positive side, this example does suggest that we can fill some gaps in the data by referring to the Bibliothèque Nationale's catalogues. The other main category of underrecorded works is that of provincial publications. Series T of departmental archives provides a record of titles submitted to the office of the local prefect, fulfilling the requirement to make a legal deposit of all new titles published. But many of them do not appear in the *Bibliographie de la France*. Like titles imported from Belgium, provincial publications slip through the net, and can only be detected in the Bibliothèque Nationale catalogue.

Handling the registers which contain the summaries of the printers' declarations is not a job for the faint-hearted. They are large and dusty and take a daily toll on the laundry bill. They bear eloquent material testimony to the expansion of the book trade and of the reading public in the early nineteenth century. In the first years after 1815, they consisted of thin tomes, drawn up annually. As book production expanded and records became more thorough, the green registers grew fatter. By the 1830s, so many declarations were being made that two volumes of registers were needed each year and, in the 1840s, quarterly registers became necessary to accommodate increased production. Altogether, the declarations for the years 1815–50 are housed in forty volumes. Having combed through them personally twice and, in some cases, three times over, I can claim that any print-run missing from this study is unlikely to have been overlooked through human error.

Several remarks have to be made about the value of the printers' declarations as a historical source. A printer's declaration, first, is not necessarily evidence of actual publication. It was essentially a declaration of intention to publish, and perhaps a few plans did not reach fruition. Second, several declarations had to be altered, because plans changed, and thus many declarations cancel previous declarations. When details change, like a book's format, this can usually be verified in the *Bibliographie de la France*. A third problem arises when different parts of the same book were contracted out to several printers, all of whom were legally obliged to lodge a separate declaration. This kind of duplicate entry is most common in the 1840s, when many Parisian publishers would give the cover and title page to one printer, and the bulk of the manuscript to another. Very often, the printers were based in the suburbs and, as a result, their declaration is difficult to trace. Since many works were sold unbound, I have not taken print-runs for covers and title pages as accurate guides to the total number of copies put into circulation.

The excellent series of Parisian printers' declarations is usually more generous with information than provincial equivalents. In the departments, the *tirage* of a title is not automatically given. Even in the Parisian printers' declarations, however, there are a few important gaps. The register for 1821 stops prematurely at 17 December, and the 1830 register similarly stops at 21 December.[2] But these lacunae are trivial compared to the inexplicable loss of the entire volumes for 1835, 1836, and 1837. For the late 1830s, therefore, I rely a little more on editions published, and a little less on actual *tirages,* than for other periods.

The printers' declarations do not always identify the author of the work to be printed, which makes it difficult to match the declared *tirage* with an edition listed in the *Bibliographie de la France.* For example, a declaration to print *Don Quichotte* may refer to Cervantes' novel; but more likely it refers to a periodical of the same name. Similarly, *La Salamandre* is a novel by Eugène Sue, but it was also the name of an insurance company, which issued prospectuses and brochures. If we confuse the two we may get a rather distorted idea of the demand for life insurance in Paris in the 1840s.

Printers sometimes declared an intention to print an entire series of novels, of the kind which French publishers have traditionally favoured. Unless we know the contents of the series, such a declaration appears to be of little use. Take the example of the printer Boulé, who launched a series entitled *Mille et un Romans,* to be published with a print-run of 2000. This information can be turned to advantage, because at one stroke, Boulé has in fact revealed the print-runs of dozens of novels in his series. If we know an author was published in this series, then we know the print-run. The series in fact included some rather obscure novelists, together with a few better-known writers like Frédéric Soulié and Alphonse Karr. Thanks to Boulé's declaration, we do not need to speculate about the print-run of every title. We know it was 2000 copies, until the revolutionary year of 1848, when it dropped to 1000.[3]

After the 1840s, the printers' declarations cease to be such a lucrative goldmine. For one thing, the serialization of novels in the press means that calculating the circulation of books cannot tell the whole story of a title's impact. Another reason lies in an increasing tendency towards decentralization in the printing industry in Paris. The decentralization did not go very far, but it went as far as the suburbs. That, however, was just enough to take many printing workshops out of the administrative jurisdiction of the Seine department, which means that many valuable printers' declarations do not survive. In the 1830s and even more so in the 1840s, publishers sent novels to be printed outside the metropolis, to Crété at Corbeil, to Vialat at Lagny or to Dépée at Sceaux. The declarations for Paris survive; but those for the Seine-et-Oise department are very fragmentary.[4] At the end of the period I have covered, the *tirages* for many titles lie just outside the historian's reach.

The tables in chapter 2 provide the 'minimum known *tirage*' for individual titles. This is a basic minimum. The remaining unlocated print-runs must be calculated or projected on the basis of existing knowledge and experience. Such a projection forms the basis of the figures in the final column of the tables, giving the 'total known or estimated *tirage*.' The figures in this column were achieved by adding (1) the 'minimum known *tirage*' in the previous column, with (2) an estimate or projection of the missing *tirages* for the remaining editions known. This projection proceeded confidently, if approximately, using the known average print-run for a given author in a given format at the time of publication. In the early part of the period, novels were rarely printed in runs exceeding 1000 or 1500 copies. In the 1830s, the average print-run rose to perhaps 1500–2000 copies for novels. In the 1840s, it went higher to between 2000 and 5000 copies.

Exceptions and nuances must be accommodated. Many editions were clearly likely to exceed or fall below the average, and the total estimated *tirage* accounted for this likelihood whenever it presented itself. We know, for instance, that Hachette produced Madame de Saint-Ouen's *Histoire de France* in an edition of 15,000 in 1835, one of 20,000 in 1843, and another of 40,000 in 1847. There is no reason to suppose that the intervening editions had print-runs any smaller than these. Similarly, Moronval produced editions of *Télémaque* in runs of 4000 or 6000, falling to 3000 in 1848. These figures must be taken into account when estimating the *tirages* of other Moronval editions of *Télémaque*. The format, too, is an important consideration in estimating print-runs. We can expect a multivolume octavo edition to have a print-run below the average, especially if the price was pushed up by engravings or illustrations. A single-volume novel in the very portable duodecimo or in-18o format (known as Grand Jésus, or the 'Charpentier format' after the publisher who pioneered it) can be reasonably expected to have had an above average print-run. The titles in Charpentier's own series normally had runs of 3000 copies. The place of publication may also be important: provincial editions almost never exceeded 1500 copies before 1830, or 2000 or 3000 thereafter. With these considerations in mind, the print-runs of all editions could be projected, and added to the known print-runs, to produce an estimate of the aggregate.

Even as a sum of copies produced, the aggregate in my final column must be regarded as a minimum since, as has been suggested, several provincial editions no doubt escaped detection by the *Bibliographie de la France*. Pirate Belgian editions were certainly not recorded there, but it is reasonable to suggest that Belgian publishing piracy echoed existing trends in France, rather than altering them. The Belgians, in other words, preferred to produce titles which were already proven successes, or else were works by authors with established reputations. So the figures in this column do not represent the total readership of the titles investigated. To achieve this, we would have to know more than we do about Belgian print-runs, as well as having some way of guessing how many readers actually read each copy produced. I have not, however, attempted the impossible, nor do I want to try to conjure hypothetical coefficients of readership out of thin air. The statistics presented in chapter 2 are designed to provide a sound basis for comparison between titles and authors, and to indicate general trends and a few eminent successes.

Five-year periods have been chosen, starting in 1811. There were some practical reasons for this decision. Calculations over a shorter period, say a single year, would have been difficult, and some very erratic fluctuations would no doubt have been recorded. Publication of the complete works of a prolific author like Voltaire commonly stretched over several years, and their print-runs cannot be counted on an annual basis. In such difficult cases, the year in which publication of a set of complete works commenced has been taken as the year which determined in which quinquennium the work was included. Calculations over a longer period might have been interesting, but a broader survey may have submerged many short-term or medium-term literary successes. A five-year period seemed short enough to permit the detection of significant fluctuations, but long enough to avoid the most freakish annual variations.

Notes

1 Introduction: The Importance of the Nineteenth Century

1 Lyons, *Le Triomphe du Livre*, 73–4.
2 Lyons, *Readers and Society in 19th-Century France*.
3 Michel Vovelle, *Piété baroque et déchristianisation en Provence au 18ᵉ siècle* (Paris: Plon, 1973); and see the Vovelle symposium in *FH*, 19.2 (2005): 145–88, especially the article by Timothy Tackett.
4 François Furet and Alphonse Dupront, eds, *Livre et société dans la France du 18ᵉ siècle* (Paris: Mouton, 1965).
5 Robert Darnton, *The Literary Underground of the Old Regime* (Cambridge, MA: Harvard University Press, 1982), and his *The Kiss of Lamourette: Reflections on Cultural History* (New York: Norton, 1990).
6 See Iser, *The Implied Reader*, and Brombert, *The Hidden Reader*.
7 Radway, *Reading the Romance*, 5.
8 Roger Chartier, *The Order of Books: Readers, Authors and Libraries in Europe*, (Cambridge: Polity, 1994), ch. 1, and his 'Labourers and Voyagers: From the Text to the Reader,' in *The Book History Reader*, ed. Finkelstein and McCreery, ch. 5.
9 Carlo Ginzburg, *The Cheese and the Worms: The Cosmos of a 16th-Century Miller*, trans. J. and A. Tedeschi (London: Routledge and Kegan Paul, 1980).
10 De Certeau, *L'Invention du Quotidien*.
11 See Lejeune, *Le Pacte autobiographique*, and *On Autobiography*, among many other titles.
12 Lucien Febvre and Henri-Jean Martin, *L'Apparition du Livre* (Paris: Albin Michel, 1958 and 1971).
13 Fish, *Is There a Text in This Class?*
14 Radway, *Reading the Romance*.

15 Robert Darnton, *The Forbidden Best-Sellers of Pre-Revolutionary France* (New York and London: Norton, 1995), 186.
16 Darnton, *Forbidden Best-Sellers*, and *Literary Underground*; Roger Chartier, *The Cultural Origins of the French Revolution*, trans. Lydia G. Cochrane (Durham, NC: North Carolina UP, 1991).

2 In Search of the Bestsellers of Nineteenth-Century France, 1815–1850

 1 *Bibliographie de la France* (originally *Bibliographie de l'Empire français*), ed. Pillet, first series, 45 vols., 1810–1856; Archives Nationales (henceforth AN) F18*. II.1 to 40, *déclarations des imprimeurs* for Paris, and AN F 18. 120–56 and 168–73 for the departments.
 2 AN F18.120–56 and 168–73.
 3 Archives départementales (AD) de Vaucluse 2 T 10–14; AD du Nord 1 T 232; AD de Maine-et-Loire 82 T 1 and 82 T 8.
 4 Orecchioni, 'Eugène Sue.'
 5 AN F 17. 9146.
 6 See the *Bulletin de la Société Franklin.*
 7 Lyons, 'The Audience for Romanticism.'
 8 See Kalifa, *L'Encre et du sang.*
 9 Mollier, *Le Camelot et la rue.*
10 AD du Maine-et-Loire, 82 T 8.
11 AN F18.126.
12 Touchard, *La Gloire de Béranger,* 1:436, 522–3, and ch. 12.
13 David H. Pinckney, *The French Revolution of 1830* (Princeton, NJ: Princeton University Press, 1972), 293–4.
14 Tannenbaum, 'The Beginnings of Bleeding-Heart Liberalism.'
15 Allen, *In the Public Eye,* 276–82.
16 Orecchioni, 'Eugène Sue,' 161–2.
17 See Lyons, 'Fires of Expiation.'
18 Daniel Mornet, 'Les Enseignements des bibliothèques privées, 1750–1780,' *Revue d'histoire littéraire de la France* 17 (1910): 460–4.
19 See Iknayan, *The Idea of the Novel in France,* and 'The Fortunes of *Gil Blas* during the Romantic Period.'
20 Mornet, 'Les Enseignements des bibliothèques privées,' 466.
21 Abbé J.-J. Barthélemy, *Voyage du jeune Anacharsis en Grèce,* 5 vols (Paris: Ledoux, 1830).
22 Mollier, *Louis Hachette,* chs 6–7.
23 François Furet and Alphonse Dupront, eds, *Livre et société dans la France du 18ᵉ siècle* (Paris: Mouton, 1965), 1:48–9.

24 Christophe von Schmid, *Sept nouveaux contes pour les enfants*, trans. E. Raybois (Nancy: Grimblot, Thomas, and Raybois, 1838).
25 Girard, 'Le Triomphe de *La Cuisinière bourgeoise*.'
26 *La Cuisinière bourgeoise* (Paris: Moronval, 1836), see *avis*.
27 [Joseph-Marie Audin-Rouvière], *La Médecine sans médecin* (Paris: the author, 1823).

3 Towards a National Literary Culture in France

 1 Weber, *Peasants into Frenchmen*.
 2 Nicole Herrmann-Mascard, *La Censure des livres à Paris à la fin de l'Ancien Régime, 1750–1789* (Paris: Presses universitaires de France, 1968).
 3 Madeleine Cerf, 'La Censure royale à la fin du 18e siècle,' *Communications*, 9 (1967): 6; and see Robert Darnton and Daniel Roche, eds, *Revolution and Print: The Press in France, 1775–1800* (Berkeley, CA: University of California Press, 1989).
 4 Lamoignon de Malesherbes, *Mémoires sur la librairie*, ed. Roger Chartier (Paris: Imprimerie Nationale, 1994).
 5 Suzanne Tucoo-Chala, 'Capitalisme et lumières au 18e siècle: La double réussite du libraire Ch. J. Panckoucke, 1736–1798,' *Rfhl* 13 (1976): 646–7.
 6 Robert Darnton, 'L'Imprimerie de Panckoucke en l'An 2,' *Rfhl* 23 (1979): 359–69.
 7 George B. Watts, 'Charles-Joseph Panckoucke, "l'Atlas de la librairie française,"' in *Studies on Voltaire and the 18th Century*, ed. T. Besterman, 68: 67–205 (Oxford: Voltaire Foundation, 1969); and Robert Darnton, *The Business of Enlightenment: A Publishing History of the* Encyclopédie, *1775–1800* (Cambridge, MA: Belknap, 1979), 66–75.
 8 Darnton, *Business of Enlightenment*, 541.
 9 Mollier, *L'Argent et les lettres*, 227, 233.
10 Mollier, *Louis Hachette*, 225.
11 Ibid., 326.
12 Mollier, *L'Argent et les lettres*, 236–47.
13 Ibid., 356–79.
14 Weber, *Peasants into Frenchmen*.
15 Thabault, *Education and Change in a Village Community*.
16 AD du Maine-et-Loire, 83 T 1.
17 AN F18.567, dossier 375, *rapport sur la situation des imprimeurs de Paris, octobre 1835*.
18 Ellen Constans, 'La Librairie à Saintes de 1815 à 1914,' in *Le Commerce de la Librairie*, ed. Mollier, 123–34.

19 Frédéric Barbier, 'La diffusion de l'imprimerie en Eure-et-Loir au XIXe siècle,' in *Commerce de la librairie*, ed. Mollier, 156.

20 AD de la Haute-Garonne 6 T 1, *état nominatif des imprimeurs et des librairies dans le département de la Haute-Garonne, juillet 1822.*

21 Jean-Baptiste Dumay, *Mémoires d'un militant ouvrier du Creusot (1841–1905)*, ed. Pierre Ponsot (Grenoble: Maspéro, 1976), 298–303.

22 AN F18. 2295–2309.

23 Lyons, *Triomphe du Livre*, ch. 10.

24 Marie-Claire Boscq, 'L'Implantation des librairies à Paris, 1815–1848,' in *Commerce de la librairie*, ed. Mollier, 27–50.

25 Savart, 'La Liberté de la librairie et l'évolution du réseau des libraires,' 102–3.

26 Ibid., 91–121.

27 See Fleury and Valmary, 'Les Progrès de l'instruction élémentaire de Louis XIV à Napoléon III, d'après l'enquête de Louis Maggiolo (1877–9)'; and Furet and Ozouf, *Lire et écrire*, ch. 1.

28 Furet and Sachs, 'La Croissance de l'alphabétisation en France, 18e–19e siècle.'

29 Darmon, *Le Colportage de Librairie en France sous le second Empire*, 102–5.

30 Michael B. Palmer, 'Some Aspects of the French Press during the Rise of the Popular Daily, c.1860 to 1890,' Oxford University DPhil thesis, 1972, 381.

31 Ibid., 45.

32 Mollier, *Louis Hachette*, ch. 11; on railway bookstalls see Parinet, 'Les bibliothèques de gare,' and DeMarco, *Reading and Riding*.

33 Parinet, 'Les bibliothèques de gare,' 101.

34 Soriano, *Jules Verne*, 107–10.

35 Naf. 17007, Hetzel Archives. I have calculated 1,100 copies for each 'edition.' There were several 'editions' in each '*tirage.*'

36 *Saga* 1 (February 1978), cited by Soriano, *Jules Verne*, 326.

37 Daniel Compère, *La Vie amiénoise de Jules Verne* (Amiens: Centre régional de documentation pédagogique de Picardie, 1985), 46.

38 Naf. 17004, Verne to Hetzel, 1865, pp. 15 and 24.

39 Jean Glénisson, 'Le Livre pour la Jeunesse,' in *Histoire de l'Edition française*, ed. Chartier and Martin, 3:426–30.

40 Naf. 17004, Verne to Hetzel, early 1867, pp. 48, 67–8, and spring 1869, pp. 103, 105, 109; Vierne, *Jules Verne et le roman initiatique*, 97 note 4.

41 Olivier Dumas, 'Hetzel, Censeur de Verne,' in *Un Editeur et son siècle*, ed. Robin, 127–36.

42 Naf. 17006, no.9, Hetzel to Jules Hetzel, 19 April 1877; all translations are mine unless otherwise noted.

43 Naf. 17004, letter from Grand Rabbi, 3 June 1877, no. 370.

44 Huet, *L'Histoire des voyages extraordinaires*, 191.
45 Jan, *La Littérature Enfantine*, 150.
46 Compère, *Vie amiénoise du Jules Verne*, 41–2.
47 Milo, 'La Bourse mondiale de la traduction.'
48 Cited in Cesar Grana, *Bohemian versus Bourgeois: French Society and the French Man of Letters in the 19th Century* (New York: Basic Books, 1964), 113.
49 Mollier, *Le Camelot et la rue*.

4 Fires of Expiation

1 Francisco M. Gimeno Blay, *Quemar libros ...! qué extraño placer!* [Eutopías, documentos de trabajo vol. 104], (Valencia: University of Valencia, 1995).
2 L. Lowenthal, *I Roghi dei libri* (Geneva: n.p. 1991).
3 Cervantes, *Don Quixote*, Part 1, chapter 6.
4 AN F7.9792–4.
5 B. de Sauvigny, *La Restauration* 3rd ed. (Paris: Flammarion, 1974).
6 Gérard Cholvy and Yves-Marie Hilaire, *Histoire religieuse de la France contemporaine*, vol. 1, *1800–1880* (Toulouse: Privat, 1990).
7 Ernest Sevrin, *Les Missions Religieuses en France sous la Restauration (1815–1830)*, vol. 1 (Paris: Vrin, 1948).
8 Acts 19:19.
9 Gimeno Blay, *Quemar libros*, 12–14.
10 Sauvigny, *Restauration*, 307.
11 Cholvy and Hilaire, *Histoire religieuse*, 1:14.
12 Ibid., 1:40.
13 *ARR*, 'Sur les Missions' 22. 552 (24 November 1819): 49–60.
14 AN F7.9793, Prefect of Meurthe to Ministre de l'Intérieur, 8 jan. 1824.
15 *ARR* 24.610 (14 June 1820), 159–60.
16 *ARR*, 10.260 (5 February 1817), 392–3.
17 AN F7.9794, Commissaire de police to Prefect of the Var, déc. 1818.
18 AN F7.9792, Prefect of Allier to Min. de la Police générale, 4 avril 1818.
19 AN F7.9794, Conseiller de la préfecture, Vaucluse, to Min. de l'Intérieur, 7 nov. 1819.
20 AN F7.9792, Prefect of Charente-Inférieure to Min. de Police, 17 jan. 1818; AN F7.9793, Prefect of Hérault to Min. de Police, 24 mars 1821.
21 AN F7.9792, mission at Briançon, Hautes-Alpes, 1818.
22 Ibid., and AN F7.9792, mission at Sederon, Drôme, among others.
23 *ARR* 19.482 (24 March 1819), 186.
24 See AN F7.9792, Prefect of Allier to Min. de la Police, 14 avril 1818.
25 AN F7.9792, mission at Briançon, Hautes-Alpes, 1818.

26 *ARR* 11.343 (22 November 1817), 57–8.
27 *ARR* 24.602 (17 May 1820), 24; *ARR* 15.372 (4 Mar. 1818), *ARR* 15.90 (La Rochelle).
28 AN F7.9792, Commandant de la Gendarmerie, Bouches-du-Rhône, to Min. de la Police, 4 jan. 1820.
29 AN F7.9793, Prefect of Isère to Min. de la Police, 7 jan. 1818.
30 *Relation de la mission qui a eu lieu au Mans pendant le Carême, année 1818* (Le Mans, 1818), 12.
31 AN F7.9792, mission at Eyguières (Bouches-du-Rhône), 1819, among others.
32 AN F7.9793, Prefect of Isère to Min.de la Police, 3 fév. 1818.
33 *ARR* 22.552 (24 Nov. 1819), 50.
34 *Chronique religieuse*, vol. 2 (Feb. 1819), 29.
35 AN F7.9794, rapport particulier, Vaucluse, 1819.
36 AN F7.9794, rapport particulier, Nîmes, 19 avril 1819.
37 AN F7.9794, dossier Var.
38 AN F7.9793, Prefect of Loire-Inférieure to Min. de l'Intérieur, 20 avril 1827.
39 AN F7.9794, Conseiller de la préfecture, Vaucluse, to Min. de l'Intérieur, 21 avril 1819.
40 AN F7.9792, Bouches-du-Rhône; *ARR* 27.686 (7 Mar. 1821), 105.
41 Cholvy and Hilaire, *Histoire religieuse*, 1:130–1.
42 *Gazette des Cultes* 1.37 (15 Sept. 1829), 3.
43 AN F7.9794, dossier Seine-Inférieure.
44 *ARR* 19.477 (6 Mar. 1819), 112.
45 AN F7.9793, mayor of Toulouse, 10 mars 1819.
46 *ARR* 31.794 (20 Mar. 1822), 168–9.
47 AN F7.9792, Prefect of Charente-Inférieure to Min. de la Police, 17 jan. 1818.
48 AN F7.9792, Prefect of Bouches-du-Rhône to Min. de la Police, 8 déc. 1819.
49 AN F7.9793, Prefect of Haute-Garonne to Min. de la Police, 18 jan. 1830.
50 AN F7.9792, Conseiller de la préfecture, Drôme, to Min. de la Police, 15 avril 1817.
51 AN F7.9792, Gendarmerie, Drôme, to Min. de la Police, 21 mai & 25 avril 1821.
52 AN F7.9792, Prefect of Bouches-du-Rhône to Min. de l'Intérieur, 3 jan. 1820.
53 AN F7.9792, Prefect of Côte-d'Or to Min. de la Police, 4 jan. 1825.
54 For the significance of *Tartuffe* battles, see Kroen, *Politics and Theater*.
55 AN F7.9794, dossier Hautes-Pyrénées.
56 Robert Darnton, *The Great Cat Massacre and Other Episodes in French Cultural History* (New York: Basic Books, 1984), ch. 2.
57 See, for example, *Chronique Religieuse*, vol. 2, fev. 1819, pp. 26–8.
58 *ARR* 10.259 (1 Feb. 1817), 376.

59 Eustace Hargrave, ed., *The Heart's Memory: Pages from the Diary of Madame de Lamartine* (London: Dent, 1951), 73–4.

60 *ARR* 11.264 (19 Feb. 1817), 33–42.

61 *ARR* 11.270 (12 Mar. 1817), 129–37.

62 *ARR* 11.280 (16 Apr. 1817), 289–97.

63 *ARR* 15.370 (25 Feb. 1818), 49–56.

64 *ARR* 15.385 (18 Apr. 1818), 289–96.

65 *ARR* 31.808 (20 Apr. 1822), 310–13.

66 *ARR* 39.995 (21 Feb. 1824), 40.

67 *ARR* 36.923 (14 June 1823), 151–4.

68 *ARR* 41.1049 (28 Aug. 1824), 70.

69 *ARR* 57.1479 (11 Oct. 1828), 279.

70 *ARR* 47.1202 (15 Feb. 1826), 11; *ARR* 48.1243 (8 July 1826), 266.

71 Cholvy and Hilaire, *Histoire religieuse*, 1:75.

72 *ARR* 44.1129 (4 June 1825), 97–103.

73 Lyons, *Triomphe du Livre*, ch. 5. The printers' declarations are registered in AN F18*.II.1 to 182.

74 Lyons, *Triomphe du Livre*, ch. 5.

75 Kroen, *Politics and Theater*, 188–9.

76 Daniel Roche, *Le Peuple de Paris: Essai sur la culture populaire au 18e siècle* (Paris: Aubier, 1981), 206–11.

77 Stendhal, *Le Rouge et le Noir*, part 2, chs. 2 and 3.

78 Charles de Rémusat, *Mémoires de ma vie*, vol. 1, *Enfance et Jeunesse, la Restauration libérale, 1797–1821*, ed. C. Pouthas (Paris: Plon, 1958), 27, 67, 100, 104.

79 See Roger Chartier, *Les Origines Culturelles de la Révolution française* (Paris: Seuil, 1990), ch. 4.

80 *ARR* 11.285 (3 May 1817), 377–81; Sevrin, *Missions*, ch. 20; *Le Constitutionnel*, 31 Mar. and 10 Apr. 1817.

81 *ARR* 12.302 (2 July 1817), 235–7.

82 *ARR* 14.343 (22 Nov. 1817), 57–8.

83 *ARR* 16.395 (23 May 1818), 58–61; *La Minerve française* 2.18, (1818), 242.

84 *La Minerve française* 5.65 (April 1819), 632. But there is no mention of an *auto-da-fé* at Avignon in the anonymous *Relation de la mission d'Avignon en mars et avril 1819* (Avignon, 1819).

85 *Mission donnée à Orange en novembre et décembre 1819, par MM. les Missionnaires de France* (Orange, 1819), 13–17.

86 *ARR* 35.888 (12 Feb. 1823), 10 and 35.907 (19 Apr. 1823), 311.

87 *Souvenirs de la mission de Vendôme en mars et en avril 1824* (Vendôme, 1824), 21–5.

88 *ARR* 43.1107 (19 Mar. 1825), 170.

89 *ARR* 43.1102 (2 Mar. 1825), 87.

90 Renan, *Souvenirs*, 97.
91 *ARR* 56.1457 (26 July 1828), 345.
92 *Gazette des Cultes* vol. 1, no. 4, 23 May 1829, p. 3 and vol. 1, no. 27, 11 Aug. 1829, p. 2.
93 Réné-Théophile Châtelain, *Le Seizième Siècle en 1817* (Paris: Brissot-Thivars, 1818), 72–9.
94 David H. Pinkney, *La Révolution de 1830 en France* (Paris: Presses universitaires de France, 1988), 166 and 318.

5 Literary Commemoration and the Uses of History

1 Elizabeth L. Eisenstein, *The Printing Press as an Agent of Change: Communications and Global Transformations in Early Modern Europe* (Cambridge: Cambridge University Press, 1979).
2 Albert Kapr, *Johann Gutenberg, the Man and His Invention*, trans. D. Martin (Aldershot, UK: Scolar Press, 1996), 286.
3 Kapr, *Gutenberg*, 286; Jean-Daniel Schöpflin, *Vindiciae Typographicae* (Strasbourg, 1760). This publication took on even greater importance after some of the originals were destroyed in the bombardment of the city during the Franco-Prussian War of 1870.
4 See Martin, 'Le Sacre de Gutenberg,' 23–4; Elizabeth L. Eisenstein, *Grub Street Abroad: Aspects of the French Cosmopolitan Press from the Age of Louis XIV to the French Revolution (the Lyell lectures 1989–90)* (Oxford: Clarendon, 1992), 75.
5 Paul Lehr, *A la mémoire de Gutenberg*, AD du Bas-Rhin 15 M 35.
6 David Miller would regard the full title of Dava Sobel's recent book as a good illustration of the phenomenon – *Longitude: The True Story of a Lone Genius who Solved the Greatest Scientific Problem of His Time* (New York: Walker, 1995).
7 Anon, *Gutenberg erfinder der buch* (Strasbourg, 1840) (BN Ln27.9448).
8 Lucien Febvre and Henri-Jean Martin, *L'Apparition du livre* (Paris: Albin Michel, 1958 and 1971); Kapr, *Gutenberg*; Guy Bechtel, *Gutenberg et l'invention de l'imprimerie: une enquête* (Paris: Fayard, 1992).
9 Kapr, *Gutenberg*, 88, 98–9; Bechtel, *Gutenberg*, 274.
10 Eusebius Caesariensis, *Chronica a S.Hieronymo latine versum et ab eo Prospero Britannico et Mattheo Palmerio continuatum* (Venice: Ratdolt, 1483); and see Bechtel, *Gutenberg*, 20.
11 *Chronik der Stadt Köln*, 1499: see Febvre and Martin, *L'Apparition du livre*, 74.
12 Jacob Wimpheling, *Epithoma Germanorum* (Strasbourg: Johann Prüss, 1505), ch. 65, folios 38 verso + 39 recto; and see Bechtel, *Gutenberg*, 25.
13 Schöpflin, *Vindiciae Typographicae*; and see Kapr, *Gutenberg*, ch. 3, and Bechtel, *Gutenberg*, 32–3.

14 Bechtel, *Gutenberg*, 39–40.

15 Margaret B. Stillwell, *The Beginning of the World of Books, 1450–1470* (New York: Bibliographical Society of America, 1972); Bechtel, *Gutenberg*, 92–108.

16 Kapr, *Gutenberg*, 189, 196, 240. These included the indulgences sold in the 1450s to raise money for the defence of Cyprus against the infidel Turks, and the so-called Neuhausen Indulgences in 1461–2.

17 Bechtel, *Gutenberg*, 86–7; Kapr, *Gutenberg*, 121–2.

18 Anon., *Gutenberg à Strasbourg, ou l'invention de l'imprimerie, divertissement en un acte, mêlé de chant et de danses, pour l'inauguration de la statue de Gutenberg* (Strasbourg: Silbermann, 1840), 25–6.

19 Martin Nadaud, *Mémoires de Léonard, ancien garçon maçon*, intro. by M. Agulhon (Paris: Hachette, 1976), 374.

20 AD du Bas-Rhin 3 M 192, souscription pour l'érection à Strasbourg d'un monument à la mémoire de Jean Gutenberg, inventeur de l'imprimerie, prospectus.

21 Auguste Luchet, *Récit de l'inauguration de la statue de Gutenberg et des fêtes données par la ville de Strasbourg les 24, 25 et 26 juin 1840* (Paris: Pagnerre, 1840), 45–8.

22 Adrian Johns, *The Nature of the Book: Print and Knowledge in the Making* (Chicago: University of Chicago Press, 1998), 374.

23 A. Cloots, *Oeuvres*, tome 3, *Ecrits et discours de la période révolutionnaire* (Munich: Klaus reprint. 1980; and Paris: Editions d'Histoire Sociale, 1980), *Discours prononcé à la barre de l'Assemblée Nationale au nom des imprimeurs, 9 septembre 1792*; and see Eisenstein, *Grub Street Abroad*, 158.

24 David S. Kerr, *Caricature and French Political Culture, 1830–1848: Charles Philipon and the Illustrated Press* (Oxford: Clarendon, 2000), 52, 133.

25 Maurice Agulhon has drawn attention to the intense 'statuomania' of this period, and the vogue for 'didactic monumentalism.' See his 'Imagerie civique et décor urbain' and 'Le "statuomanie" et l'histoire,' in his *Histoire vagabonde* vol. 1 (Paris: Gallimard, 1988), 101–85.

26 Stéphane Gerson, 'Town, Nation, or Humanity? Festive Delineations of Place and Past in Northern France, ca. 1825–1865,' *JMH* 72.3 (2000): 628–81.

27 AD du Bas-Rhin 1 N 74, conseil-général du Dept. du Bas-Rhin, procès-verbal of meeting of 24.08.1836. The archival sources do not indicate how the deficit of several thousand francs was eventually covered.

28 AD du Bas-Rhin 3 M 179.

29 Luchet, *Récit de l'inauguration*.

30 AD du Bas-Rhin 3 M 179, no. 23, Prefect to Min. of Interior, 16.06.1840.

31 AD du Bas-Rhin 3 M 179, no. 17, 12.06.1840.

32 Robert Darnton, 'A Bourgeois Puts His House in Order: The City as a Text,' in his *Great Cat Massacre*, ch. 3.

33 Luchet, *Récit de l'inauguration*, 69.
34 AD du Bas-Rhin 3 M 179, no. 41, Prefect to Min. of Interior, 25.06.1840.
35 AD du Bas-Rhin 3 M 179, no. 23, Prefect to Min. of Interior, 16.06.1840.
36 Georges Foessel, 'Le Règne des Notables: Strasbourg et la Monarchie Consti-
    tutionnelle (1815–1848),' in *Histoire de Strasbourg des origines à nos jours*, ed.
    Georges Livet and Francis Rapp (Strasbourg: Dernières Nouvelles d'Alsace,
    1982), 4:48.
37 Anon., *Gutenberg à Strasbourg*, 3–5; Luchet, *Récit de l'inauguration*, 12–17.
38 Luchet, *Récit de l'inauguration*, 31–8.
39 Martin, 'Le Sacre de Gutenberg,' 22; for an illustrated description of these
    and other Gutenberg celebrations in Germany from the Reformation to the
    Third Reich, see the exhibition catalogue edited by Monika Estermann, *'O
    werthe Druckerkunst/ Du Mutter aller kunst': Gutenbergfeiern im Laufe der Jahrhun-
    derte* (Mainz: Gutenberg-Museum, 1999).
40 AD du Bas-Rhin 3 M 192, no. 123, official circular to prefects, 30.05.1835.
41 Victor Hugo, *Notre-Dame de Paris: 1482* (Paris: Gallimard-Folio, 1974), book 5,
    ch. 2, 237.
42 Ibid., 237.
43 Ibid., 246.
44 Dagmar Herzog, *Intimacy and Exclusion: Religious Politics in Pre-Revolutionary
    Baden* (Princeton, NJ: Princeton University Press, 1996).
45 Barbier, *L'Empire du livre*, 128–9.
46 Foessel, 'Le Règne des notables,' 32; AD du Bas-Rhin 3 M 56, irritation causée
    à Strasbourg, parmi les catholiques et les protestants par le bas-relief du mon-
    ument de Gutenberg, sur lequel figure l'effigie de Martin Luther, Min. of
    Interior to Prefect, 6.10.1842.
47 AD du Bas-Rhin 3 M 179, nos 3 and 4, letters of 25.05.1840 and 1.06.1840.
48 AD du Bas-Rhin 3 M 56, Prefect to Min. of Interior, 10.10.1842. and
    25.10.1842.
49 AD du Bas-Rhin 3 M 179, no. 1, Cartier to Min. of Interior, 29.05.1834.
50 AD du Bas-Rhin 3 M 179, nos 8, 9, and 15, correspondence of June 1840.
51 AD du Bas-Rhin 2 M 179, no. 28, Prefect to Min. of Interior, 19.06.1840.
52 AD du Bas-Rhin 3 M 179, no. 35, Prefect to Min. of Interior, 23.06.1840.
53 AD du Bas-Rhin 3 M 179, no. 55, Prefect to Min. of Interior, 27.06.1840.

**6 The Reading Experience of Worker-Autobiographers in Nineteenth-Century
    Europe**

1 Rose, 'Rereading the English Common Reader,' 70.
2 John Burnett, David Vincent, and David Mayall, eds, *The Autobiography of the*

Working Class: An Annotated, Critical Bibliography, 2 vols (Brighton, UK: Harvester, 1984–7). vol. 1.

3 *Grand Dictionnaire Larousse*, 1866 ed., 1:979.

4 See Vincent, *Bread, Knowledge and Freedom*.

5 See Bourdieu, *La Distinction*.

6 Edward Lillie Craik, *The Pursuit of Knowledge under Difficulties*, rev. ed. (London: George Bell, 1876).

7 Hannah Mitchell, *The Hard Way Up: The Autobiography of Hannah Mitchell, Suffragette and Rebel*, ed. Geoffrey Mitchell (London: Virago, 1977), 43–54.

8 Norbert Truquin, *Mémoires et aventures d'un prolétaire à travers la révolution, l'Algérie, la République argentine et le Paraguay* (Paris: Librairie des Deux Mondes, 1888), 14. On Truquin, see Ragon, *Histoire de la littérature prolétarienne en France*, 100–3; Michelle Perrot, 'A Nineteenth-Century Work Experience as Related in a Worker's Autobiography: Norbert Truquin', in *Work in France*, ed. Kaplan and Koepp, chapter 10; Paule Lejeune, introduction to the 1977 edition of Truquin's *Mémoires et aventures*, published by Maspéro in Paris; Traugott, *The French Worker*, chapter 5.

9 Truquin, *Mémoires et aventures*, 144 and 231.

10 Ibid., 72–3.

11 Ibid., 225–7 and 235–6.

12 Ibid., 294–5.

13 Ibid., 447–8. Truquin spent seven years in Algeria, 1848–55.

14 Ibid., 451.

15 John James Bezer, 'Autobiography of One of the Chartist Rebels of 1848,' in *Testaments of Radicalism*, ed. Vincent, 157.

16 Gabriel Gauny, *Le Philosophe plébéien*, ed. Jacques Rancière (Paris: La Découverte/Maspéro, 1983), 27. Gauny believed that the soul could be reincarnated many times in different bodies, which made possible a kind of evolution, transmitted by heredity, towards human perfection.

17 Bourdieu, *La Distinction*, 378.

18 Richter, *La Conversion du mauvais lecteur et la naissance de la lecture publique*, 9–22.

19 Thomas Cooper, *The Life of Thomas Cooper, Written by Himself* (London: Hodder and Stoughton, 1872 and 1897), 57, 59.

20 Sebastien Commissaire, *Mémoires et Souvenirs*, 2 vols (Lyon: Méton, 1888), 1:121.

21 Rose, *Intellectual Life*, 60.

22 Clark, *Schooling the Daughters of Marianne*, 11.

23 Purvis, 'The Experience of Schooling for Working-Class Boys and Girls, in 19th-century England,' 106–10; and Purvis, 'The Double Burden of Class and Gender,' 103–4.

24 Hurt, *Elementary Schooling and the Working Classes*, 25–7.

25 Mitchell, *Hard Way Up*, 43.

26 Susan Grogan, *French Socialism and Sexual Difference: Women and the New Society* (London: Macmillan, 1992), esp. chapter 5.

27 Marianne Farningham, *A Working Woman's Life: An Autobiography* (London: J. Clarke, 34).

28 Ibid., 49.

29 Ibid., 19.

30 Ibid., 71.

31 Margaret Penn, *Manchester Fourteen Miles*, 1947 (Sussex, UK: Caliban reprint, 1979), 191–2.

32 Flint, *The Woman Reader*, chapter 4.

33 Adelheid Popp, *La Jeunesse d'une ouvrière* (Paris: Maspéro, 1979), 13 (first published in 1909 as *Die Jugendgeschichte einer Arbeiterin*).

34 Richter, *Conversion du mauvais lecteur*, 9–22.

35 Duveau, *La Pensée ouvrière*, 302–7; and Henri Tolain, 'Le Roman Populaire,' *La Tribune ouvrière* 1.3 (18 June 1865), 9–10.

36 Lyons, *Readers and Society in Nineteenth-Century France*, chapters 2–3.

37 Fish, *Is There a Text in This Class?*

38 Louis-Arsène Meunier, 'Mémoires d'un ancêtre ou tribulations d'un instituteur percheron,' *Cahiers percherons* 65–6 (1981), 38–44. Meunier's memoirs were first published as supplements to the teachers' journal *L'Ecole Nouvelle* in 1904.

39 Victorine Brocher, *Souvenirs d'une morte vivante*, 1909 (Paris: Maspéro, 1976), 34.

40 James Dawson Burn, *The Autobiography of a Beggar Boy*, ed. David Vincent (London: Europa, 1978), 198.

41 George Henry Roberts, 'How I Got On,' *Pearson's Weekly*, 17 May 1906, 806c. This was one in a series of life histories by the new contingent of Labour Members of Parliament.

42 Brocher, *Souvenirs*, 62.

43 Suzanne Voilquin, *Souvenirs d'une fille du peuple ou la Saint-simonienne en Egypte*, 1866, introduction by Lydia Elhadad (Paris: Maspéro, 1978), 65, 77.

44 Rose, *Intellectual Life*, 180, 201.

45 Bourdieu, *La Distinction*, 91–2.

46 Alphonse Viollet, *Les Poètes du peuple au XIXe siècle*, ed. M. Ragon (Paris: Librairie française et étrangère, 1846); and François Gimet, *Les Muses Prolétaires* (Paris: Fareu, 1856).

47 Avrom Fleishman, *Figures of Autobiography: The Language of Self-Writing in Victorian and Modern England* (Berkeley CA: University of California Press, 1983),

58–69 and 104. My summary seems to differ from the view of Regenia Gagnier, who states inexplicably, 'Most working-class autobiographies do not have crises and recoveries just as they do not have climaxes'; See R. Gagnier, 'Social Atoms: Working-Class Autobiography, Subjectivity and Gender,' *Victorian Studies* 30.3 (1987), 344.

48 Linda H. Petersen, *Victorian Autobiography: The Tradition of Self-Interpretation* (New Haven, CT: Yale University Press, 1986), 1–10.

49 Jocelyn Bety Goodman, ed., *Victorian Cabinet-Maker: The Memoirs of James Hopkinson, 1819–1894* (London: Routledge Kegan Paul, 1968), 3–5.

50 Ibid., 39.

51 William Edwin Adams, *Memoirs of a Social Atom*, 2 vols (London: Hutchinson, 1903), 1:154, first published in 1901–2 in the *Newcastle Weekly Chronicle* edited by Adams from 1864 to 1900.

52 William James Linton, *Memories* (London: Lawrence and Bullen, 1895).

53 Thomas Burt, *Thomas Burt, MP, Pitman and Privy Councillor: An Autobiography* (London: T. Fisher Unwin, 1924); John Hodge, *Workman's Cottage to Windsor Castle* (London: Sampson, Low, and Marston, no date ?1927); and William Cobbett, *The Autobiography of William Cobbett*, ed. William Reitzel (London: Faber, 1967).

54 Jacques Laffitte, *Mémoires de Laffitte, 1767–1844*, ed. Jacques Duchon (Paris: Firmin-Didot, 1932).

55 Farningham, *A Working Woman's Life*, 44.

56 Brocher, *Souvenirs*, 113–16.

57 Lejeune, *Le Pacte autobiographique*; and his *On Autobiography*, ed. P.J. Eakin.

58 Rémi Gossez, ed., *Un Ouvrier en 1820: manuscrit inédit de Jacques-Etienne Bédé* (Paris: Presses universitaires de France, 1984), 45–9.

59 Christopher Thomson, *The Autobiography of an Artisan* (London: Chapman, 1847), vi–vii.

60 Charles Manby Smith, *The Working Man's Way in the World, Being the Autobiography of a Journeyman Printer* (London: W. and F. Cash, no date ?1853), 2.

61 J.W. Taylor, 'How I Got On – Life Stories by the Labour M.P.s,' *Pearson's Weekly*, London, 1906, 771c.

62 Adams, *Memoirs of a Social Atom* 1:xiii.

63 Gossez, *Un Ouvrier en 1820*, 73. See the review by Michael Sonenscher in *History Workshop Journal* 21 (summer 1986), 173–9.

64 Among them Traugott, *The French Worker*, 47–8.

65 Ellen Johnston, *Autobiography, Poems and Songs, by E.J., the Factory Girl* (Glasgow: Love, 1867), 7.

66 Ibid., 5–6.

67 Brocher, *Souvenirs*, 115–16.

68 Thomson, *Autobiography of an Artisan*, 24 and 169.
69 Burn, *Autobiography of a Beggar Boy*, 197.
70 Agricol Perdiguier, *Mémoires d'un compagnon* (Moulins: Cahiers du Centre, 1914), 87.
71 Jean-Baptiste Arnaud, *Mémoires d'un compagnon du Tour de France* (Rochefort: Giraud, 1859), 50.
72 Martin Nadaud, *Mémoires de Léonard, ancien garçon maçon*, 1895, introduction by Maurice Agulhon (Paris: Hachette, 1976), 282.
73 Cited in Ragon, *Histoire de la littérature prolétarienne*, 82.

7 Oral Culture and the Rural Community

1 I am grateful to Roger Chartier for correcting some of my own misconceptions, as well as for some useful references.
2 Robert Mandrou, *De la culture populaire aux 17e et 18e siècles: La Bibliothèque bleue de Troyes* (Paris: Stock, 1964 and 1975), 18.
3 Weber, *Peasants into Frenchmen*.
4 See Devos and Josten, *Moeurs et coûtumes*.
5 Ibid., 303.
6 Louise Michel, *Mémoires*, vol. 1 (Paris: F. Roy, 1886).
7 Eugène Leroy, *Le Moulin du Frau* (Paris: Fasquelle, 1905).
8 Ibid., 147.
9 Daniel Fabre and Jacques Lacroix, *La Vie quotidienne des paysans du Languedoc au 19ᵉ siècle* (Paris: Hachette, 1973); Georges Rocal, *Le Vieux Périgord* (Toulouse: Guitard, 1927), 13–19; Roger Béteille, *La Vie quotidienne en Rouergue au 19ᵉ siècle* (Paris: Hachette, 1973), 131–3; G.-Michel Coissac, *Mon Limousin* (Paris: A. Lahure, 1913; reprinted Marseille, 1978), 285–7; Devos and Josten, *Moeurs et coûtumes*; Suzanne Tardieu, *La Vie domestique dans le Mâconnais rural pré-industriel* (Paris: Institut d'ethnologie, 1964), 154–62; Emile Guillaumin, *La Vie d'un simple* (Paris: Livre de poche, 1979), 82, 191; Michel, *Mémoires*, 1:52; Eugène Bougeâtre, *La Vie rurale dans le Mantois et le Vexin au 19ᵉ siècle*, ed. M. Lachiver (Meulan: Persan, 1971), 172–6 and 195–7; Pierre-Jakez Hélias, *Le Cheval d'Orgeuil: mémoires d'un breton au pays bigouden* (Geneva: Famot, 1979), 1:92.
10 Devos and Josten, *Moeurs et coûtumes*. There is room for some disagreement about the exact figure. Not every gathering mentioned is specifically called a *veillée*.
11 AD Seine-et-Oise 2 V 25–6, visites paroissiales, diocèse de Versailles, 1859.
12 Fabre and Lacroix, *Vie quotidienne des paysans du Languedoc*, 250–3.
13 Tardieu, *Vie domestique dans le Mâconnais*, 155; Gabriel Jeanton, *Le Mâconnais traditionaliste et populaire*, 4 vols (Mâcon: Protat, 1920–2), 3:15–20.

14 Fabre and Lacroix, *Vie quotidienne des paysans du Languedoc*, 250–3; Tardieu, *Vie domestique dans le Mâconnais*, 158; Emile Violet, *Les Veillées en commun et les réunions d'hiver,* 9e enquête de folklore, de l'Académie des Arts, Sciences et Belles-Lettres de Mâcon (Mâcon: 1942), 4.

15 Fabre and Lacroix, *Vie quotidienne des paysans du Languedoc*, 250–3; Tardieu, *Vie domestique dans le Mâconnais*, 159; Bougeâtre, *Vie rurale dans le Mantois,* 174, 195.

16 Violet, *Les Veillées en commun*, 6.

17 Ibid., 2; Jeanton, *Le Mâconnais traditionaliste*, 15; Michel, *Mémoires*, 1:52.

18 Tardieu, *Vie domestique dans le Mâconnais*, 158–9; Violet, *Les Veillées en commun*, 3; Yann Brékilien, *La Vie quotidienne des paysans de Bretagne au 19e siècle* (Paris: Hachette, 1966), 94–7; Devos and Josten, *Moeurs et coûtumes;* Fabre et Lacroix, *Vie quotidienne des paysans du Languedoc*, 250–3.

19 Rocal, *Vieux Périgord*, 13–14.

20 Tardieu, *Vie domestique dans le Mâconnais*, 159.

21 Bougeâtre, *Vie rurale dans le Mantois*, 174, 195–7.

22 Leroy, *Moulin du Frau*, 133–6.

23 Fabre and Lacroix, *Vie quotidienne des paysans du Languedoc*, 390.

24 Devos and Josten, *Moeurs et coûtumes*, 261 (St Nicolas-la-Chapelle).

25 Bougeâtre, *Vie rurale dans le Mantois*, 176.

26 Gérald Duverdier, 'La Pénétration du livre dans un société de culture orale: Le cas de Tahiti,' *Rfhl* (1971): 27–53.

27 Jean-Pierre Piniès, 'Du choc culturel à l'ethnocide: La pénétration du livre dans les campagnes languedociennes du 17e au 19e siècles,' *Folklore* 44.3 (1981), 15, 20; Fabre and Lacroix, *Vie quotidienne des paysans du Languedoc*, 253.

28 Béteille, *Vie quotidienne en Rouergue*, 131.

29 Tardieu, *Vie domestique dans le Mâconnais*, 161; Violet, *Les Veillées en commun*, 5; Leroy, *Moulin du Frau*, 144; Devos and Josten, *Moeurs et coûtumes*, passim; Fabre and Lacroix, *Vie quotidienne des paysans du Languedoc*, 250–3; Rocal, *Vieux Périgord*, 18–19.

30 Béteille, *Vie quotidienne en Rouergue*, 131–3; Tardieu, *Vie domestique dans le Mâconnais*, 160.

31 Bougeâtre, *Vie rurale dans le Mantois*, 195.

32 Fabre and Lacroix, *Vie quotidienne des paysans du Languedoc*, 250–3.

33 Michel, *Mémoires* 1:52; Devos and Josten, *Moeurs et coûtumes*, at Fumet and Vailly for example.

34 Bougeâtre, *Vie rurale dans le Mantois*, 195.

35 Guillaumin, *La Vie d'un Simple*, 82.

36 Jeanton, *Le Mâconnais traditionaliste*, 15–20; Tardieu, *Vie domestique dans le Mâconnais*, 160; Violet, *Les Veillées en commun,* 7.

37 Devos and Josten, *Moeurs et coûtumes*, 307.

38 Leroy, *Moulin du Frau.*

39 Devos and Josten, *Moeurs et coûtumes*, 200, and see replies to bishop's questions from Chatel and Mégevette, 306.

40 Marie-Hélène Froeschlé-Chopard and Marcel Bernos, 'Entre peuple et hiérarchie: l'échec d'une pastorale,' *Dix-huitième siècle* 12 (1980): 271–92.

41 Violet, *Les Veillées en commun*, 2.

42 Bougeâtre, *Vie rurale dans le Mantois*, 176, 195.

43 Devos and Josten, *Moeurs et coûtumes*, see replies from e.g. Sarraval, Publier, Reyvroz and St Cergues.

44 Maurice Agulhon et al, *Histoire de la France rurale*, vol. 3, *Apogée et crise de la civilisation paysanne, 1789–1914* (Paris: Seuil, 1976), 354.

45 Jeanton, *Le Mâconnais traditionaliste*, 15–20.

46 Guillaumin, *La Vie d'un Simple*, 291.

8 Why We Need an Oral History of Reading

1 See Nora, *Les Lieux de Mémoire*; Philippe Joutard and Patrick Cabanel, eds, *Les Camisards et leur mémoire, 1701–2002* (Montpellier: Presses du Languedoc, 2002); and Philippe Joutard et al, 'Archives orales: une autre histoire?' *AESC* 35.1 (1980): 124–99.

2 Thiesse, *Le Roman du quotidien*; and her two articles, 'Imprimés du pauvre, livres de fortune,' and 'Mutations et permanences de la culture populaire.

3 Ponsard, 'Lectures ouvrières au XXe siècle' in Jean-Yves Mollier, ed., *Histoires de lecture, 19ᵉ–20ᵉ siècles*, and her 'Quand l'histoire socioculturelle est aussi histoire orale.'

4 Radway, *Reading the Romance.*

5 Lyons and Taksa, *Australian Readers Remember.*

6 Iser, *The Implied Reader*; and Brombert, *The Hidden Reader.*

7 Luisa Passerini, *Fascism in Popular Memory* (Cambridge: Cambridge University Press, 1987).

8 For more on the history of reading as a cultural practice, see the works of Roger Chartier, for example, *Histoire de la lecture*, and Mauger, 'Ecrits, lecteurs, lectures.'

9 Radway, *Reading the Romance*, 221.

10 Fish, *Is There a Text in This Class?*

11 Ponsard, 'Lectures ouvrières,' 141–6.

12 Hall, 'The Uses of Literacy in New England, 1600–1850.'

13 Engelsing, *Der Burger als Leser.*

14 Mary Gilmore, *Old Days, Old Ways: A Book of Recollections* (Sydney: Angus and Robertson, 1934), 58.

15 Interview with the author, 27 February 1986.
16 Mary MacLeod Banks, *Memoirs of Pioneer Days in Queensland* (London: Heath Cranton, 1931), 40.
17 Radway, *Reading the Romance*, 55–80.
18 Thiesse, 'Mutations,' 73–4.
19 Lyons and Taksa, *Australian Readers Remember*, 77.
20 Ibid., 163.
21 John Murphy, 'The Voice of Memory: History, Autobiography and Oral Memory,' *Historical Studies* 22 (1986): 157–75.
22 Ponsard, 'Quand l'histoire socioculturelle est aussi histoire orale,' 112.
23 Ibid., 109–10; Thiesse, 'Mutations,' 71–2.
24 Martyn Lyons and Lucy Taksa, '"If Mother caught us reading ...!": Impressions of the Australian Woman Reader, 1890–1933,' *Australian Cultural History* 11 (1992): 39–50.
25 Eileen McC., interviewed by the author, 7 November 1986, and subsequent correspondence.
26 Ponsard, 'Quand l'histoire socioculturelle est aussi histoire orale,' 109.
27 Lyons and Taksa, '"If Mother caught us reading ...!,"' 44.
28 Thiesse, *Roman du quotidien*, 32–5 and 40–1.
29 Ibid., 62–6.
30 On this familiar problem see the refreshingly frank Ponsard, 'Quand l'histoire socioculturelle est aussi histoire orale,' 106.
31 Thiesse, *Roman du quotidien*, 22–3.
32 Thiesse, 'Imprimés du pauvre,' 106.
33 Lyons and Taksa, *Australian Readers Remember*, chapter 5.
34 Fussell, *The Great War and Modern Memory*, chapter 5.
35 Bogacz, 'A "Tyranny of Words."'
36 Lyons and Taksa, *Australian Readers Remember*, 68–9.
37 Interview with the author, 2 May 1986.
38 Daisy B., interview with the author, 16 July 1986.

9 Reading Practices, Writing Practices

1 According to Jacob Presser, ego-documents are 'texts in whatever form or size which hide or reveal the self deliberately or accidentally.' See Dekker, *Autobiographical Writing in Its Social Context since the Middle Ages*.
2 Chartier, *La Correspondance*.
3 Dauphin et al, *Ces Bonnes Lettres*.
4 Ibid., 78.
5 Annabella Boswell, *Some Recollections of My Early Days, Written at Different Periods* (?Sydney: n.p. [?1908]), 19.

6 Lucile Le Verrier, *Journal d'une jeune fille Second Empire, 1866–78*, ed. Lionel Mirisch (Cadeilhan: Zulma, 1994), entry of 21 March 1869.

7 Didier, *Le Journal intime*, 11.

8 Martine Reid, 'Ecriture intime et Destinataire,' in *L'Epistolarité à travers les siècles*, ed. Bossis and Porter, 24–5.

9 Lejeune, *'Cher Cahier ...,'* 69–70.

10 Simonet-Tenant, *Le Journal intime*, 36–7.

11 Lynn Z. Bloom, '"I Write for Myself and Strangers": Private Diaries as Public Documents,' in *Inscribing the Daily*, ed. Bunkers and Huff, 23.

12 Leleu, *Les Journaux intimes*.

13 Simonet-Tenant, *Le Journal intime*, 78–80.

14 Examples of this genre include Bunkers and Huff, *Inscribing the Daily*; Harriet Bodgett, *Centuries of Female Days: Englishwomen's Private Diaries* (New Brunswick, NJ: Rutgers University Press, 1988); Lorely French, *German Women as Letter Writers: 1750–1850* (Madison, WI: Fairleigh Dickinson University Press, 1996).

15 J.-P. Albert, 'Ecritures domestiques,' in *Ecritures ordinaires*, ed. Fabre, 78–9.

16 Didier, *Le Journal intime*, 115.

17 Chartier, *La Correspondance*, 369.

18 Dauphin, 'Pour une histoire de la correspondance familiale,' 92–3.

19 Chartier, *La Correspondance*, 87.

20 Ibid., 42–60.

21 Ibid., 39; David Vincent, *Literacy and Popular Culture in England*, 39; New South Wales PMG's Annual Report, 1901.

22 Michelle Perrot, 'Le Secret de la Correspondance au XIXe siècle,' in *L'Epistolarité à travers les siècles*, ed. Bossis and Porter, 184–8.

23 Maguy de St-Laurent, 'Cent Lieues et Dix-Huit Jours: Lettres d'Amour en 1844,' in *Les Correspondances*, ed. Bonnat et al., 81.

24 Dauphin et al, *Ces Bonnes Lettres*, 161–77.

25 Jean Hébrard, 'La Lettre representée: Les pratiques épistolaires populaires dans les récits de vie ouvriers et paysans,' in *La Correspondance*, ed. Chartier, 305.

26 Dauphin, *Ces Bonnes Lettres*.

27 Wanda Bannour, 'La Correspondance de P.I. Tchaikowski avec la baronne Von Meck: un pacte étrange,' in *Les Correspondances*, ed. Bonnat et al, 418–25.

28 See also Lisa Jardine, 'Reading and the Technology of Textual Affect: Erasmus' Familiar Letters and Shakespeare's *King Lear*,' in *The Practice and Representation of Reading in England*, ed. Raven et al, chapter 5; Choderlos de Laclos, *Liaisons Dangereuses*, letter CV : 'Vous voyez bien que, quand vous écrivez à quelqu'un, c'est pour lui et non pas pour vous: vous devez donc moins chercher à lui dire ce que vous pensez, que ce qui lui plaît davantage.'

29 Jean-Louis Cornille, 'L'Assignation, analyse d'un pacte épistolaire,' in *Les Correspondances*, ed. Bonnat et al, 34.

30 Roland Barthes, 'La Lettre d'Amour,' in *Fragments d'un Discours Amoureux* (Paris: Seuil, 1977), 187–9.

31 Dauphin, *Ces Bonnes Lettres*, 106–7.

32 Foley, '"J'avais tant besoin d'être aimée … par correspondance,"' 157–8.

33 Ibid., 158.

34 Grassi, 'Des Lettres qui parlent d'amour.' 23–32.

35 Bernard Bray, 'Treize Propos sur la lettre d'amour,' in *L'Epistolarité*, ed. Bossis and Porter, 40–7.

36 Dauphin, *Ces Bonnes Lettres*, 70–1.

37 Chotard-Lioret, 'Correspondre en 1900,' 65.

38 Ibid., 64–5.

39 Dauphin, *Ces Bonnes Lettres*, 118–19.

40 Ibid., 155–60.

41 Ibid., 170.

42 Eugénie de Guérin, *Journal*, 60th ed. (Albi: Ateliers professionnels de l'Orphelinat St.-Jean, 1977). For a discussion of Eugénie's reading, see Lyons, *Readers and Society in 19th-Century France*, 103–8.

43 Didier, *Le Journal intime*, 56–9.

44 Lejeune, *Le Moi des demoiselles*, 18–20.

45 Marie Lenéru, *Journal* with *Journal d'Enfance*, ed. Fernande Dauriac (Paris: Grasset, 1945), entry of 30 November 1886.

46 Ibid., entry of 21 August 1888.

47 Marie-Claude Penloup, 'Literary Temptations and Leisure-Time Copying: Spontaneous Adolescent Writing in Contemporary France,' in *Ordinary Writings, Personal Narratives*, ed. Lyons, 191–206.

48 Lejeune, *Le Moi des demoiselles*, 11.

49 Michelle Perrot and Georges Ribeill, eds, *Le Journal Intime de Caroline B.* (Paris: Montalba, 1985).

50 Ibid., 207.

51 Jean-Pierre Baylac, 'Journal Intime,' *Les Temps Modernes* 71 (Sept. 1951): 495–508.

52 Henri-Frédéric Amiel, *Journal Intime*, 12 vols (Lausanne: L'Age d'homme, 1976–94; and, in contrast, Brussels: Complexe, 1987).

53 Leleu, *Les Journaux intimes*, 274.

54 Henri Troyat, *Tolstoy* (Harmondsworth, UK: Penguin, 1970), 903–19; Didier, *Le Journal intime*, 79–81.

55 Penloup, *La Tentation du littéraire*.

56 Lejeune, *'Cher cahier.'*

10 French Soldiers and Their Correspondence

1 Chartier, *La Correspondance*; Dauphin et al, *Ces Bonnes Lettres*; Fabre, *Ecritures ordinaires*; Lyons, 'Love Letters and Writing Practices.'

2 Jean-Jacques Becker, *The Great War and the French People* (Leamington Spa, UK: Berg, 1985).

3 Annick Cochet, '*L'Opinion et le moral des soldats en 1916, d'après les archives du contrôle postal*,' unpublished 3e cycle thesis (Paris-X-Nanterre, 1985). In the same vein, see Filipe Ribeiro de Maneses, '"All of Us are Looking Forward to Leaving": The Censored Correspondence of the Portuguese Expeditionary Corps in France, 1917–1918,' *European History Quarterly* 30.3 (2000): 333–55.

4 David Englander, 'The French Soldier, 1914–1918,' *FH* 1.1 (1987): 49–67.

5 Guy Pedroncini, *Les Mutineries de 1917* (Paris: Presses universitaires de France, 1967 and 1983).

6 Stéphane Audoin-Rouzeau and Annette Becker, *14–18, Retrouver la Guerre* (Paris: Gallimard, 2000), 127–8.

7 John Horne, 'Soldiers, Civilians and the Warfare of Attrition: Representations of Combat in France, 1914–1918,' in *Authority, Identity and the Social History of the First World War*, ed. Frans Coetzee and N. Shenn-Coetzee (Oxford and Providence, RI: Berghahn, 1995). Hanna, 'A Republic of Letters,' adopts an approach similar to my own, but the author finds in the letters a frankness and a determination to tell the truth which I believe was rarer than she suggests.

8 Patrick O'Farrell, *Letters from Irish Australia, 1825–1929* (Sydney: University of New South Wales Press and Belfast: Ulster Historical Foundation, 1984), 1–4.

9 Bacconnier, Minet, and Soler, *La Plume au Fusil*, 18–19.

10 Ibid., 17.

11 Ibid., 29.

12 Ibid., 19.

13 Jules Maurin, *Armée, Guerre, Société: Soldats languedociens, 1889–1919* (Paris: Sorbonne, 1982), 118.

14 Jean-François Kahn, ed., *Journal de Guerre d'un Juif Patriote, 1914–18* (Paris: Hachette, 1979), 285.

15 Service historique de l'Armée de Terre (SHAT), 16 N 292, Anonymous note of 21.5.1916; and 16 N 1424, 7th Army, report of 13.8.1916.

16 SHAT 16 N 1424, 7th Army, report of 14.5.1916.

17 SHAT 16 N 1424, 7th Army, report of 14.5.1916, quoting soldier to Madame L.B. in Tarn, 343rd Infantry Regiment, 8.5.1916.

18 SHAT 16 N 1553, Officier-interprète Laporte to Lt. Col. Zopff, 20.7.1917.

19 SHAT 16 N 292, *Rapport sur les échanges de correspondance entre marraines de guerre et filleuls*, by Commission de Contrôle Postal (CCP) de Pontarlier, 1.2.1916.
20 SHAT 16 N 292, Minister of War to C-in-C, 13.7.1916.
21 SHAT 16 N 1553, Officier-interprète Laporte to Lt. Col. Zopff, 26.12.1917, and enclosure.
22 SHAT 16 N 292, *Rapport sur les échanges de correspondance entre marraines de guerre et filleuls*, by CCP de Pontarlier, 1.2.1916.
23 SHAT 16 N 1380, note to Minister of War, 15.5.1919.
24 SHAT 16 N 292, *Rapport sur les échanges de correspondance entre marraines de guerre et filleuls*, by CCP de Pontarlier, 1.2.1916.
25 See Jeanneney, 'Les Archives des Commissions de Contrôle Postal aux Armées, 1916–1918; Liens, 'La Commission de Censure et la Commission de Contrôle Postal à Marseille'; and Cochet, 'L'Opinion et le moral.'
26 SHAT 16 N 1425, reports of March 1916.
27 SHAT 16 N 292, orders of 20.1 and 21.3.1916.
28 SHAT 16 N 1425, 7th Army, report of 3.9.1916.
29 SHAT 16 N 1381, Order of 28.6.1916. In 1916, an infantry regiment consisted of about 2,500 men.
30 SHAT 16 N 1380, Admin of CCP, report from Gare régulatrice, 4th Army, 3.10.1916, and Statistical summary for 10th Army, 2.10.1916.
31 Jeanneney, 'Les Archives,' 212, and Cochet, 'L'Opinion et le moral,' 56.
32 SHAT 16 N 1551 and 1552.
33 SHAT 16 N 1381, Note from GQG to all CCPs on 14.11.1917 ordering 'Il ne sera plus donné d'extraits ayant uniquement une valeur pittoresque. Dans les extraits, on ne devra citer que les faits intéressants en éliminant toutes les phrases superflues.'
34 SHAT 16 N 1554, Note sur l'Envoi des cartes postales illustrées, 9.2.1918.
35 SHAT 16 N 1551, lettres saisies.
36 SHAT 16 N 1381, rapport special, CCP de Beauvais, 20.2.1918.
37 SHAT 16 N 292, Note concernant la correspondance postale, 24.6.1916.
38 SHAT 16 N 1424, report of 25.6 to 8.7.1916.
39 Bacconnier, *Plume au fusil*, 25.
40 SHAT 16 N 1425, 100th Infantry Regiment, report of 24.3.1917; 16 N 1414, 214th Regiment, *sondage* of 2.2.1918.
41 SHAT 16 N 1414, report on foreign correspondence, 5–11.1.1918.
42 SHAT 16 N 1551, lettres saisies, Lauzier to Maria in Seine-et-Marne, 2.2.1917.
43 SHAT 16 N 1391, 2nd Army, anon extract cited in report of 18.10.1916.
44 Ephraïm Grenadou, *Grenadou, paysan français (propos receuillis par Alain Prévost)* (Paris: Rombaldi, 1980), 136, first published by Seuil in 1966.

45 Jacques Lovie, ed., *Poilus Savoyards (1913–1918): Chronique d'une famille taren-taise* (Chambéry: self-published, 1981).

46 Maurice Genevoix, *Ceux de 14* (Paris: Seuil, 1984), 125.

47 J.H. Lefebvre, *Verdun* (Paris: Durassié, 1961), cited by Cochet, 'L'Opinion et le moral,' 199–200.

48 Cochet, 'L'Opinion et le moral,' 46.

49 Bacconnier, *Plume au Fusil,* 23.

50 Ibid., 22.

51 Ibid., 43.

52 Ibid.

53 Ibid., 44.

54 Ibid.

55 SHAT 16 N 1424, 7th Army, report of 10.9.1916, letter of 5.9.1916.

56 Maurin, *Armée, Guerre, Société,* 668.

57 Georges Rigol, 'La Poste pendant la Guerre de 1914–1918,' *Revue des Postes et Télécommunications de France* 20.3 (May–June 1965), 32.

58 SHAT 16 N 1391, 2nd Army, *sondage special,* 8th Infantry Division, 13.7.1916.

59 SHAT 16 N 1391, 2nd Army, weekly report of 25.6.1916.

60 SHAT 16 N 1424, 7th Army, report of 21.5.1916, intercepted letter from soldier in 401st Infantry Regiment to a friend in the Hautes-Pyrénées, May 1916.

61 SHAT 16 N 1424, 7th Army, report of 9.7.1916.

62 SHAT, 2nd Army, 8.6.1916, quoted by Cochet, 'L'Opinion et le moral,' 455.

63 SHAT 16 N 1391, 2nd Army, weekly report, 20.10.1916.

64 Cochet, 'L'Opinion et le moral,' 460.

65 Weber, *Peasants into Frenchmen.*

66 Becker, *The Great War and the French People.*

67 On letters by third parties, see Cochet, 'L'Opinion et le moral,' 21.

68 Bacconnier, *Plume au fusil,* 20, 49, and 52–3.

69 Ibid., 64.

70 SHAT 16 N 1391, 2nd Army, *sondage spécial,* 11.7.1916.

71 SHAT 16 N 1551, lettres saisies, Louise to Louis Lemaire, 23rd Infantry Regiment, 1.2.1916.

72 Bacconnier, *Plume au fusil,* 47.

73 Marc Bloch, *Souvenirs de Guerre, 1914–1915* (Paris: cahiers des annales no. 26, 1969), 45.

74 Jean-Yves Naour, 'La Faute aux "Midis": la légende de la lâcheté des méridionaux au feu,' *Annales du Midi* 112.232 (Oct.–Dec. 2000), 499–515.

75 Khan, *Journal de Guerre,* 155.

76 Richard Cobb, *French and Germans, Germans and French* (Hanover and London: Brandeis University Press, 1983).

Appendix

1 Philarète Chasles, 'Statistique littéraire et intellectuelle de la France pendant l'année 1828,' *Revue de Paris* (1829): 191–243; David Bellos, 'Le Marché du livre à l'époque romantique: recherches et problèmes,' *Rfhl* 47.20 (1978): 647–60, and the same author's 'The *Bibliographie de la France* and its Sources,' *The Library*, 5th ser. 28 (1973): 64–7.
2 AN F18* II. 8 and 20.
3 Paris printers' declarations for 16 March 1847, 28 May 1847, 18 September 1847, and 27 January 1848.
4 AN F 18. 153.

Select Bibliography

This select bibliography lists works of importance for the history of reading and writing practices in France and Britain in the 'long nineteenth-century' (1815–1918). It also includes a few additional works referring to a later period or to other countries, which are included because they are of special interest to historians of reading and writing. More detailed references on specific topics can be found in the notes to individual chapters.

Allen, James Smith. *Popular French Romanticism, Authors, Readers and Books in the 19th Century*. Syracuse, NY: Syracuse University Press, 1981.

– *In the Public Eye: A History of Reading in Modern France, 1800–1940*. Princeton, NJ: Princeton University Press, 1991.

Altick, Richard D. *The English Common Reader: A Social History of the Mass Reading Public, 1800–1900*. Chicago: University of Chicago Press, 1957.

Bacconnier, Gérard, André Minet, and Louis Soler, eds. *La Plume au Fusil: Les poilus du Midi à travers leur correspondance*. Toulouse: Privat, 1985.

Barbier, Frédéric. *L'Empire du livre: Le livre imprimé et la construction de l'Allemagne contemporaine, 1815–1914*. Paris: Editions du Cerf, 1995.

Barton, David, and Nigel Hall, eds. *Letter Writing as a Social Practice*. Amsterdam: John Benjamins, 1999.

Bibliographie de la France [originally *Bibliographie de l'Empire français*]. Ed. Pillet. 1st ser., 45 vols. Paris, 1810–56.

Bogacz, Ted. 'A "Tyranny of Words": Language, Poetry and Anti-Modernism in England in the First World War.' *JMH* 58.3 (1986): 643–68.

Bonnat, Jean-Louis, et al, eds. *Les Correspondances: Problématique et économie d'un genre littéraire (Actes du colloque de Nantes 1982)*. Nantes: Université de Nantes Press, 1983.

Bossis, Mireille, and Charles A. Porter, eds. *L'Epistolarité à travers les siècles: Actes du colloque de Cérisy*. Stuttgart: Franz Steiner, 1990.

Bourdieu, Pierre. *La Distinction: Critique sociale du jugement.* Paris: Minuit, 1979.

Brombert, Victor. *The Hidden Reader: Stendhal, Balzac, Hugo, Baudelaire, Flaubert.* Cambridge, MA: Harvard University Press, 1988.

Bulletin de la Société Franklin, journal des bibliothèques populaires, 1868–1933.

Bunkers, Suzanne L, and Cynthia A. Huff, eds. *Inscribing the Daily: Critical Essays on Women's Diaries.* Amherst. University of Massachusetts Press, 1996.

Burnett, John, David Vincent, and David Mayall, eds. *The Autobiography of the Working Class: An Annotated, Critical Bibliography.* 2 vols. Brighton, UK: Harvester, 1984–7.

Chartier, Anne-Marie, and Jean Hébrard. *Discours sur la lecture, 1880–1980.* Paris: Bibliothèque publique d'information, Centre Georges Pompidou, 1989.

Chartier, Roger, ed. *Pratiques de la lecture.* Marseilles: Rivages, 1985.

– *La Correspondance: Les usages de la lettre au XIXe siècle.* Paris: Fayard, 1991.

– *Histoire de la lecture: Un bilan de recherches.* Paris: IMEC, Editions de la Maison des Sciences de l'Homme, 1995.

Chartier, Roger, and Henri-Jean Martin, eds. *Histoire de l'Edition française.* Vol. 3. Paris: Promodis, 1985; and Paris. Fayard/Cercle de la librairie, 1990.

Chotard-Lioret, Caroline. 'Correspondre en 1900, le plus public des actes privés, ou la manière de gérer un réseau de parenté.' *Ethnologie française,* new ser., 15.1 (1985): 63–72.

Clark, Linda. *Schooling the Daughters of Marianne: Textbooks and Socialization of Girls in Modern French Primary Schools.* Albany: State University of New York Press, 1984.

Cuvillier, A. *Un journal d'ouvriers:* L'Atelier, *1840–1850.* Paris: Félix Alcan, 1914.

Darmon, Jean-Jacques *Le Colportage de Librairie en France sous le second Empire: Grands colporteurs et culture populaire.* Paris: Plon, 1972.

– 'Lecture rurale et lecture urbaine.' *Europe* 542 (1974): 63–8.

Dauphin, Cécile. 'Pour une histoire de la correspondance familiale.' *Romantisme* 90 (1995): 89–99.

Dauphin, Cécile, et al, eds. *Ces Bonnes Lettres: Une correspondance familiale au XIXe siècle.* Paris: Albin Michel, 1995.

De Certeau, Michel. *L'Invention du Quotidien* [*The Practice of Everyday Life*]. Vol. 1, *Arts de Faire.* Paris: Gallimard, 1990.

Dekker, Rudolf, ed. *Autobiographical Writing in Its Social Context since the Middle Ages.* Hilversum: Verloren, 2002.

DeMarco, Eileen S. *Reading and Riding: Hachette's Railroad Bookstore Network in 19th-Century France.* Bethlehem, PA: Lehigh University Press, 2006.

Devos, Roger, and Charles Josten. *Moeurs et coûtumes de la Savoie du Nord au 19e siècle: L'enquête de Mgr Rendu.* Annecy and Grenoble: Centre alpin et rhodanien d'ethnologie, 1978.

Didier, Béatrice. *Le Journal intime*. Paris: Presses universitaires de France, 1976.

Dolfi, Anna, ed. *'Journal intime' e letteratura moderna*. Rome: Bulzani, 1989.

Duveau, Georges. *La Pensée Ouvrière sur l'éducation pendant la Seconde République et le Second Empire*. Paris: Domat Montchrestien, 1948.

Engelsing, Rolf. *Der Burger als Leser: Leser geschichte in Deutschland, 1500–1800*. Stuttgart: Metzlersche Verlagsbuchhandlung, 1974.

Fabre, Daniel, ed. *Ecritures ordinaires*. Paris: POL/Centre Georges Pompidou, 1993.

Felkay, Nicole. *Balzac et ses éditeurs, 1822–1837: Essai sur la librairie romantique*. Paris: Promodis/Cercle de la Librairie, 1987.

Finkelstein, David, and Alistair McCreery, eds. *The Book History Reader*. London: Routledge, 2002.

Fish, Stanley. *Is There a Text in This Class? The Authority of Interpretive Communities*. Cambridge, MA: Harvard University Press, 1980.

Fleury, M., and A. Valmary. 'Les Progrès de l'instruction élémentaire de Louis XIV à Napoléon III, d'après l'enquête de Louis Maggiolo (1877–9).' *Population* 12 (1957): 71–92.

Flint, Kate. *The Woman Reader, 1837–1914*, Oxford: Clarendon, 1993.

Foley, Susan. '"J'avais tant besoin d'être aimée ... par correspondance": Les discours de l'amour dans la correspondance de Léonie Léon et Léon Gambetta, 1872–1882.' *Clio – histoire, femmes, et sociétés* 24 (2006): 149–69.

Furet, François, and Jacques Ozouf, eds. *Lire et écrire: L'alphabétisation des français de Calvin à Jules Ferry*. 2 vols. Paris: Editions de Minuit, 1977.

Furet, François, and W. Sachs. 'La Croissance de l'alphabétisation en France, 18e–19e siècle.' *AESC* 29 (1974): 714–37.

Fussell, Paul. *The Great War and Modern Memory*. Oxford: Oxford University Press, 1977.

Girard, Alain. 'Le Triomphe de *La Cuisinière bourgeoise*. Livres culinaires, cuisine et société en France au 17e et 18e siècle.' *Rhmc* 24 (1977): 497–523.

Gosselin, Ronald. *Les Almanachs républicains: Traditions révolutionnaires et culture politique des masses populaires de Paris, 1840–1851*. Paris: L'Harmattan, 1992.

Grassi, Marie-Claire. 'Des Lettres qui parlent d'amour.' *Romantisme* 68 (1990): 23–32.

Hall, David D. 'The Uses of Literacy in New England, 1600–1850.' In *Printing and Society in Early America*, ed. William L. Joyce et al, 1–47. Worcester MA: American Antiquarian Society, 1983.

Hanna, Martha. 'A Republic of Letters: The Epistolary Tradition in France during World War 1.' *American Historical Review* 108.5 (2003): 1338–61.

Hassenforder, Jean. *Développement comparé des bibliothèques publiques en France, en*

Grande-Bretagne et aux Etats-Unis, dans la seconde moitié du 19ᵉ siècle, 1850–1914. Paris: Cercle de la Librairie, 1967.

Hélias, Pierre-Jakez. *Le Cheval d'Orgeuil: Mémoires d'un breton au pays bigouden.* 2 vols. Geneva: Famot, 1979.

Hoggart, Richard. *The Uses of Literacy: Aspects of Working-Class Life.* Harmondsworth, UK: Penguin, 1958.

Hooke-Demarle, Marie-Claire. 'Reading and Writing in Germany.' In *A History of Women.* Vol. 4, *Emerging Feminism from Revolution to World War,* ed. Geneviève Fraisse and Michelle Perrot, 145–65. Cambridge, MA: Belknap, 1993.

Huet, M.-H. *L'Histoire des voyages extraordinaires: Essai sur l'oeuvre de Jules Verne.* Paris: Lettres modernes, 1973.

Hurt, J.S. *Elementary Schooling and the Working Classes, 1860–1918.* London: Routledge and Kegan Paul, 1979.

Iknayan, Marguerite. 'The Fortunes of *Gil Blas* during the Romantic Period.' *French Review* 31 (1958): 370–7.

– *The Idea of the Novel in France: The Critical Reaction, 1815–1848.* Geneva: Droz, 1961.

Iser, Wolfgang. *The Implied Reader: Patterns of Communication in Prose Fiction from Bunyan to Beckett.* Baltimore: Johns Hopkins University Press, 1974.

Jan, Isabelle. *La Littérature Enfantine.* Paris: Editions Ouvrières, 1977.

Jeanneney, Jean-Noël. 'Les Archives des Commissions de Contrôle Postal aux Armées, 1916–1918: Une source précieuse pour l'histoire contemporaine de l'opinion et des mentalités.' *Rhmc* 15 (1968): 209–33.

Kalifa, Dominique. *L'Encre et du sang: Récits de crime et société à la Belle Epoque.* Paris: Fayard, 1995.

Kaplan, Steven J., and Cynthia J. Koepp, eds. *Work in France: Representations, Meaning, Organization and Practice.* Ithaca: Cornell University Press, 1986.

Kerr, David S. *Caricature and French Political Culture, 1830–1848: Charles Philipon and the Illustrated Press.* Oxford: Clarendon, 2000.

Kroen, Sheryl. *Politics and Theater: The Crisis of Legitimacy in Restoration France, 1815–1830.* Berkeley and Los Angeles: University of California Press, 2000.

Lejeune, Philippe. *Moi Aussi.* Paris: Seuil, 1975.

– *Le Pacte autobiographique.* Paris: Seuil, 1975.

– *On Autobiography,* ed. P.J. Eakin. Minneapolis: University of Minnesota Press, 1989.

– *'Cher Cahier ...': Témoignages sur le journal personnel.* Paris: Gallimard, 1989.

– *Le Moi des demoiselles: Enquête sur le journal de jeune fille.* Paris: Seuil, 1993.

Leleu, Michèle. *Les Journaux intimes.* Paris: Presses universitaires de France, 1952.

Liens, Georges. 'La Commission de Censure et la Commission de Contrôle

Postal à Marseille pendant la première guerre mondiale.' *Rhmc* 18 (1971): 649–67.

Liljewall, Britt. '"Self-written Lives" or Why did Peasants Write Autobiographies?' In *Writing Peasants: Studies on Peasant Literacy in Early Modern Northern Europe*, ed. Klaus-Joachim Lorenzen-Schmidt and Bjørn Poulsen, 210–38. Odense: Landbohistorisk Selskab, 2002.

Lyons, Martyn. 'The Audience for Romanticism: Walter Scott in France, 1815–51.' *European History Quarterly* 14.1 (1984): 21–46.

– 'Oral Culture and Rural Community in Nineteenth-Century France: The *veillée d'hiver.*' *Australian Journal of French Studies* 23.1 (1986): 102–14.

– *Le Triomphe du Livre; Une histoire sociologique de la lecture dans la France du 19e siècle.* Paris: Promodis, 1987.

– 'Fires of Expiation: Book-Burnings and Catholic Missions in Restoration France.' *FH* 10.2 (June 1996): 240–66.

– 'New Readers in the Nineteenth Century: Women, Children and Workers.' In *A History of Reading in the West*, ed. Guglielmo Cavallo and Roger Chartier, 313–44. Oxford: Polity, 1999.

– 'Love Letters and Writing Practices: On *Ecritures Intimes* in the Nineteenth Century.' *Journal of Family History* 24:2 (April 1999): 232–9.

– *Readers and Society in Nineteenth-Century France: Workers, Women, Peasants.* Basingstoke, UK: Palgrave, 2001.

– 'La culture littéraire des travailleurs: Autobiographies ouvrières dans l'Europe du XIXe siècle.' *Annales: Histoire, sciences sociales* 56.4–5 (June–Oct. 2001): 927–46.

– 'French Soldiers and Their Correspondence: Towards a History of Writing Practices in the First World War.' *FH* 17.1 (2003): 79–95.

– 'La experiencia lectora y escritora de las mujeres trabajadoras en la Europa del siglo XIX.' *Cultura Escrita y Sociedad* 1.1 (2005): 158–76.

– *Ordinary Writings, Personal Narratives.* Bern: Peter Lang, 2007.

Lyons, Martyn, & Lucy Taksa. *Australian Readers Remember: An Oral History of Reading, 1890–1930.* Melbourne: Oxford University Press, 1992.

– '"If Mother caught us reading ...!": Impressions of the Australian Woman Reader, 1890–1933.' *Australian Cultural History* 11 (1992): 39–50.

Martin, Henri-Jean. 'Le Sacre de Gutenberg.' *Revue de Synthèse.* 4th ser., 1–2 (Jan.–June 1992): 15–27.

Mauger, Gérard. 'Ecrits, lecteurs, lectures.' *Genèses* 34 (March 1999): 144–61.

Milo, D. 'La Bourse mondiale de la traduction: Un baromètre culturel?' *AESC* 39 (1984): 92–115.

Mollier, Jean-Yves. *Michel et Calmann Lévy, ou la naissance de l'édition moderne, 1836–91.* Paris: Calmann-Lévy, 1984.

– *L'Argent et les lettres: Histoire du capitalisme d'édition, 1880–1920*. Paris: Fayard, 1988.
– ed. *Le Commerce de la Librairie en France au XIXe siècle, 1789–1914*. Paris: IMEC/ Maison des Sciences de l'Homme, 1997.
– *Louis Hachette, 1800–1864, le fondateur d'un empire*. Paris: Fayard, 1999.
– *Le Camelot et la rue: Politique et démocratie au tournant des XIXe et XXe siècles*. Paris: Fayard, 2004.
– ed. *Histoires de lecture, XIXe–XXe siècles*. Bernay: Société d'histoire de la lecture, 2005.
Nora, Pierre, ed. *Les Lieux de Mémoire*. 3 vols. Paris: Quarto-Gallimard, 1997.
Oliveiro, Isabelle. *L'Invention de la collection: De la diffusion de la littérature et des savoirs à la formation du citoyen au XIXe siècle*. Paris: IMEC/ Maison des Sciences de l'Homme, 1999.
Orecchioni, Pierre. 'Eugène Sue: Mesure d'un succès.' *Europe* 60.643–4 (1982): 157–66.
Parent-Lardeur, Françoise. *Les cabinets de lecture: La lecture publique sous la Restauration*. Paris: Payot, 1982.
Parinet, Elisabeth. 'Les bibliothèques de gare, un nouveau réseau pour le livre.' *Romantisme* 80 (1993): 95–106.
Penloup, Marie-Claude. *La Tentation du littéraire*. Paris: Didier, 2000.
Piniès, Jean-Pierre. 'Du choc culturel à l'ethnocide: La pénétration du livre dans les campagnes languedociennes du 17e au 19e siècles.' *Folklore* 44.3 (1981): 1–24.
Ponsard, Nathalie. 'Lectures ouvrières au XXe siècle.' In *Histoires de lecture, 19e–20e siècles*, ed. Jean-Yves Mollier, 141–50. Bernay: Société d'histoire de la lecture, 2005.
– 'Quand l'histoire socioculturelle est aussi histoire orale: L'exemple des pratiques de lectures dans une communauté d'ouvriers des années trente à nos jours.' *Genèses* 48 (2002): 100–14.
Purvis, June. 'The Double Burden of Class and Gender in the Schooling of Working-Class Girls in 19th-Century England, 1800–1870.' In *Schools, Teachers and Teaching*, ed. L. Barton and S. Walker, 106–10. Lewes: Falmer, 1981.
– 'The Experience of Schooling for Working-Class Boys and Girls in 19th-Century England.' In *Defining the Curriculum: Histories and Ethnographies*, ed. I.F. Goodson and S.J. Ball, 89–115. Lewes: Falmer, 1984.
Quéffelec, Lise. 'Le Lecteur du roman comme lectrice: Stratégies romanesques et stratégies critiques sous la Monarchie de Juillet.' *Romantisme* 16.53 (1986): 9–21.
Radway, Janice. *Reading the Romance: Women, Patriarchy and Popular Literature*. London: Verso, 1987.

Ragon, Michel. *Histoire de la littérature prolétarienne en France*. Paris: Albin Michel, 1974.

Raven, James, et al, eds. *The Practice and Representation of Reading in England*. Cambridge: Cambridge University Press, 1996.

Richter, Nöé *La lecture et ses institutions: La lecture populaire, 1700–1918*. Le Mans: Plein Chant, 1987.

– *La Conversion du mauvais lecteur et la naissance de la lecture publique*. Marigné: Editions de la Queue du Chat, 1992.

Robin, Christian, ed. *Un Editeur et son siècle: Pierre-Jules Hetzel, 1814–1886*. Paris: ACL, 1988.

Rose, Jonathan 'Rereading the English Common Reader: A Preface to the History of Audiences.' *Journal of the History of Ideas* 53.1 (1992): 47–70.

– *The Intellectual Life of the British Working Classes*. New Haven, CT: Yale University Press, 2001.

Savart, Claude. 'La Liberté de la librairie et l'évolution du réseau des libraires.' *Rfhl* 22 (1979): 91–121.

Simonet-Tenant, Francoise. *Le Journal intime: Genre littéraire et écriture ordinaire*. Paris: Téraèdre, 2004.

Soriano, Marc. *Jules Verne [le cas Verne]*. Paris: Julliard, 1978.

Tannenbaum, Edward. 'The Beginnings of Bleeding-Heart Liberalism: Eugène Sue, *Les Mystères de Paris*.' *Comparative Studies in History and Society* 16 (1981): 491–507.

Thabault, Roger. *Education and Change in a Village Community: Mazières-en-Gâtine, 1848–1918*. London: Routledge and Kegan Paul, 1971.

Thiesse, Anne-Marie. 'Imprimés du pauvre, livres de fortune.' *Romantisme* 43 (1984): 91–109.

– 'Mutations et permanences de la culture populaire: La lecture à la Belle Epoque.' *AESC* 39.1 (1984): 70–91.

– *Le Roman du quotidien: Lecteurs et lectures populaires à la Belle Epoque*. Paris: Le Chemin Vert, 1984.

Touchard, Jean. *La Gloire de Béranger*. 2 vols. Paris: A. Colin, 1968.

Traugott, Mark, ed. *The French Worker: Autobiographies from the Early Industrial Era*. Berkeley, CA: University of California Press, 1993.

Varry, Dominique, ed. *Histoire des bibliothèques françaises*. Vol. 3, *Les bibliothèques de la Révolution et du XIXe siècle, 1789–1914*. Paris: Promodis/Cercle de la Librairie, 1991.

Vierne, Simone. *Jules Verne et le roman initiatique: Contribution à l'étude de l'imaginaire*. Lille: Presses de l'Université de Lille, 1972.

Vincent, David. *Bread, Knowledge and Freedom: A Study of Nineteenth-Century Working-Class Autobiography*. London: Methuen, 1982.

– *Literacy and Popular Culture in England, 1750–1914.* Cambridge: Cambridge University Press, 1989.
– ed. *Testaments of Radicalism: Memoirs of Working-Class Politicians, 1790–1885.* London: Europa, 1977.
Webb, R.K. *The British Working-Class Reader, 1790–1848: Literacy and Social Tension.* London: Allen and Unwin, 1987.
Weber, Eugen. *Peasants into Frenchmen: The Modernisation of Rural France, 1870–1914.* London: Chatto and Windus, 1977.

Index

Adams, William E., 130, 133
Agulhon, Maurice, historian, 148
Allier department, 85, 141
almanacs, 28–9, 42, 49, 50, 55, 61, 145
Alsace, 70, 102, 172, 195
Amiel, Henri-Frédéric, 170, 181–2, 183
Ancien Regime book trade, 44–6
Angers. *See* Maine-et-Loire department
Angers, David d', sculptor, 97, 100, 101, 105, 106
Annales School, 6
Anquetil, *Histoire de France*, 19, 21, 23, 24–5, 27
anticlericalism, 29, 35, 50, 67, 73–6, 77, 84, 90–1, 104, 107, 113, 114
anti-Semitism, 59, 61, 123
Arabian Nights, Tales of. See Mille et Une Nuits
Ardèche department, 152, 160
Ariège department, 51
Association des Bons Livres, 78
Audoux, Marguerite, 119
Australian readers, 152–3, 157–9, 160, 161, 162, 163, 164
autobiographies, 7, 8, 9, 111–38, 151, 154, 159
autodidacts, 111–38

Avignon. *See* Vaucluse department

Balzac, Honoré de, 15, 18, 28, 33, 40, 125
Barthélemy, *Voyage du jeune Anacharsis*, 20, 21, 22, 23, 24, 26, 36
Bashkirtseff, Marie, 170, 183
battle of the books, 11, 35, 67, 77–8, 84, 85
Baylac, Jean-Pierre, 180–1
Bechtel, Guy, historian, 94
Becker, Jean-Jacques, historian, 184, 196
Bédé, Jacques-Etienne, 133, 134
Belgium, 19, 202, 204–5
Béranger, 18, 22, 23, 25, 26, 27, 29–30, 55, 82
Bérenger, *La Morale en Action*, 19, 20, 22, 23, 24, 25, 26, 38, 39, 41
bestsellers, 6, 11, 15–42, 79, 201–5
Bezer, James, 115
Bible, 33–4, 43, 94, 95, 96, 120, 121, 129, 145, 156, 157; family, 120, 157
Bibliographie de la France, 16–17, 19, 32, 34, 35, 36, 38, 79, 82, 201–5
Bibliothèque bleue. See colportage literature

Bonapartism, 28, 29, 30, 32, 55, 96, 144, 147
bons livres, campaign for, 74, 78
book production, 3–4, 6, 16, 92, 96
bookshops, 6, 43–62
Bordeaux, 51–2, 69, 78
Bossuet, 78, 105–6
Bourdieu, Pierre, sociologist, 9, 112, 128
Bourges diocese, 68, 69, 84, 85
Brame, Caroline, 178–9, 180
Brest, 74, 75
brevet de libraire, 49
Brillat-Savarin, *Physiologie du goût*, 27, 28
Brittany, 49, 51, 52, 55, 74, 85, 88, 141, 146, 172, 197
Brocher, Victorine, 126–7, 131–2, 135
Buffon, 20, 22, 23, 34, 35, 36, 45
Bunyan, John, *Pilgrim's Progress*, 125, 129
Burn, James, 126, 136
Burt, Thomas, 130
Byron, 18, 23, 34, 41, 170

Cabet, Etienne, *Voyage en Icarie*, 27, 113
cabinets de lecture, 48, 127
Calmann-Lévy, publisher, 47. *See also* Lévy, Michel
Carlyle, Thomas, 125
catechisms, 37, 40, 41, 42, 43, 61, 145
censorship, 44, 45, 55, 65–91, 97, 105, 120, 121; postal, 172–3, 184–99
centre (region of France), 51, 52, 55, 69, 85
Certeau, Michel de, sociologist, 8, 9
Charpentier, publisher, 4, 46, 83, 204

Chartier, Roger, historian, 7, 9, 11
Chartism, 116, 125, 128, 130, 133
Chateaubriand, 18, 23, 24, 25, 28, 29, 125
Cholvy, Gérard, historian, 66, 69, 73, 78, 79
classicism, seventeenth-century, 16, 34, 40, 42, 125
Cochet, Annick, historian, 185, 189, 192
colportage literature, 37, 43, 48, 55–6, 61, 139
communist reading, 155–6
communities of readers, 10, 125, 137, 155–8, 162
Constant, Benjamin, 77
conversion of the bad reader, 116, 123
Cooper, Thomas, 116–17
Corneille, Pierre, 34, 97
correspondence, 9, 167–9, 171–3, 173–5, 184–99; family, 167–8, 174, 175–7, 182, 185–6, 191, 192
Corsica, 51, 52, 55, 197
Cottin, Sophie, 19, 21, 25, 30–1, 32, 127
Creuse department, 55, 88, 136–7, 141
Cuisinière bourgeoise, 21, 23, 39

dancing, 66, 72, 74, 75, 89, 142–3, 145, 146, 147
Darnton, Robert, historian, 6, 10, 11, 46, 76, 101
Dauphin, Cécile, historian, 173, 176
Defoe, Daniel, *Robinson Crusoe*, 22, 24, 25, 26, 27, 34, 36, 40, 41, 45, 121, 126, 201
diary. See *journal intime*
Dickens, Charles, 126, 160, 163

dictionaries, 33
Diderot, 35, 77, 81, 86, 89
Didier, Béatrice, literary critic, 177
Didot, printer, 35, 47, 100
Don Quixote, 20, 22, 26, 36, 65, 66, 88, 90, 99, 203
Dreyfus affair, 59, 61
Ducray-Duminil, 20, 26, 27, 32, 134
Dumas, Alexandre, 15, 18, 27, 31, 32, 33, 46, 59, 61; *Le Comte de Monte Cristo*, 27; *Les Trois Mousquetaires*, 27, 43
Dumay, Jean-Baptiste, 50
Duruy, Victor, 18–19

east (region of France), 38, 43, 51, 52, 73. *See also* Alsace; Strasbourg
education, 4, 43, 46, 62, 92, 112, 113, 114–15, 116, 122, 135–6, 138, 155, 186, 196, 199
educational books, 36–7, 38, 40, 41, 46, 47, 49
Eisenstein, Elizabeth, historian, 92, 97
Engelsing, Rolf, historian, 156–7
Enlightenment, 11, 16, 34, 35, 37, 39, 76–84, 85, 89, 96, 97, 104, 106, 136
epistolary pact, 173–5
Erasmus, 97, 106
Erckmann-Chatrian, 15

Fabre, Daniel, ethnologist, 145
faits divers, 28, 57, 144
Farningham, Marianne, 120–1, 122, 131
Fayard, publisher, 4, 46
Fénelon, *Télémaque*, 20, 21, 22, 23, 24, 25, 27, 34, 36, 40, 41, 78, 204
Fish, Stanley, literary critic, 10, 125, 155

Flammarion, publisher, 4, 46, 57
Flaubert, Gustave, 15, 61
Fleury, *Catéchisme historique*, 19, 20, 21, 22, 23, 24, 25, 27, 34, 37, 40, 41
Florian, 20, 21, 22, 23, 25, 26, 27, 34, 36, 38, 41
Foley (formerly Grogan), Susan, historian, 120, 175
Franco-Prussian War, 141, 176
Frayssinous, abbé, 77–8
French Revolution of 1789, 11, 44, 45, 52, 68, 70–1, 73, 76, 84, 85, 89, 90, 96, 141, 172, 191

Garnier brothers, publishers, 47
Gauny, Gabriel, 115
Genevoix, Maurice, novelist, 192
Gerson, Stéphane, historian, 99, 102, 107
Gimeno Blay, Francisco, historian, 65–6, 67, 89
Ginzburg, Carlo, historian, 8
Grenadou, Ephraïm, 191, 195
Grenoble, 71, 72, 78, 86
Guérin, Eugénie de, 177, 181, 183
Guillaumin, *La Vie d'un Simple*, 146, 149
Guizot law of 1833, 37, 46, 99
Gutenberg, Johannes, 3, 92–107

Hachette, Louis, publisher, 37, 46–7, 56, 57, 92, 204
Hall, David, historian, 156
Hardy, Thomas, *Tess of the D'Urbervilles*, 121
Haute-Marne department, 141, 143, 145
Helvétius, 71, 77, 82, 86, 89
Hetzel, Jacques-Louis, publisher, 57, 58, 59

Hoggart, Richard, sociologist, 154
Hopkinson, James, 129
Hugo, Victor, 4, 18, 20, 31, 32, 33, 40,
    104, 125, 126, 127, 161, 169; *Les
    Misérables*, 127; *Notre-Dame de Paris*,
    24, 27, 31, 43, 104, 125

illiteracy, 5, 49, 113, 114, 121, 122,
    152, 161, 187, 196
imperialism, 59–60
intensive reading, 156–7

Jane Eyre, 121–2
Jesuits, 30, 66–7, 69, 75, 88, 114
Johns, Adrian, historian, 96
Johnston, Ellen, 134–5
journal intime, 7, 9, 167–71, 177–8,
    178–83
July Monarchy, 20, 30, 36–7, 47, 93,
    96–7, 107
Jussieu, *Simon de Nantua*, 24, 26

Kock, Paul de, 24, 32, 123

Laffitte, Jacques, 131, 136
La Fontaine, *Fables*, 20, 21, 22, 23, 24,
    25, 26–7, 34, 36, 40, 41, 42
Lamartine, Alphonse de, 18, 22, 24,
    27, 29, 33, 34, 38, 40, 41, 77, 92, 99–
    100, 141, 181
Lamennais, *Paroles d'un Croyant*, 18,
    24, 28, 33, 132
Languedoc. *See* southwest
Lascases, *Mémorial de Sainte-Hélène*, 22,
    26
Laval diocese, 68, 71, 84, 85, 87
Lejeune, Philippe, 9, 132–3, 169,
    170–1, 173, 178, 183
Lenéru, Marie, 177–8, 180, 183
Léon, Léonie, 175

Leroy, Eugène, *Le Moulin du Frau*,
    141, 144, 145, 146
Lesage, *Gil Blas*, 18, 20, 21, 22, 23, 24,
    25, 26, 35, 88
Lettres d'Héloïse et d'Abelard, 22, 25, 33
Le Verrier, Lucile, 168–9, 179–80
Lévy, Michel, publisher, 4, 46. *See also*
    Calmann-Lévy
Liaisons Dangereuses, 174
libraries, public, 4, 6, 19, 48, 121, 164,
    181
Limoges. *See* Creuse department
literacy rates, 4, 5, 6, 11, 43, 49, 52,
    83, 167, 185, 187
Loire valley, 68, 69, 87, 172
London, Jack, 156
Loti, Pierre, 15, 34
love letters, 167, 173–5
Lovett, William, 130
Luther, Martin, 95, 102, 104–6
Lyon, 38, 52, 96, 106, 113, 114

Mâconnais, 141, 142, 143, 145, 146,
    148
magazines, 55, 58, 158, 160, 188
Maggiolo line, 52, 55
Maine-et-Loire department, 17, 29,
    49
Mainz, 92, 94, 103, 104
Mandrou, Robert, historian, 139–40,
    145, 148
marraines de guerre, 187–8
Marseille, 71, 74
Martin, Henri-Jean, historian, 9, 94,
    104
Massif Central, 49, 55, 172
Massillon, *Petit carême*, 19, 20, 21, 22,
    26, 37, 41, 71
Meunier, Arsène, 67, 126
Michel, Louise, 141, 146, 181

Michelet, Jules, 27, 29
Mille et Une Nuits, 19, 25, 26, 27
Milton, John, 97, 117, 125
Mitchell, Hannah, 113, 118–19, 122
Molière, 20, 21, 23, 24, 26, 34, 40, 97; *Tartuffe*, 75, 76
Mollier, Jean-Yves, historian, 28, 37, 61
Montesquieu, 35, 97, 106
Montpellier, 51, 70, 73, 101
Mornet, Daniel, historian, 35
Moronval, printer, 37, 38, 204

Nadaud, Martin, 96, 136–7
Nancy, 38, 69
Napoleon, 16, 28, 29, 96; *See also* Bonapartism
Nevers diocese, 68, 69, 85
newspapers, 3, 10, 18, 32, 45, 49, 56–7, 61, 62, 67, 76, 77, 89, 96–7, 105, 111, 115, 117, 123, 124, 126, 133, 145, 149, 156, 158–9, 160, 162–3, 190, 198; cartoons, 96–7. *See also* press freedom
Nord department. *See* north (region of France)
Normandy, 51, 52, 71
north (region of France), 17, 43, 51, 52, 172, 198
novels, 4, 15, 16, 17–18, 30–3, 41, 43, 44, 45, 46, 48, 50, 57–61, 88, 89, 115, 121, 122, 123, 124–7, 134–5, 137, 153, 156, 171, 203; crime, 156; English, 45 (*see also* Scott, Walter); picaresque, 35 (*see also* Lesage); romance, 152, 155, 158; of sensibility, 35, 40. See also *roman-feuilleton*

Orecchioni, Pierre, historian, 18, 31–2

pamphlets, 28, 45, 61, 67, 93, 101
Panckoucke, publisher, 45–6, 47
Paris, 16, 17, 19, 28, 29, 31, 35, 37, 38, 40–2, 48, 51, 52, 74, 77–8, 83, 90, 96–7, 100, 101, 106, 114, 115, 124, 131, 132, 134, 136–7, 152, 169, 170–1, 179, 188, 190, 193, 195, 198, 202, 203
Paris Commune, 126, 131–2
Passerini, Luisa, historian, 154
peasants' reading, 4, 18–19, 29, 43, 57, 61, 139–50, 152, 160, 181
peasants' writing, 5, 119, 180–1, 195–6
Pellico, Sylvio, *Mes Prisons*, 24, 25, 26, 33
Penloup, Marie-Claude, educationalist, 178, 183
Penn, Margaret, 121–2
Perdiguier, Agricol, 136
Périgord, 141, 144
Perrault, *Contes des fées*, 20, 21, 22, 24, 25, 26, 27, 34, 40, 41
Pigault-Lebrun, 15, 18, 32, 82
Pinckney, David, historian, 30
poetry, 33, 41, 50, 112, 117, 127, 128, 137, 163
Ponsard, Nathalie, historian, 152, 155–6, 160, 162
Popp, Adelheid, 122–4
Postal Control Commission, 184, 185, 188–91
postal service, 171–2, 193, 194
postcards, 188–90
post-mortem inventories, 6, 151
press freedom, 28, 45, 89, 97, 102, 105
printers' declarations, 16, 17, 19, 33, 38, 79, 201–5
printing, invention of, 92–5, 96, 102, 103, 105, 107

Privat, Edouard, publisher, 49
Protestantism, 70, 75, 95, 102, 104,
    105, 106, 120, 121, 125, 129, 156–7,
    158
Provence, 6, 198
publishing industry, 44–5, 47, 55,
    203
Pyrénées, 52, 75, 172, 180–1

Racine, 20, 21, 23, 25, 26, 27, 34, 41, 97
Radway, Janice, historian, 7, 10, 152,
    155, 158, 162
railway bookstalls, 47, 56, 57, 92
reading aloud, 113, 121, 124, 139,
    145, 147, 148, 157, 162, 163, 173,
    176, 177, 186
reception theory, 7, 153
religious books, 37, 40, 41, 50, 78,
    117, 126, 156. *See also* Bible; cate-
    chisms; Fleury; Massillon
Rémusat, Charles de, 83–4
Renaissance, 95, 97, 99
Renan, Ernest, 68, 88
Rennes, 70, 72
Restoration, Bourbon, of 1815–30, 7,
    18, 20, 29, 30, 31, 35, 37, 50, 55, 65–
    91
Revolution of 1789. *See* French Revo-
    lution of 1789
Revolution of 1830, 30, 77, 90–1, 96,
    104, 105
Revolution of 1848, 4, 16–17, 18, 28,
    30, 55, 105, 132, 141
Reybaud, *Jérôme Paturot*, 19, 26, 27
Rhône valley, 43, 52, 172
Richter, Noé, historian, 116, 123
roman-feuilleton, 17, 31, 32, 33, 46, 55,
    161, 162
romanticism, 11, 16, 18, 33, 41, 42,
    82, 127, 134

Rose, Jonathan, historian, 111, 127
Rouen, 74, 152, 155, 178
Rousseau, Jean-Jacques, 21, 22, 23,
    34, 35, 40, 67, 71, 76–84, 86, 87, 88,
    89, 96, 99, 125; *La Nouvelle Héloïse*,
    24, 25, 35, 40, 77, 82
Rouvière, *La Médecine sans médecin*,
    22, 39–40
Ruskin, John, 125

Saint-Ouen, *Histoire de France*, 19, 23,
    24, 25, 26–7, 36–7
Saint-Pierre, Bernardin de, *Paul et Vir-
    ginie*, 21, 23, 24, 26, 27, 34, 35
Saint-Simonians, 115, 119–20, 127
Sand, George, 18, 33, 168, 170
Sarthe department, 71, 74, 194
Savoy, 140, 141–2, 145, 146, 147, 148,
    192
Schmid, *Contes*, 19, 20, 25, 27, 38–9
Scott, Walter, 15, 18, 19, 23, 24, 26,
    31, 32, 33, 34, 40, 61, 134–5
Second Empire, 32, 39, 47, 48, 50, 51,
    55, 118, 132, 179
Seine-et-Oise department, 51, 203
serialized fiction. See *roman-feuilleton*
Sevrin, abbé, historian, 66, 67
Shakespeare, 61, 97, 117, 121, 127,
    160, 163
socialism, 5, 31, 113, 114, 119–20,
    122–4, 125, 127, 185. *See also* Cabet,
    Etienne; Saint-Simonians
southern crescent, 43, 52
southwest (region of France), 43, 51,
    52, 75, 141, 142, 144, 145, 146,
    198
Staël, Germaine de, 18, 21, 25, 127
Stendhal, *Le Rouge et le Noir*, 4, 15, 18,
    19, 32–3, 169, 170
Strasbourg, 92–107

Sue, Eugène, 15, 18, 27, 31, 32, 33, 46, 55, 61, 125, 203; *Le Juif errant*, 25, 27, 30, 31, 32; *Les Mystères de Paris*, 26, 27, 31, 32
Sunday schools, 115, 121, 129, 131

Tasso, *Jérusalem délivrée*, 19, 21, 22, 23, 24, 25, 26, 33, 41
Tchaikovsky, 173–4
Thabault, Roger, 49
Thiers, Adolphe, *Histoire de la Révolution française*, 24, 25
Thiesse, Anne-Marie, historian, 152, 158, 160, 161, 162
Third Republic, 47, 50, 152, 173, 186, 196, 199
Tocqueville, Alexis de, 169
Tolain, Henri, 124–5, 126
Tolstoy, Leo, 170, 182–3
Toulon. *See* Var department
Toulouse, 49, 50, 51, 145
Tours diocese, 68, 87–8
Truquin, Norbert, 113–14

Var department, 69, 70, 72
Vaucluse department, 17, 40, 68, 70, 72, 85, 86, 94
Verne, Jules, *Voyages extraordinaires*, 15, 34, 44, 57–61, 156, 161
Versailles, 51, 142

Vigny, Alfred de, 18, 29, 33
Vincent, David, historian, 111
Volney, *Les Ruines*, 21, 22, 23, 82, 89, 125
Volquin, Suzanne, 119–20, 127
Voltaire, 18, 21, 22, 34–5, 40, 45, 55, 67, 71, 73, 76–84, 86, 87, 88, 89, 96, 97, 105, 125, 205

Weber, Eugen, historian, 43, 48, 61–2, 148, 196, 199
west (region of France), 43, 51, 52. *See also* Brittany
women's autobiographies, 111, 113, 118–24, 126, 131–2
women's education, 118, 177
women's reading, 4, 10, 11, 39, 118–24, 126, 155, 158–9, 160–1, 162
women's writing, 9, 118–24, 170, 173, 174–5, 176, 177–80, 181
workers' autobiographies, 9, 111–38, 151
workers' reading, 4, 5, 10, 43, 50, 111–38, 151, 152, 155–6
World War, First, 5, 163, 184–99; mutinies of 1917, 185, 190

Young, *Les Nuits*, 23, 41

Zola, Emile, 15, 56, 156, 161

STUDIES IN BOOK AND PRINT CULTURE

General Editor: Leslie Howsam

Hazel Bell, *Indexes and Indexing in Fact and Fiction*

Heather Murray, *Come, bright Improvement! The Literary Societies of Nineteenth-Century Ontario*

Joseph A. Dane, *The Myth of Print Culture: Essays on Evidence, Textuality, and Bibliographical Method*

Christopher J. Knight, *Uncommon Readers: Denis Donoghue, Frank Kermode, George Steiner, and the Tradition of the Common Reader*

Eva Hemmungs Wirtén, *No Trespassing: Authorship, Intellectual Property Rights, and the Boundaries of Globalization*

William A. Johnson, *Bookrolls and Scribes in Oxyrhynchus*

Siân Echard and Stephen Partridge, eds, *The Book Unbound: Editing and Reading Medieval Manuscripts and Texts*

Bronwen Wilson, *The World in Venice: Print, the City, and Early Modern Identity*

Peter Stoicheff and Andrew Taylor, eds, *The Future of the Page*

Jennifer Phegley and Janet Badia, eds, *Reading Women: Literary Figures and Cultural Icons from the Victorian Age to the Present*

Elizabeth Sauer, *'Paper-contestations' and Textual Communities in England, 1640–1675*

Nick Mount, *When Canadian Literature Moved to New York*

Jonathan Carlyon, *Andrés González de Barcia and the Creation of the Colonial Spanish American Library*

Leslie Howsam, *Old Books and New Histories: An Orientation to Studies in Book and Print Culture*

Deborah McGrady, *Controlling Readers: Guillaume de Machaut and His Late Medieval Audience*

David Finkelstein, ed., *Print Culture and the Blackwood Tradition*

Bart Beaty, *Unpopular Culture: Transforming the European Comic Book in the 1990s*

Elizabeth Driver, *Culinary Landmarks: A Bibliography of Canadian Cookbooks, 1825–1949*

Benjamin C. Withers, *The Illustrated Old English Hexateuch, Cotton Claudius B.iv: The Frontier of Seeing and Reading in Anglo-Saxon England*

Mary Ann Gillies, *The Professional Literary Agent in Britain, 1880–1920*

Willa Z. Silverman, *The New Bibliopolis: French Book-Collectors and the Culture of Print, 1880–1914*

Lisa Surwillo, *The Stages of Property: Copyrighting Theatre in Spain*

Dean Irvine, *Editing Modernity: Women and Little-Magazine Cultures in Canada, 1916–1956*

Janet B. Friskney, *New Canadian Library: The Ross-McClelland Years, 1952–1978*

Janice Cavell, *Arctic Exploration in British Print Culture*

Elspeth Jajdelska, *Silent Reading and the Birth of the Narrator*

Martyn Lyons, *Reading Culture and Writing Practices in Nineteenth-Century France*